ALSO BY JORDAN ROMERO

The Boy Who Conquered Everest:
The Jordan Romero Story

No Summit out of Sight

The True Story of the Youngest Person to Climb the Seven Summits

Jordan Romero

with Linda LeBlanc

SIMON & SCHUSTER BFYR

NEW YORK LONDON TORONTO SYDNEY NEW DELHI

SIMON & SCHUSTER BFYR

An imprint of Simon & Schuster Children's Publishing Division
1230 Avenue of the Americas, New York, New York 10020

For information about special discounts for bulk purchases, please contact
Simon & Schuster Special Sales at 1-866-506-1949
or business@simonandschuster.com.
The Simon & Schuster Speakers Bureau can bring authors to your live event.
For more information or to book an event, contact
the Simon & Schuster Speakers Bureau at 1-866-248-3049
or visit our website at www.simonspeakers.com.
Jacket design by Chloë Foglia
Interior design by Hilary Zarycky
The text for this book is set in Electra.
Manufactured in the United States of America
2 4 6 8 10 9 7 5 3 1
Library of Congress Cataloging-in-Publication Data
Romero, Jordan, 1996–
No summit out of sight : the true story of the youngest person to climb the seven
summits / Jordan Romero with Linda LeBlanc. — First Edition.
pages cm
Summary: "The story of Jordan Romero, who at the age of 13 became the youngest
person ever to reach the summit of Mount Everest. At age 15, he reached the
summits of the world's 7 highest mountains"—Provided by publisher.
ISBN 978-1-4767-0962-8 (hardback) — ISBN 978-1-4767-0963-5 (eBook)
1. Romero, Jordan, 1996– —Juvenile literature. 2. Mountaineers—United States—
Biography—Juvenile literature. 3. Mountaineering—Juvenile literature. I. Title.
GV199.92.R66A3 2014
796.522092—dc23
[B]
2013031296

FIRST
EDITION

To every person young and old who
strives to Find Your Everest

ACKNOWLEDGMENTS

This book is dedicated to every person who supported me throughout the years and made my dream come true. If you bought a T-shirt, a taco, or a movie ticket, donated to the website, cheered me on, followed the red dot to the last two summits, or sent an encouraging e-mail, you know who you are and you have my sincerest gratitude.

To my family who supported me every step of the way, I love you from the bottom of my heart. To my dad, who didn't say no from the beginning, I love you and thank you for everything you've done for me. To Karen, who made everything happen and helped me with my math homework up at 21,000 feet, I love you like a mom of my own and cannot express enough gratitude for everything you've done for me. To my mom and my little sister, Makaela, who cheered me on all the way from home when I was missing you the most, I love you both.

A special thanks to Linda LeBlanc, the real writer of this book; I feel lucky to have had this opportunity to get to know you while putting this all together. This book would not exist without you.

I also want to acknowledge and thank the following people, who all played an important role in the success of this project: Thank you to Grandpa Alex Romero, Grandpa Robert Drake, Ang Pasang Sherpa and the Everest team, Samuel Kusamba, Terry Torok, Glenn Staack, Rob Bailey, Allan Laframboise and ESRI, Mike Baker, Katherine Blanc, Cathy Mills, King Richard, Steve Renecker, Neal Drake, the many sponsors and partners who joined our team, and the community of Big Bear.

Ad alta!

—Jordan

Denali
Continent: North America (United States)
Elevation: 20,320 feet

Aconcagua
Continent: South America (Argentina)
Elevation: 22,837 feet

Vinson
Continent: Antarctica
Elevation: 16,050 feet

The Seven Summits*

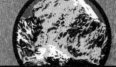

Elbrus
Continent: Europe (Russia)
Elevation: 18,510 feet

Everest
Continent: Asia (Nepal)
Elevation: 29,029 feet

Carstensz Pyramid
Continent: Australia (Indonesia)
Elevation: 16,024 feet

Kilimanjaro
Continent: Africa (Tanzania)
Elevation: 19,341 feet

Kosciuszko
Continent: Australia
Elevation: 7,310 feet

PROLOGUE

April 26, 2010—Mount Everest

I heard only my labored breathing and the crunch of my crampons biting into snow as I traversed a nearly vertical slope on the north face of Mount Everest. Below us the slope continued steeper and steeper until it spilled over into a bottomless cliff, but I was securely attached to a safety line that was anchored to the mountain. My stepmother, Karen, and our Sherpa guides, Ang Pasang and Karma, were ahead of me; my father, Paul, just behind. The weather was perfect, with clear blue sky everywhere I looked. It was a beautiful day for climbing.

I took one step, then another. Suddenly a thunderous roar ripped through the air. The earth rumbled and shifted beneath my feet.

I looked up and saw a ten-story wall of ice and snow break

free from the mountain and explode into an enormous cloud of white that hurtled downward, building higher and higher as it gained speed. Snow dust billowed in the air.

The avalanche was coming straight at me.

My mind froze, paralyzed with fear. I couldn't think, couldn't react fast enough.

Snow and ice sliced through what had been our trail.

Freezing air burned my throat all the way to my lungs.

The wave slammed into me and sucked me under. Everything was white, whirling around me, tossing me. I was tumbling out of control and couldn't breathe. Where was the sky, the earth? I kicked desperately, trying to sink my crampons into snow, ice, anything to keep from sliding toward the deadly cliff.

I tried to scream but no sound left my lips.

I was still clipped in to the safety line that kept me anchored to the mountain. With a jolt that ran through my body, the rope snapped and zipped past my head. Would the rest of the rope hold me in place or yank me away?

I clung to what was left of the line as a second wave of falling snow and ice swept me toward the bottomless cliff. "Dad!" I screamed. Had I lost him? Where were Karen and the others?

The thunderous roar died down, replaced by a cold, whipping wind. The ground finally stopped moving as the ice and snow began to settle on the mountainside. I sank my crampons into solid ice, but I was still surrounded by a cloud of snow blocking my vision. My head spinning and heart racing, I searched for Dad, Karen, and our guides. I sucked the burning cold air into my lungs and screamed, "Dad!"

No answer. Only the frozen breath of Everest against my face.

I desperately clung to the side of the mountain as the dream that had been the focus of my entire existence for the past four years slipped away. It couldn't end like this, not with losing people I loved, not with losing the Sherpas who'd been risking their lives to help me reach my goal. I screamed again and again until the cold shredded my throat.

If anything had happened to them, it would be my fault. I'd brought us to this mountain where more than two hundred climbers had died—one death for every ten successful attempts to reach the top. I wished I could go back to the beginning, to the very first time I had said the words "I want to climb the Seven Summits," and rethink everything.

Maybe this whole journey had been one huge mistake.

CHAPTER 1

It was the first day of fourth grade when I told my dad I had decided to climb the highest peak on each of the seven continents: the Seven Summits.

I was nine, and all summer long I'd been thinking about a mural on the wall of my elementary school, which laid out each of the Seven Summits and their elevations. I'd passed it every day on my way to and from recess, all through third grade. Other kids hardly seemed to notice it in their rush to play soccer or basketball, but I often stopped and stared, mesmerized by those mountains. What would it be like to stand on their summits and gaze across entire continents? I wanted to find out.

One thing you should know about me: When I get interested in something, I become a fanatic and learn everything I can about it. When I was younger and got interested in reptiles, I learned everything there was to know about every species. Now my interest turned to mountains.

I've always jumped into new interests with both feet, especially if they have to do with the outdoors. I've never been into playing video games or watching TV. Practically from the moment I could walk, I was outdoors—chasing lizards, riding my bike, skateboarding, and skiing. Especially skiing. That was my passion.

But I couldn't stop thinking about those mountains. Over the summer between third and fourth grades, I did Internet searches to read about the summits. I made lists of their locations, their elevations, and the best routes to the top of each. Along the way I discovered that there were people who had made it a goal to climb all seven.

I decided I could do that.

I was the ultimate goal setter, so at that age I already understood that things didn't always happen instantly.

But that was okay. I was also extremely patient.

And frankly, I didn't think the idea would shock my dad that much. My dad and my stepmom, Karen, are professional athletes. They compete in extreme adventure races all over the world. It's a crazy sport. They race nonstop on foot, on bicycles, in kayaks and canoes, and even on horses and camels. And they do it all in some of the most wild and remote places in the world. Our home has always been open to a never-ending stream of competitive athletes who are driven to enter the most brutal contests on the planet.

Dad and Karen thought outside the box, set huge goals,

and grabbed life with both hands. So why couldn't I?

Seeing that mural again on the first day of fourth grade help sharpen my resolve. My dad picked me up from school that day, and I sprang it on him.

He was going on and on about this killer endurance event he and Karen were training for. They'd been preparing non-stop for weeks. They were always going, going, going. They believed you should live your life, not watch it. Their motto hung on the front of the house: GO FAST. TAKE CHANCES.

And I intended to.

"Hey, Dad, you ever heard of the Seven Summits?"

He glanced at me. "Sort of, Little J," he said, using his nickname for me.

I paused, took a deep breath, and exhaled slowly. "I want to climb them."

His jaw dropped, and he stared at me openmouthed for a minute.

"Oookaaay," he said. My dad has this way of stretching an "okay" out for a mile. This one went for two miles.

I could tell he thought this was a *someday* kind of goal. But I wanted to do it sooner. "Not when I'm older, but, like, right now."

That *really* surprised him.

"What made you decide *that*?"

I told him about the mural, and about how I had been looking at it for years and thinking about what it would be like to stand on top of each of those mountains and look at the world.

"You really know about all this?" he asked.

That was it, bang. I told him about all the stuff I'd learned — where and how high each summit was, what countries they were in, the best routes to the top of each summit.

My dad has a huge smile, one that can light up a whole room. And nothing makes him happier than the idea of an athletic challenge. I watched his face closely, waiting for that smile. I guess I half expected him to say, *Okay. Let's buy tickets for every corner of the world and leave tomorrow.*

He didn't.

"Mountaineering is long, hard, and dirty," he said. "It's not all fun. You'd need weeks and even months of training before you could even think of climbing even the smallest ones."

"I don't care. I can do it," I answered.

Dad thought about it for a minute. He didn't say yes, but he didn't exactly say no, either.

"Let's get Super K," he said, using his nickname for Karen, "and go for a hike."

CHAPTER 2

That afternoon Dad and Karen strapped a pack on me and we headed out for that hike.

Dad and Karen's house is in Big Bear Lake, California, on the edge of the San Bernardino National Forest. Our altitude of just under seven thousand feet above sea level is nothing compared to Everest, but it's way higher than the average elevation in the United States, which is about 2,500 feet. All we had to do to go for a hike was take a left outside the front door and head up into the San Bernardino Mountains. It was something Dad and Karen did all the time.

I was never that much of a hiker. Maybe that's why my dad wanted me to hike with my Seven Summits goal in mind. I loved being outdoors, but hiking for hiking's sake had never really worked for me. I needed a goal to shoot for to keep me interested. This time was no different. After ten minutes on the trail I was panting and my heart was pounding.

"I'm tired. Can we go back?" I asked.

"No lizards, bugs, or snakes today?" Karen said.

When I did hike with them, it was mostly to search for reptiles.

"Haven't seen any," I answered.

"There!" Dad said as a lizard skittered across our path.

"A western fence lizard. Sweet." I darted after it, just wanting to hold it a minute to look at its bright blue belly.

From then on I got caught up in looking for snakes and bugs and didn't realize I'd been climbing uphill for forty-five minutes straight until we reached the top. I decided if I could make it that far on such a boring hike, I could handle this whole mountain-climbing thing. It would be way more fun on *real* mountains. Right?

Back home I opened a world atlas on the breakfast counter. Dad and Karen looked over my shoulder while I pointed out the location of each of the Seven Summits, going from lowest to highest.

"Here's Kosciuszko in Australia," I said. "There are reptiles all over the place down there."

Karen smiled. "Maybe you'd run into Steve Irwin."

When I was nine, I loved Steve Irwin. His television show, *The Crocodile Hunter*, was one of the few I watched. I had every single one of his videos and watched them over and over until they were practically worn out. Inspired by him, I had a collection of snakes, horny toads, lizards, and other assorted cold-blooded creatures living in my room.

"The next tallest is Vinson in Antarctica," I said, flipping to that page. "You guys ever raced down there?"

Dad shook his head. "No. But I know they have an annual marathon."

"Elbrus is the highest summit in Europe, but it's in Russia," I said, shrugging. I hadn't realized that Russia was considered part of Europe. "Who figures these things out?"

"Got me," Karen said. "I would've thought it was Mont Blanc in the Alps."

I turned to Africa and pointed to the country of Tanzania. "Next is Kilimanjaro. The summit used to be covered by ice, but the glaciers are melting. They'll be gone sometime in the next twenty years. I want to see them before they disappear."

Karen nodded. "We've been talking about going to Africa anyway."

"The next tallest is Denali in Alaska. That shouldn't be too hard to get to," I said. "It's right here in our own country."

"But it's extremely difficult to climb, Jordan," Dad said. "It's not that far from the North Pole. We're talking seriously nasty weather."

I was too busy imagining myself standing on all these mountaintops to worry about weather. "What about this one?" I asked. "Did you know Aconcagua in Argentina is the highest peak in the world outside of the Himalayas?"

Dad looked impressed. "I did not."

I sat back, grinning. "And now the big one, Mount Everest. Think about standing on the highest point on earth and seeing forever. I am so stoked!"

"Easy, Little J," Karen said. "Let's look at this one mountain at a time."

I glanced at Dad out of the corner of my eye. Did that mean we were actually going? If we were, it was time for me to drop another bomb.

"There are two lists of the Seven Summits," I told them. "To do it right you actually have to climb eight mountains, not seven."

"You have to climb *eight* mountains to climb the *Seven* Summits? Somebody missed a math lesson," Dad joked.

I don't know if my dad really didn't know this stuff, or if he just enjoyed seeing how excited I was. He listened while I rattled off one fact after another—practically everything I had learned in my research over the summer. The more I talked about it, the more excited I got.

I told Dad and Karen all about Dick Bass, a businessman who came up with the idea of climbing the Seven Summits. He'd included Australia's Mount Kosciuszko on his list and conquered the last of his seven mountains with Everest in 1985. Then in 1986 another famous climber, Reinhold Messner, climbed the Seven Summits, but he claimed that the Carstensz Pyramid on the island of New Guinea should be the seventh because it was more technically difficult and

challenging than Kosciuszko and had a much higher elevation. And the Carstensz Pyramid is considered part of the
continent Oceania, which includes the Australian continent.

I'd leave that part up to the geographers of the world, but
I was sure about one thing. "I want to do a combined list of all
eight," I announced.

"How many people have climbed all these summits?" Dad
asked.

I'm sure the number is higher today, but back then around
eighty-seven people had climbed the Carstensz list, and just
over a hundred people had climbed the list that included
Kosciuszko. A much smaller number of people had climbed
all eight—people tended to do one list or the other.

"That's a hefty undertaking," Dad said.

I still didn't know if I had his go-ahead. But one thing for
sure—I had his and Karen's attention. It was time to push for
my first mountain.

CHAPTER 3

Every year we made a list of the amazing places we wanted to go on vacation. Karen would put them all together on a makeshift spinner made of poster board, and I'd spin an arrow to see where it landed. That year it had pointed to Africa, and we all wanted to go on a safari. We were planning to go over my spring break from school.

"While we're in Africa, maybe we could climb Kilimanjaro," I suggested.

Karen gave an appreciative little chuckle. "Good move, Little J." Then she got serious. "If we really are going to climb Kilimanjaro, you'll have to train for it. Hike at least three times a week, climbing higher and steeper each time. And carrying heavier loads."

"And you'll have to prepare mentally, too," Dad said. "You'll have to drive yourself until you're cold, miserable, and tired, until you're tough as nails." He smiled and leaned back with his hands clasped behind his head. He always came home from adventure races full of stories about people who pushed themselves beyond anything they thought they could ever achieve. I think he loves seeing other people succeed as much as he loves winning himself. It's all about being your own personal best.

I wanted him to have stories like that to tell about me. "I can do it," I insisted.

Dad looked at Karen. "What do you think?"

"It makes sense to try Kilimanjaro if we're going there anyway," she said.

I jumped to my feet and gave them each a high five. "Kilimanjaro, here we come!" I shouted. *I'm on my way*, I thought. *I'm going to climb my first summit.*

I could hardly sleep that night, thinking about it. I pulled the covers to my chest and closed my eyes, imagining myself standing on top of Kilimanjaro and looking out over all of Africa.

I was still flying high when I got home from school the next afternoon. Then Karen delivered the bad news. She had read online that you had to be ten years old to even set foot in the Kilimanjaro National Park. That meant spring break was out. I'd have to wait until July. Like any kid, I wanted things to happen now, not wait nine whole months!

Sunday night I returned to my mom's house, where I lived half the time with her and my half sister, Makaela, who is six years younger than I am. I alternated weeks between my mom's house and my dad's, and I hated having to split time between them. It was hard going back and forth and having to keep stuff in both places. Every Sunday night I'd have to pack for the next week, and sometimes I'd forget what I needed. Life would have been so much easier if my parents had never split up, but I do love being a big brother to Makaela.

I was excited to tell Mom about Kilimanjaro, even if I did have to wait nine months to go. She has a big heart. Like all moms she wants to know where I am and what I'm doing, but she isn't the overly protective type. I knew I'd need her permission to make this dream come true, and I hoped she'd be happy for me.

I brought it up over my favorite afternoon snack of apples and peanut butter. "We're planning this trip to Africa this summer, and we're going to climb Kilimanjaro while we're there."

She raised her eyebrows. "Really, Jordan? Is this your idea or your father's?"

"All mine," I told her. "You know that mural at school about the highest mountains on each continent?"

"Yes."

"I thought about it all summer. Wouldn't it be awesome to stand on the top of each one?"

"So you want to climb all *seven*?"

I nodded, not quite ready to tell her there were actually eight mountains to climb.

Then I swore she looked straight into my heart. "Do you feel ready for something that big? You've never hiked more than a mile without whining. Don't you remember going up Butler Peak last spring? About halfway up, you were lying on the ground, exhausted and crying, 'Leave me here. I can't do this. Leave me here to die.'"

That was true, but like I said before, hiking for the sake of hiking had never done much for me. But hiking to reach the summit of the tallest mountain in Africa? That was something I could get behind. Mom knew that I liked to set goals. Especially challenging ones. I tried to explain that reaching the summit of Kilimanjaro would be like taking on the ultimate challenge.

"I'm going to put everything I have into achieving this."

"And you feel strong enough?" she asked.

"I'll *get* strong enough," I promised her. "Dad and Karen have time to train me. I can't even get into the Kilimanjaro National Park until I'm ten."

Mom pulled me in close for a hug. "You know people can get hurt climbing mountains."

I nodded. "I'll be careful," I promised. "It's not a mountain with crevasses or steep cliffs. It's just a long hike. Dad says we won't even need an ice axe or ropes."

A worried look crossed Mom's face. "Your dad and Karen are racers, not mountain climbers."

That was true. Dad and Karen had participated in every kind of extreme race there was, but they had never actually scaled a mountain like Kilimanjaro. Still, they had more than enough experience hiking, rock climbing, high-altitude mountaineering, and surviving on extreme expeditions. And on top of that, Dad was an air-rescue paramedic.

"Dad knows more about emergencies than anybody," I pointed out.

She nodded. "Yes, he probably does. He and Karen have taken care of themselves in all kinds of extreme situations."

"And they'll take care of me, too," I said. "They'll make sure I'm ready."

Mom thought about that for a minute. She knew Dad and Karen would do everything possible to make sure I didn't get hurt. I could tell I was winning her over when she stopped worrying about my safety and brought up the subject of money.

"How's your father going to make this happen? He doesn't have that kind of cash."

I hadn't thought about the expense of a trip like this, and we hadn't talked about it. "I don't know," I admitted.

Dad and Karen had a number of sponsors for their adventure racing, companies that provided gear and even money in exchange for publicity and advertising. I hoped they would be able to gain some sponsors for our mountain climbing as well. Trips like the ones I was thinking about were expensive.

Mom sighed. "I'm sure he'll figure it out. I don't want to stand in your way, but promise me you'll be careful."

"I promise."

CHAPTER 4

As much as I'd learned about the summits, serious mountain climbing was still a big mystery. I had no idea how many miles I'd have to carry a heavy pack or how hard it would be to walk up super steep hills. I didn't think much about any of those things; I just wanted to get to the top of those eight mountains.

Mountain climbing is one of those sports that can be defined a lot of different ways. Some mountains are an easy hike to the top and don't require any special equipment beyond a backpack filled with water and snacks. Steeper peaks can call for special mountain-climbing shoes, hiking poles, and even snowshoes and ice axes in the winter. And then there are the technical mountains, which call for rock-climbing skills — the ability to find handholds and footholds and make your way to the top using ropes and other tools. Over the course of my mountain-climbing career I'd have to learn about all those things, but right now I was focused on training to climb Kilimanjaro.

I'd never been a long-distance kind of kid, not like Dad and Karen. I thought of myself more as a sprinter. Endurance was Dad's thing. But if I was going to scale *any* summit, I needed endurance too.

For the first few weeks, the three of us hiked trails in the hills and valleys above the house to help me get fit enough for Mount Kilimanjaro. I had to learn to carry a pack and to pull out snacks while we were moving. I especially had to let Dad and Karen know when my feet were hurting so that I wouldn't get blisters. We used hiking poles when the climbs were steep and wore snowshoes in the winter. I had been walking in snowshoes for practically my whole life, so I was used to them.

I knew that in Africa I'd have to hike for three or four or even five hours at a time without stopping, and I definitely worked up to that in my training.

Gradually, my day pack got heavier. Sometimes we filled it with water and canned food. Once I even lugged a medicine ball up a mountain. I carried first ten, then twenty pounds in my pack to help build my strength and endurance. I think Dad saw that as a measure of my fitness and how much mental strength I was building, because one afternoon a few months into my training he announced, "It's time to move your training a notch higher on Snow Summit tonight."

We walked to the base of the mountain from our house,

wearing our packs. When we got there, Dad handed me a pair of crampons. Crampons are metal spikes that get attached to the bottoms of your shoes with straps that hold them in place. They make it possible to walk on hard, slippery snow and ice. Crampons are a must-have for a serious mountain climber.

"Why do we need these?" I asked.

Dad grinned. "We're going to hike thirteen hundred feet right up the ski slope."

I knew Snow Summit well. It was one of the best ski mountains around, and I had climbed up it and skied down it many, many times. But the difference this time was that I'd be hiking at night and in full mountaineering gear with a rope, ice axe, helmet, and crampons.

I couldn't believe it—my first time hiking on serious snow and ice!

"You want to climb big mountains?" Dad asked.

"Yes!"

"Then you have to be able climb on that," he said pointing to the ski run called Westridge. "And I think it's time to add some interval training to your workouts too."

Interval training means going all out—climbing as fast as you possibly can—for a short period of time, thirty seconds or a full minute, followed by a minute at a normal pace to recover before rocketing up your speed again. It's a great training tool for building strength and endurance. But doing that for an entire mountain was more than a little intimidating.

"You want me to do that all the way to the top?" I asked.

"Yes," he answered.

I'd said I wanted a goal, and here was a big one. It was the hardest thing I'd ever done. I had to learn to walk flat-footed and slightly duck-footed to sink all ten spikes on my crampons into the snow for traction, or they'd get caught on my pant legs. Not only that, but I was climbing practically straight up the ski slope with freezing cold wind blowing into my face. I was so frustrated that tears streamed down my cheeks. I took out my anger by sprinting during my speed intervals. That tired me out faster, making the training even more intense. Karen tried to keep me calm and keep me moving.

It took about an hour and a half to reach the top. When we got there, Dad gave me a big hug. "Way to go, Little J." Then he saw the furious look on my face and laughed. "Those sprints of yours are going to make you stronger and stronger."

I knew he was right, and that helped me let go of my frustration and even feel a little bit proud. But I was also exhausted. If Snow Summit had kicked my butt, I wondered how I would make it all the way to the top of Kilimanjaro.

When I said so, Karen came back with one of her encouraging speeches.

"Climbing a mountain is like facing an adventure race," she said. "If you told yourself, 'I've got to make six hundred miles in the next five days,' you wouldn't even start. But if you break it down into little goals and achieve each one as it comes along, it's a lot less overwhelming. And when you do finish, you realize that you've done something much bigger than you set out to do."

Seeing the look on my face, Karen smiled. "Don't get discouraged, Jordan. When you're climbing, aim for the next rock or tree, and then the one after that, until you reach the top. You're doing great. But you have to be one hundred percent ready before we head off for something big, like Kilimanjaro."

About six weeks later we hiked to a forest-fire outlook in the San Bernardino Mountains, and I started to see a difference in my strength and endurance—all thanks to my daily training. My thighs didn't burn as much and my heart wasn't pounding so hard that I thought it would burst through my ribs. I leaned forward in to the hill and imagined I was climbing to the summit of Everest. When Dad and Karen stepped onto the fire lookout platform at about eight thousand feet, I was right behind them.

I guess I proved something to them and to myself that day, because from the top Karen pointed to San Gorgonio—the highest peak in Southern California, at 11,503 feet. "So, Jordan, should we make it our goal to climb that on Christmas Day?"

"Are you kidding?" I asked. "I can't wait!" Finally, I thought, I was going to climb a mountain with a *real* summit. I was only sorry I had to wait until Christmas.

• • •

We started out at three a.m. Christmas morning. Other nine-year-olds were still asleep and dreaming of Santa, but I was getting ready to scale a mountain. Dad said we could open a few presents before heading out, and he handed me a long skinny package. I had no clue what to expect and tore the paper off.

"An ice axe!" I shouted. I turned it over in my hands. Mountain climbers use ice axes to cut footholds in the ice and to stop themselves if they start to fall. I fell crazy in love with it. I could hardly wait to try it out.

We headed to the trailhead with Bernardo, a Brazilian friend of ours who was coming along to take photographs. We hiked for several hours, crossing a number of creeks and climbing a series of long switchbacks to the back of the mountain. Switchbacks are 180-degree bends in a path that make it easier to hike up a mountain. Instead of going straight up, you walk in a kind of zigzag pattern.

Dad turned to me with a grin. "With all this great snow," he said, "it'd be more fun to climb three thousand feet straight up the slope, wouldn't it?"

Yes! Up until now we had been hiking, but now we would be doing some real mountain climbing. Anybody could hike, but actual mountain climbing required skill, endurance, and special equipment.

I slid my crampons on over my shoes. Karen helped me get them on tight so they wouldn't budge when the mountain got really steep. With my new axe in hand, I was ready to conquer the mountain! Karen went first, with me second and Dad behind Bernardo. The ice was hard as concrete at times and really tested my crampons. One of Karen and Dad's sponsors, Salomon, had donated a pair of trail shoes that were light and allowed me to move fast, but about halfway up I still ran out of gas.

Bernardo was struggling too, even more than me. He was a little out of shape, so the higher we went, the harder it was on him. He was totally wiped out, but we couldn't leave him behind. I tried to encourage Bernardo as Dad carried his massive backpack. For the first time, I wasn't lagging behind everyone else. That felt good, and it seemed to make the hiking easier. I liked not being the person everyone was waiting for. It gave me a chance to breathe.

I kept my eye on the summit. Seeing my goal within reach gave me a boost of energy. When we climbed off the face and onto the ridge, there was a trail to the summit. I charged right on up, past Karen, even though just minutes before I had nearly been falling down from exhaustion.

Reaching the summit was the greatest feeling I'd ever experienced. "Yes!" I shouted, thrusting my axe into the air and turning in a complete circle. I was on the top of Southern California and could see all the way to the ocean on one side and the desert on the other. If I could get up here, I could climb anything. "Bring on Kilimanjaro!" I shouted.

Dad's smile was as big as mine. "Jordan, go to the box over there and add all our names to the logbook."

Many mountains have a logbook at the top where climbers can add their names to the list of people who've summited to prove they actually made it. Still bursting with confidence, I raised the lid, ready to record my accomplishment. There was an envelope lying on top with *my* name on it.

I glanced at Dad and Karen, totally confused.

"What is it?" Karen asked.

I shrugged. They were the only ones, aside from Mom, who'd known where I'd be this morning.

"Well, look," Dad said.

My fingers were so cold that I could barely open the envelope. A card inside read:

Dear Jordan,
Congratulations on reaching the summit of your first big
mountain. Merry Christmas.
Love, Santa.

Santa had found me at 11,503 feet.

Tanzania wouldn't give anyone a permit to climb the mountain unless you hired the country's approved porters and guides to lead the climb and carry your equipment up the mountain. As much as we would have preferred to go alone, we had no choice in the matter.

"Hiring guides isn't our style," Dad said. "Super K and I

are used to racing fast and light all over the world."

"The porters and guides add a lot to the cost, too," Karen added. "To get all three of us to Africa, pay to climb, *and* do a safari will run way more than we can afford."

Dad was an athlete and helicopter paramedic, not a CEO of a major company. He couldn't simply write a big check to make my dream come true.

Karen searched for the cheapest guide services, the most affordable flights, and rock-bottom hotels, but the trip still seemed out of reach. Then we got lucky. Some family friends from the endurance-competition circuit had just returned from climbing Kili—the mountain climbers' nickname for Mount Kilimanjaro—and they put us in touch with the less expensive guide they'd used. Plus they showed us pictures and told us what to expect. They knew me pretty well and believed I'd make it. I was more excited than ever, but money was still an issue.

Dad and Karen already had a few sponsors, like Salomon and SOLE custom footbeds, who agreed to help us by providing gear as long as we photographed their banners on the summit. But that wasn't nearly enough to cover costs. We had to get creative.

Karen designed a T-shirt with a list of the summits printed on the back and boxes so folks could mark off each one as we conquered the mountain. We sold a lot of those T-shirts in Big Bear and online through a website Karen put together just for me: www.jordanromero.com.

Karen had an idea for me, too. She suggested a lemonade stand.

I stood for hours in front of our friend's bike shop, Bear Valley Bikes, selling lemonade at fifty cents a cup. But I wanted to do more than just fund my dream. New Orleans had just been practically wiped out by Hurricane Katrina, so I set up two cans for collecting money. One said KILIMANJARO and the other said KATRINA. I sent half the money I earned to the Red Cross for hurricane victims and put the other half aside for our trip to Africa. I told anyone who'd listen about my dream and what I needed to make it happen. And pretty soon everybody in Big Bear got to know me.

And almost all of them bought at least two cups, and I earned a few hundred dollars from really nice people who believed in me. It inspired me to keep going.

THE FIRST CLIMB:

AFRICA'S

MOUNT

KILIMANJARO,

19,341 FEET

AVERAGE NUMBER OF CLIMBERS
PER YEAR: 25,000

JULY 22, 2006, AGE 10

WORLD RECORD

CHAPTER 5

Just over ten months after I announced my big goal on the first day of fourth grade, I boarded a plane to Africa.

The first thing I did when we got off the plane was check my new watch. It had both a thermometer to measure temperature and an altimeter to measure altitude. We were at 5,500 feet in hot, muggy, 80-degree air.

Our journey to Kilimanjaro would begin with a long drive from Nairobi, Kenya, to the neighboring country of Tanzania. We made our way through crowds to catch a local bus leaving from the airport. While we waited, a few local women approached. They had shaved heads and wore enormous beaded necklaces and dresses made from brightly colored cloth. They carried baskets full of all sorts of stuff for sale, like beads, pictures made out of banana leaves, and bottles of water. They pushed their wares in our faces and wouldn't let up.

"I wish they'd quit pressuring me to buy something," I told Karen.

"They're only trying to make a living. They probably have hungry kids at home."

Suddenly I started thinking about them as moms who were trying to take care of their kids instead of as pushy salespeople. "Can we buy some bottled water?"

"Sure," Karen agreed. She handed me some Kenyan money, and it felt good to be able to buy something.

We finally got onto a bus packed with people and packages. The only open seats were the second to the last row, where wheel wells stole all the legroom. Dad's knees were up around his chin. I was totally squished next to the window.

Nairobi was a bustling city filled with honking horns, the smell of roadside trash and diesel fumes, and a constant flow of families, kids, animals, scooters, and workers all on the move. The bus ride was long and slow. We hit a bump every two minutes and everything flew into the air—baskets of produce, eggs, even a goat on a leash. Everything, that is, except the squawking chicken in front of me. It was tied down and wouldn't shut up. I gave it my best cobra stare, but the chicken was unfazed.

As we left the busy city, everything started to look brown and beige. It was the dry season in Kenya. One roadside village after another was filled with rickety wooden stalls where people sold fruit and vegetables and chickens and goats. Barefoot kids in rags chased in and out among the stalls, kicking up dust and watching buses like ours go by.

Just as I'd thrown myself into learning the details of every species of reptile, I'd studied Kilimanjaro and the people who lived nearby. There was a tribe of nomadic cattle herders called the Masai who pierced and stretched their earlobes so big that they hung down to their chins. The men walked along the road wearing red-checkered blankets draped over one shoulder. Their hair was dyed red from clay and animal fat.

"The color red means power to them," I told Dad. "And the only thing a lion fears is a Masai warrior holding a spear."

We reached the border crossing at the village of Namanga, Kenya, in just over two hours. The road was packed with huge trucks, vans, and buses passing between Kenya and Tanzania. Broken-down metal stalls painted in bright reds and yellows lined both sides of the road with food for sale. I wanted a piece of fruit, but Karen warned me not to eat anything I couldn't peel and to drink only bottled water. Our bodies weren't accustomed to the bacteria in the local water, so drinking it, or anything washed in the local water, could have made us very ill.

The bus stopped next to the building where we had to register for entry cards and visas for Tanzania. We got our papers, crossed the border on foot, and boarded our dilapidated bus again. Next stop Arusha—the city closest to Kilimanjaro.

"If the sky clears, you might see the mountain," Karen said.

I pulled the window down and leaned on my arms across the sill, wind blowing in my hair. I wasn't searching for Kilimanjaro on the Internet. I was here—living it!

All of a sudden I felt a sharp sting on my neck. I jerked back inside the bus and stared at the nasty-looking kamikaze dung beetle I had swatted to the floor.

Dad was craning his head to see over the suitcases, goat, and chicken. "There's Kili!"

Holding my sore neck and keeping my lips squeezed tight against any other flying creatures, I leaned out the window again and gazed upward. There was the world's tallest freestanding mountain, all 19,341 feet of it. Clouds hovered around its base, just like they had in Internet pictures, and above them was the summit.

Unlike the rest of the Seven Summits, Kili isn't part of a mountain range. It's a dormant volcanic mountain with three volcano cones. Standing alone like that makes it look even more enormous than it is. By comparison, San Gorgonio, Southern California's tallest peak, suddenly seemed like a foothill. I knew that about a third of the people who tried to climb Kilimanjaro didn't make it to the summit. Could I really climb all the way to the top, or would I have to turn back?

Karen, who had been shooting pictures, sensed my hesitation and set the camera in her lap. "Don't think of tackling the whole mountain all at once," she reminded me. "Take one small step at a time."

To ease my worries, I thought about everything I had learned about the mountain. Africans used to believe that an evil spirit on the mountain killed everyone who tried to climb it. It wasn't until the mid-1800s that a missionary realized that what they called a cloud on the top of Kili was actually snow, and that it was the extreme cold that killed the visitors, not an evil spirit. The locals didn't even have words for snow and ice in their language.

The fact that the summit is covered in snow and ice is kind of amazing when you think about the fact that the mountain is just ninety miles south of the equator, but the air is so thin and cold at nineteen thousand–plus feet above sea level that average temperatures are below freezing.

Once Westerners found out about the mountain, they wanted to climb it. A German officer and a British geologist first tried in 1861, but even with fifty porters helping them they only got as far as 8,200 feet before they had to turn back because of the weather. The German officer tried again the next year and made it all the way to fourteen thousand feet before a snowstorm sent him back down the mountain.

It was another German, Hans Meyer, who finally reached the summit in 1889. On his first attempt he didn't have the equipment to handle the ice and snow and was forced to turn back. On his second he was captured and held hostage in a revolt against the German East Africa Trading Company, and he was only able to escape after a ransom was paid. You'd think he'd give up after that, but he didn't. Meyer was the one who finally figured out that if he used porters to set up camps with food and shelter along the way, he wouldn't have to go all the way back to the bottom every time he needed something, and he finally summited on his third attempt.

Thinking about all those failed attempts to reach the summit didn't exactly calm all my fears, but I decided that I would be just like Hans Meyer. I wouldn't give up until I reached the summit.

We finally arrived in Arusha three hours after crossing the border into Tanzania and took a taxi to our one-star hotel. The beds were draped with nets to prevent mosquitoes from getting in at night and passing along malaria or yellow fever—a real problem in many African countries. Dad and Karen didn't seem too concerned, but I made sure to spread the netting around my bed and theirs. We'd traveled far to climb Kilimanjaro, and the last thing we needed was for a potentially deadly disease to get in our way.

Our guide, Samuel Kusamba, met us at the hotel in the morning. He was bald, wore reading glasses, was maybe forty years old, and had a very round, smiling face. I liked him right away, but like most of the adults we talked to, he doubted my ability to climb the mountain. He'd climbed Kilimanjaro about eighty times and said it usually took six days, but with a kid like me along it would probably take seven or more. We didn't argue with him, but I decided then and there that I would make it to the top in six days—or fewer.

There are six routes to the top of Kili, and after doing a lot of research I had settled on the Umbwe Route for Dad, Karen, and me.

"The Umbwe Route is the most difficult," Samuel said. "It's only recommended for the most experienced climbers."

I knew that too. But Kilimanjaro had long, flat approaches, and I tended to daydream and lose focus on those kinds of hikes. I knew that I'd do better on a tougher climb. And besides, Umbwe had some killer rocks to scramble over.

I didn't admit any of that to Samuel. "It's supposed to be the most beautiful and least crowded," I said.

I could tell that Samuel was still skeptical, but Dad and Karen backed me up.

"All right, then," Samuel agreed. "The porters and I will meet you at the permit office in the morning."

That afternoon we wandered around Arusha, and Karen and Dad had their hair done in cornrows like the African women so that they wouldn't have to deal with it in the climb. Walking around, seeing all the people, I realized that I wouldn't just be climbing the Seven Summits. I would also be experiencing more of the world in a few years than most people do in a whole lifetime.

CHAPTER 6

The next morning, mosquito bite–free, we took a bus from Arusha to the entrance of Kilimanjaro National Park. We rode through coffee and banana plantations on our way to the Umbwe Gate, the entrance to the Umbwe Route.

Two family friends were planning to climb with us, and I was happy to see them waiting at the gate. The first was Faiz, a businessman and weekend adventurer who had a great sense of humor. It was cool having him around because he talked to me like an adult. The second was Nikki, a pretty Scandinavian-looking woman with blond hair and blue eyes. I was glad they were coming along. Not only were they new people to talk to, but I secretly hoped they'd fall behind me on the trail. Dad and Karen were always out in front. I kind of longed to not be the trail sweeper, the one in the rear who everybody else had to wait for.

We all checked in and signed the register at the Umbwe Gate and stepped onto the trailhead.

More than a hundred years after Hans Meyer had the idea to set up camps, they were well established. We only had to bring our sleeping bags and pads, personal items, and additional warm clothes for the summit. Samuel made sure we had everything else we needed. The twelve porters he hired would carry our packs, tents, tarps, food, stoves, and propane up the mountain for us. They wore cotton shirts, shorts, and flip-flops and greeted us with great big smiles.

Every load was carefully wrapped and tied together with twine. Then the porters balanced them on their heads and started up the trail like a line of leaf-cutter ants.

"Those guys are incredibly fit," Dad said, watching them go. "I've raced against the best athletes all over the world and would put them up against anybody."

With the porters carrying our heavy loads, I only had to carry my iPod, lunch, snacks, water, and a windbreaker in my familiar day pack. We'd covered a lot of miles together, and it felt comfortable on my shoulders, reminding me of the trails in Big Bear. After all my training, with only ten pounds now the straps felt relaxed and comfortable as I pulled it into place. I was ready to go.

As we began our climb, I took in the scenery around me. The trail was a single track through a rain forest of rubber trees, giant fig trees, and huge ferns. The foliage was so dense I couldn't see the sun. The humongous vegetation was my first clue that this place got a lot of rain, followed by the thick moisture in the air. Before long the rain let loose on us.

There was too much to see for me to be bothered by the rain. I imagined that every vine was the shadow of a snake; every rustle in the bushes, a lizard; every crack of a stick, an animal cruising through the trees. I saw long lines of ants, each carrying a piece of a leaf, crossing our trail in a zigzag line. I jumped over them so I wouldn't disrupt their work.

I was so busy taking it all in that I didn't watch for puddles. My shoes and socks were muddy and soaking wet, but I was smiling from ear to ear. Scrambling up steep sections of roots and boulders made me even happier.

"Now *this* is what I call mountain climbing," I told Dad.

We passed a couple of our porters sitting at the side of the trail, smoking cigarettes. *"Jambo!"* they shouted, with big smiles and sparkling white teeth set against black skin.

"That means 'hello' in Swahili," Samuel said.

"Jambo!" I yelled back

A few minutes later they sped past us again in their flip-flops, balancing loads on their heads. I tried catching up to these superhumans, but there was no way.

"Pole pole," Samuel called after me. "That means 'slowly, slowly' in Swahili. Far more than half the people on Kilimanjaro turn back because of altitude sickness."

"We're fine," Dad told him. "Just going our pace."

And it was true. It turned out our slow was faster than most climbers' normal. I liked being first and was pushing right on up. Faiz and Nikki were just a bit behind when we started out, but lagged more and more behind as we climbed.

I felt great. Not only was I super excited to be climbing my first of the Seven Summits, but the scenery was like nothing I had seen before. The last stretch to our first camp was so cool—we climbed a narrow trail, pushing our way through thick trees and vines, scrambling over massive roots and boulders.

Not only that, but I was proving Samuel wrong. In four hours, instead of his projected six or seven, we reached the Umbwe Cave Camp, nestled in the middle of the rain forest at 9,514 feet and completely surrounded by dense vegetation. Samuel smiled and told me that I had arrived so quickly that the porters thought I must have magically flown up there.

Rain was still making its way through the canopy, and everything was cold and wet. We were supposed to spend the night at the camp and then move on toward the summit the next morning. But after hot tea and some of the best popcorn I'd ever eaten, I wasn't even tired.

"How about we keep moving toward the summit?" I asked.

With his usual gentle smile Samuel said, "It's better that you stay here tonight. The Barranco Camp is six more hours."

Karen set her cup of tea down. "I agree. Let's see how everyone feels in the morning."

Faiz and Nikki were relieved by our decision to stay. It was only then that I realized just how wiped out they were, even though they were in great physical shape. As soon I was alone with Dad and Karen, I asked them what was going on.

"Probably a little altitude sickness," Dad explained.

Then I understood. Dad, Karen, and I lived at an altitude of seven thousand feet and were more accustomed to the thinner air we breathe at high elevations. Faiz and Nikki lived closer to sea level, so the thin air on the mountain was making them feel sick.

It's hard to think of air being *thin*, but we live under an atmosphere several miles deep. At sea level its weight pushes down on you and creates pressure. As you go higher, there's less air above you and the pressure decreases. Air molecules spread out, and you get fewer in each inhale. That can make people seriously sick with headaches and nausea, not to mention cause shortness of breath. It can also make you want to sleep—a lot.

Everyone reacts differently to altitude, and nobody really knows why. But we all breathe faster at high altitude to take in larger amounts of air. After a while your body adjusts to the oxygen level by producing more red blood cells, and you end up with more oxygen in your blood.

Even so, I knew that climbing too high too fast could be deadly.

"Will they be all right?" I asked.

"They just need time," Karen said. "And if they get worse, all they have to do is go to a lower elevation."

Relieved now that we were staying at the Umbwe Cave Camp, I crawled into my tent to get out of the rain. My jacket, hat, shoes, and socks were all wet and heavy, and there was no way to dry them out. That was a drag, but my sleeping bag was warm and dry, so I climbed inside. There wasn't anything else to do.

Two of the porters looked like they were only a year older than me. They were laughing and kidding each other just like me and my friends back home. It would have been nice to hang out with them, but there seemed to be an unspoken rule that they kept to themselves instead of mingling with the climbers. They ran ahead and did everything they could to make us comfortable and then set up a separate camp for themselves.

The next morning, after a breakfast of hot porridge and tea, Faiz and Nikki were feeling better and we were ready to climb.

Shortly after we started out, the forest thinned and the trees grew shorter. Kili is only two degrees south of the equator, but you climb through five different vegetation zones to reach the summit. First there's the rain forest, with a canopy so dense the sun can hardly penetrate. That's what we had hiked through on our first day. Now we were above the forest zone, in a region of giant heather and tough scrub. For the next three hours it took both our hands and feet to scramble over the boulders in our path. I wondered how the porters were going to manage in flip-flops. My own feet were hurting. I was pretty sure a blister was forming on my right foot, so I tried to protect it.

Karen was walking behind me and noticed my funny walk. She immediately asked what was going on. "Hey, J, sit down on this rock so I can look at your foot," she said.

I removed my shoes and socks and stretched my toes. "My shoes feel kind of tight," I told her.

"You must've grown a half size last month," she said.

Before I could even think about it, Karen had exchanged shoes with me. It felt good to have some space between my toes, but I knew my shoes must have been small on her. She didn't say a word about it.

"You going to be all right, Super K?" Dad asked.

She smiled. "Let's go. I'll be fine."

Soon the landscape changed again. We were at cloud level in the third zone, called the moorlands. Twenty-foot-tall rubbery stalks with rose-shaped tufts of wide, waxy leaves sprouting from the tops bordered the trail.

The fog cleared as we hiked along a ridge that became narrower and sharp as a knife's edge. There were steep drops on both sides. I didn't dare let my thoughts wander as I focused on the path ahead.

When we came to the end of the ridge and had a little bit more room to move, Samuel touched my shoulder and pointed toward the s ummit.

"Kilimanjaro," he said with a smile. "We'll be there in two or three days."

This from the same guy who'd initially thought it'd take

me seven days or more to reach the top! At that moment I knew two things: I had won Samuel's confidence, and I would make it to the summit.

Faiz and Nikki caught up to the rest of us, breathing really hard.

"This altitude's a killer," Faiz said after he'd rested a few minutes.

I hated that he and Nikki felt so bad. I pointed up like Samuel had done. "Look, there's the summit. It's awesome."

Faiz rested his arm on my shoulder. "That it is," he said. "That it is. I just hope I make it to the top."

It was raining when we arrived in the Barranco Camp, at 12,800 feet: a wide, flat area littered with the colorful tents of hikers arriving from the longer, easier Machame Trail. Lichen-painted rocks and small shrubs covered the entire ground. A mist hung over everything.

"How you doing?" Dad asked me as we sat down for lunch.

"Wet and a little cold, but feeling good," I said.

"Shall we push on to the next camp?" Karen asked.

I stared at the enormous volcanic-rock formation ahead of us. "Do we have to go over *that*?"

Samuel nodded. "It looks steep and scary but won't be hard for you."

His confidence in me made me feel like I could do it.

Then he said something that made me even more sure: "The porters have named you Little Lion. In Africa 'lion' means you're the king."

I loved that nickname.

The rain slowed down to a fine mist, and we got going again. Samuel led the way, and I was right behind him, followed by Karen and her continual words of encouragement. Dad brought up the end of the line behind Nikki and Faiz. We snaked our way up the steep rock wall single file, in front of about twenty climbers from other groups.

It was pretty fun searching for handholds and places to put my toes as I lifted myself up and over big rocks. Sometimes I wished my legs were as long as Dad's.

We came to a narrow part of the path that dropped off about a hundred feet. Samuel told us it was called the Kissing Rock. "The ledge is so skinny that you have to flatten against the wall and almost kiss it," he explained.

"Don't look down, little buddy," Karen said. "Just focus and you'll be fine."

I hugged the wall and walked my fingers along the rock, searching for a place to grab hold. I took a small step forward and then let go with the other hand. I repeated this all the way across, but I wasn't about to let my lips touch that rock if a bunch of strangers had been kissing it.

It was definitely worth the hour climb. From the top of the rock formation we could see the snowy face of Kibo, one of the three volcanoes that make up Kilimanjaro.

Dad gave Faiz and Nikki some Diamox, a medication that helps people breathe faster and get more air. Most climbers prefer to allow their bodies to adjust naturally to higher altitudes, but our friends were seriously hurting.

Five other climbers lumbered onto the top behind them, looking pretty ragged. A young guy in a baseball cap stared at me. "Who's this kid that got up here so fast?"

"Jordan," Karen said. "And he's only ten."

"You're kidding me," the guy said.

"He's going all the way to the top," she added.

The guy was even more amazed. "I didn't think they even allowed kids on the mountain. That must be some kind of a record."

"Could be," Dad answered.

Samuel nudged me, and I flashed a big smile. "*Jambo.*"

The climbers all laughed. "*Jambo,*" they responded.

"I wish you the best of luck and hope we stand on the summit together," the first man said.

I flashed him another smile. "Thanks. I'll see you there."

We headed down the gentler side of the wall before the trail turned up again. Our porters were right behind us. It must have been hard on them to be so young and already at work on the mountain to help feed their families, but that seemed to be the norm here.

I had tried again that morning to talk to a couple of the

younger ones, but all they did was stare at me. I asked Samuel why.

"Because you're so young. They don't understand why you're here," he told me. "Give them time to know you."

We soon left vegetation behind and entered the alpine zone—above the tree line. It was an alien landscape of dirt, boulders, and volcanic gravel with no plant life of any kind. The trail went on and on, an endless expanse of gray nothing. My mind started to drift, and I missed my mom and Makaela.

"How're you doing?" Karen asked.

"This part's no fun at all," I admitted. "I'm ready to reach the summit and go home."

Samuel must have heard me, and once again he said exactly the right words to give me a boost of confidence. "You're walking faster than most grown-ups," he said. "I know you're going to make it, and so do the porters. They're proud to be working for the Little Lion."

When we passed other climbers on the trail, they all asked about the little boy walking with Samuel and how he was doing.

I greeted them with "Jambo," and they all wished me good luck. That energized me even more. I lifted my tired head and walked a little more proudly.

We reached the third camp, Karanga, at 13,123 feet, at the end of our second day of climbing. Most people stayed at the

Barranco Camp, where we'd had lunch, so Karanga wasn't very crowded. The porters had already set up our tents. The wind was ferocious and cold. After hiking all day, all I wanted to do was crawl into my sleeping bag and listen to tunes.

I had just snuggled down when Faiz yelled, "Hey, Jordan, want to fly a kite?"

Was he kidding? I peeked outside and there he was, taking advantage of the crazy-strong wind to fly a really high-tech kite that you had to steer with both hands. "Where'd you get that?"

"Brought it with me."

"No freaking way." I tied my shoes and ran out to help him.

"Here, you take it."

I grabbed the strings, but the wind was so powerful I crashed the kite three tries in a row.

"You'll get it." Faiz stayed with me every step, his hand on the back of my jacket. "You're so light the wind could pick you up and blow you off the mountain," he said, and he wasn't joking.

Everyone came out to watch us laughing and racing around. I think we lightened the mood in the whole place.

After a few more tries, Faiz bent over with his hands on his knees. He was breathing really hard. "Sorry, but I'm done now."

He looked awful. I knew that in serious cases of altitude sickness a person's lungs could fill with fluid, which was deadly. "Dad!" I yelled.

He came over to check Faiz out. "You okay, bro?" he asked, searching Faiz's face for signs of serious trouble.

Faiz stood and nodded. "Just a little winded. I shouldn't have run so much."

He'd brought that kite all the way up the mountain just for me and had flown it even though he felt awful. "Thank you so, so much," I said. "You're awesome."

Dad brought the kite in. "Pretty cool, huh?" he asked me.

"Definitely. It made me less homesick."

It had been a big day. I could hardly stay awake through dinner, but I wasn't too tired to appreciate the great view of Kilimanjaro when the sky cleared that evening. The snow on the mountain shimmered and reflected in the moonlight. Twinkling stars created an amazing light show, and I watched for a while before crawling into my warm bag. One thing I did better than anyone else was sleep. On rocks, ice, uneven ground—you name it and I was out cold.

CHAPTER 7

The next morning Dad stuck his head inside my tent and asked, "Hey, buddy, ready for the summit?"

Here it was, the biggest day of my life so far, something I'd been working toward for almost a year—the day I would reach my first of the Seven Summits.

After a breakfast of African porridge, omelets, hot cocoa, and toast, we headed out just before dawn. This was it, no turning back.

We hiked up a narrow trail on loose, flat stones similar to slate. They rang out when I hit them with the tips of my hiking poles, almost like tinkling glass. Everything was covered with gray volcanic dust as we climbed a barren slope up onto the ridge where our trail merged with the route coming up from an easier route. Both led to the highest camp, Barafu, which meant 'ice camp' in Swahili.

We were entering the fifth of the five climatic zones on

Kilimanjaro—the summit zone. Windchill dropped the temperature to below freezing. The change in climate was the same as if we had walked from the equator to the North or South Pole.

Karen tipped her face toward the warm sun. "So what's your altimeter say, Little J?"

I checked the altimeter on my watch. "Wow, 15,287 feet—the highest I've ever been."

Barafu Camp was a ragged, rocky outcropping on the side of an exposed hill. We stopped for a snack. Kilimanjaro's summit loomed straight ahead of me. I dropped onto a rock and munched popcorn while staring at the summit. I was almost there.

Something ran over my foot. I jerked my leg back, wondering what creature could possibly exist up here. My eyes darted left and right. Then I broke out laughing. Chipmunks were scurrying in and out among the rocks. One sat with a paw on the toe of my boot, begging for some popcorn. He was so cute I wanted to feed him, but I knew that wasn't the right thing to do. It's a bad move to feed wild animals human food.

Faiz and Nikki were still really struggling with the altitude.

"My head's killing me, and Nikki's already thrown up twice this morning," Faiz said.

I was beginning to get really worried about them. "We can wait here until you feel better."

Faiz shook his head. "You need to go for it."

I looked at Dad and Karen. "Waiting one day to summit won't matter," I said.

Nikki's face was as gray as the barren landscape. "I want to go down now. I knew coming in that I might not make the summit," she said.

Samuel's gentle smile and voice seemed to calm her. "Two of the porters can leave at once and take you down to the Mweka Camp at ten thousand feet. You'll feel better immediately."

"I'm going with her," Faiz said, putting his pack on. "We'll wait for you and celebrate your successful summit when you join us."

I searched Samuel's face. "Will they really be okay?" I asked.

He nodded calmly. "They'll be fine."

I hugged them both before they left.

"Summit for us, too, Jordan," Faiz said.

We watched them go, and then Samuel turned to me. "How are you feeling?" he asked.

"A little tired, but good. No headache or anything."

"You still want to go on?"

"Yes," I answered.

I was ready to push for the summit. I'd been watching videos on YouTube about Everest climbers struggling to take one step and then another. They'd lift each foot like it was covered with bricks and then let it fall like it was too heavy to hold up any longer. I decided to give it a try.

As soon as I did, Karen broke out laughing. "Okay, Jordan,

stop with the Everest steps. You're not going to make it to the top like that."

We walked single file up a path that got steeper and steeper, with endless switchbacks going up, up, up on mounds of small loose rocks called scree. As the climb to Kilimanjaro's peak became more difficult, I just kept putting one foot in front of the other. The farther along we got, the icier and snowier the climb became. The wind picked up to gale force. Suddenly this so-called easy mountain wasn't so easy after all. The higher we went, the slower we walked, having to stop more often for short rests.

Every fifteen minutes I'd ask Dad, "How much longer? Are we there yet?"

And he'd answer, "Just keep going a few more minutes."

The air was growing thinner and thinner. It was harder and harder to breathe.

At around eighteen thousand feet I hit a wall.

It was cold. I couldn't breathe well. My legs ached and my back hurt, and we weren't even near the top. This was more difficult than anything I had imagined. Exhausted, frustrated, and homesick, I tried to keep walking, but tears were suddenly streaming down my cheeks. Samuel looked back and saw that I was crying.

He stopped, walked to me, and gave me a hug. "It's okay," he said in a calm, soothing voice. "You're the strongest kid I've ever seen. You're going at an unbelievable pace. I'm extremely proud to be your guide." He leaned back and stared at me with his kind eyes. "You have shown great respect for Kilimanjaro. The mountain wants you to climb it."

I knew Samuel's job was to take care of everyone he guided up this mountain, but I could tell he genuinely wanted me to succeed. His encouragement gave me confidence and made me want to trust in myself.

"He's right, Little J," Karen said. "The mountain wants you to climb it."

Dad sat down next to me. "Nothing's ever good all the time, Jordan. If it's ninety percent good and ten percent bad, you have to keep reminding yourself about the ninety percent. It's moments like this, when you feel you can't take another step, that separate success from failure." He helped me to my feet and gave me the same upbeat smile I'd see when he'd set off on adventure races. "Time to suck it up and climb, dude."

I understood. I swallowed my tears and started out again. The final switchbacks were extra steep and really hard. We passed climbers at the side of the trail, sitting or lying down and holding their heads. But for some reason I kept getting stronger the higher we went. My heart was pounding but not from the altitude. I knew the summit was within striking distance.

I got to what I thought was the top of Kili and shouted, "We made it!"

Samuel bit his lips to keep from smiling and slowly shook

his head. "Kilimanjaro has three volcanic cones on top. We're at Stella Point on Kibo, the highest of the three volcanoes, but we have another forty minutes to the official summit—Kibo's Uhuru Peak."

I couldn't believe what I was hearing. Not only was I totally exhausted, but I felt silly for having been fooled by a false summit. Still, I'd never been a quitter and wasn't going to give up now. So I kept following Samuel, trying to match his stride.

And before long there it was—the wooden sign at the summit that I'd seen in so many Google images. Suddenly my legs weren't tired, my feet didn't hurt, and I didn't feel the wind biting my face. We were on snow now, and I was tripping in other people's footprints, but I didn't care. I headed straight for that sign. Karen ran ahead to make sure she got photos of me reaching the summit. I got to the sign next before Dad and Samuel.

Once we'd all made it, I found myself overcome with emotion. My dad and Karen were too. We all hugged each other, crying.

We were standing on the roof of Africa, at 19,341 feet, looking down on an endless ocean of white fluffy clouds. It had been less than a year since I'd told Dad I wanted to climb Kilimanjaro. Now I'd done it—by the hardest route, and faster than anyone had estimated. Once we'd hugged it out, the excitement of it all set in, and we started hopping around and laughing. It was the craziest feeling I'd ever experienced.

CHAPTER 8

It was incredibly windy and frigidly cold up at the top of Kilimanjaro—minus 5 degrees Fahrenheit. While we were hiking it hadn't seemed that cold, but as soon as we stopped, you could feel it. Shivering, we put our hats on and zipped our jackets up tight, and Samuel took a picture of us in front of that beautiful wooden sign that read CONGRATULATIONS! YOU ARE NOW AT UHURU PEAK, TANZANIA, 5895M. AMS. AFRICA'S HIGHEST POINT. WORLD'S HIGHEST FREE-STANDING MOUNTAIN. ONE OF WORLD'S LARGEST VOLCANOES. WELCOME.

"Okay, now, Jordan," Karen said, "time for sponsor pictures."

One of the things we did in exchange for the free climbing gear and financial support from our sponsors was allow them to use pictures of us with their equipment in their advertising and publicity. I held up a few banners and one of my Salomon shoes while Karen snapped photos of me, and then we were ready to head down the mountain. We descended to Barafu Camp and stopped for a quick lunch.

Descending wasn't as much fun as I'd thought it would be, and it was taking forever. So after lunch I ran and slid on the loose gravel. Dad and Karen could hardly keep up. It was dark by the time the porters dismantled the few tents they had set up for us at Barafu and caught up to us and then passed us by. They were incredible. Fifty pounds on their heads, in flip-flops, and wearing no headlamps, they raced through a maze of boulders and volcanic rock. Dad and Karen, the elite athletes, were stunned by the power and agility the porters showed running in the dark.

Coming down the mountain, we experienced the same change in vegetation zones, only in the reverse and at a much quicker pace. We didn't have to stop to acclimatize. From the glacier on the summit we descended through an alpine desert, the foggy moors, the heather zone, and finally the rain forest.

Running down more than nine thousand vertical feet took its toll. I was completely wiped out by the time we reached Mweka Camp, where Faiz and Nikki ran out to meet us.

"Did you make it?" Nikki asked.

My smile told them all they needed to know.

"Jordan amazed me," Dad said. "He was so tired and was even tempted to give up at one point, but then he managed to find something inside himself to keep going."

"I set a goal and wasn't going to quit, no matter what," I said.

Karen laughed. "As soon as he saw that summit sign, he was unstoppable. We could barely keep up."

Faiz put his arm around my shoulder as we walked into camp. "I knew you were made for great things."

"How about you?" I asked. "How do you guys feel?"

"Samuel was right," Nikki said. "As soon as we moved to a lower altitude, we were fine."

That was a huge relief, and so was the fact that not only had the porters already set up camp, but they had food waiting for us—popcorn and hot soup. I was addicted to their popcorn, which was for some reason the best popcorn I'd ever eaten, even though it had no salt or butter.

I sat there munching and taking in the hustle and bustle of the Mweka Camp. Climbers, porters, and guides headed in both directions. I was shocked to discover that people actually knew who I was. Word had spread all over the mountain about a ten-year-old climbing stronger and faster than most adults. No one could believe that I'd made it to the top and back down to Mweka Camp in three days instead of the usual six or seven days for the Umbwe Route. Everyone I met wanted a picture with me. It was kind of cool to realize that other people recognized my accomplishment.

Even better, the barrier between the porters and me disappeared. We hung out that night exchanging stories of life in Africa compared to America. It was awesome. I learned that even though they didn't have much in comparison with my life in Big Bear, they were happy and felt they were living a good life. It was an evening I knew I would never forget.

The next morning we had a two-hour walk back to the main gate through the lush rain forest. After the barren gray rock up above, I appreciated the dense, mossy, green vegetation more than I had three days earlier.

We left Mount Kilimanjaro National Park through the Mweka Gate, but first we stopped to sign the register and get our certificates to prove that we had climbed the mountain successfully. Those who made it to Uhuru received golden certificates; those who stopped at Stella Point got green ones. All our names were added into a book.

"Look at that, Little J," Karen whispered. "They listed you as the world record holder for this mountain's youngest climber, at age ten."

I hadn't really thought about setting a world record, and I suspected some younger African kid might have summited before me with his dad without anyone bothering to record it, but it was still pretty cool.

I called my mom as soon as we got back to the hotel in Arusha. I told her all about the climb, that I missed her, and that I'd be home soon. But we had one more thing to do before we left Africa, and that was visit the Ngorongoro Conservation Area.

The Ngorongoro Conservation Area is considered to be one of the seven natural wonders of Africa. Almost all the animal species native to East Africa can be found in the huge crater at its center. There are nearly thirty thousand animals living in about one hundred square miles. I had been dying to visit.

We chartered a driver and a safari bus with a removable roof and took a winding road two thousand feet down into the largest volcanic crater in the world. I leaned over the driver's seat. "There aren't any fences or gates. Don't the animals ever just walk out?"

"They could, but why would they? Everything they need is right here."

"Jordan, look," Karen said excitedly. "Zebras."

"Wow, look at that!"

"The stripes are different on every single animal, just like fingerprints," the driver explained.

We didn't go a mile without seeing some kind of herd—elephants, wildebeests, buffalo, hippos, or warthogs. It was game-viewing paradise, Noah's Ark in a giant bowl. I felt a little like my hero, Crocodile Hunter Steve Irwin, and I was still on the prowl for rhinos. They are critically endangered, and some subspecies of white rhino are already extinct. The total number of black rhinos in the wild is slowly increasing, but they're still scarce. I just had to see one, and I did—five of them!

The bus stopped to watch a pride of lions lazing near the road. A pair of male lions with full bellies walked our way and used the bus for a shade tree. I could've stuck my hand out the window to pet them, but I wanted to keep my fingers.

"What do we do now?" I asked.

"Wait until they decide to move on," the driver answered.

I didn't mind waiting. After all, I had gotten a chance to see the big five game animals—lion, leopard, Cape buffalo, elephant, and rhino—all in one day.

While we waited, thoughts of the next mountain were brewing in my head. I wanted to go to Australia, not just to climb its highest peak but also to see crocodiles, kangaroos, and koalas. Maybe I'd even get to meet Steve Irwin in person.

CHAPTER 9

After visiting the crater, we flew home and went directly to the hospital. We'd found out that my dad's father, Papa Zona, had suffered a heart attack and had undergone triple-bypass surgery while we were in Africa.

The doctor said everything was fine, and he was recovering, but it was still hard seeing my grandfather in a hospital bed with a tube in his nose. He had always been active and strong, and he'd passed down his sense of healthy mind and body to my dad, too.

While he rested, I told him all about my adventures in Africa. He always wanted to hear all the details about the things I had accomplished, and he was always proud of me. I was thankful he was going to be okay and hoped that my words would help him recover faster.

As soon as we knew Papa Zona was going to be all right, we headed back to Big Bear. Everyone welcomed me home with open arms, and it seemed like all of a sudden I was a celebrity. I got tons of attention, and Judi Bowers, the editor of the local newspaper, the *Big Bear Grizzly* did a story about me. KBHR radio interviewed me and so did Channel 6 TV news. All my friends saw me on television, and that was pretty dang cool. One of the best things was getting to travel to Los Angeles for a radio interview there. Even climbing magazines wrote articles about me.

Reaching the summit of Kili was of course a big deal to me, but I was shocked by how much other people cared too. It was pretty surreal.

Then something really wild happened. Martha Stewart had heard about me setting the record for youngest person to climb Kilimanjaro. She had climbed the mountain herself, and she asked me to be on her show to talk about the experience.

We flew to New York City for the taping. I could usually sleep anywhere, but the night before the show I lay awake in my hotel room, going over the names of the camps and their elevations, the vegetation zones we'd passed through, and details about Samuel and the incredible porters. I wanted to be prepared for my first national television appearance.

The next day we got to the studio, and before I knew it I was backstage waiting for my cue. What if I did or said something stupid? Made a total fool of myself?

I heard Martha say my name and I took in a huge breath.

The woman who'd done my makeup stood next to me. "Just wave to the audience while you walk toward Martha. Try not to look at the cameras. It's like sitting at a kitchen table and talking to a friend at home."

Martha Stewart, a friend at home? Not quite. But I exhaled slowly and strolled toward Martha's table. Out of the corner of my eye I spotted a camera pointed directly at me. Nervous sweat gathered at my temples as I smiled and said, "Hello."

Martha asked two quick questions about my climb, and I didn't screw up my answers. Then I got to relax and listen while she told the story about her climb, and then she gave me a four-season tent as a gift.

While it was cool to meet Martha, there were other celebrities I wanted to meet more—like Steve Irwin. Unfortunately, less than two months after I summited Kili, before we could even start planning our trip to Australia, the Crocodile Hunter died. I was devastated. My hero had survived encounters with poisonous snakes, crocodiles, and tigers only to be killed by a stingray while snorkeling at the Great Barrier Reef.

I was disappointed that I wouldn't get to meet him when I was in Australia, but I still wanted to make Kosciuszko our next climb.

One morning, not long after we got back from Africa, I sat at the breakfast counter as Dad whipped up a batch of his killer waffles.

"I've been thinking about Kosciuszko," I told him. "I'd like to go there next."

He poured batter into the waffle iron. "Oookaaay, and why did you think we won't?"

"It's pretty far to go just to climb a hill that just about anybody can handle."

The tallest peak on Australia wouldn't be a climb like Kilimanjaro. Mount Kosciuszko would be more like a weekend stroll. The altitude of 7,310 feet is only slightly higher than in Big Bear, and you can even drive most of the way and hike the last five miles if you want to—not that I would have ever considered driving.

Dad closed the waffle iron, leaned on the counter, and looked me in the eyes. "Listen, this is your dream, and it's an awesome adventure. Super K and I will do whatever it takes to make it happen."

"But what about your adventure races?" I asked. "Won't you have to miss out on some things while we're in Australia?"

"These are your years," Dad told me.

Dad and Karen were both willing to put their own goals and adventure racing on the back burner so that I could accomplish my dream. I knew that not many kids were so lucky.

Before I knew it, we were booking our trip to the land down under for spring break, when I had enough time off school to make it to Australia and back. And with the help of our sponsors and sales of the Seven Summit T-shirts, as well as a new Kosciuszko one Karen had designed, we had the funds to get there.

Australia, I thought, *here I come.*

THE SHORTEST CLIMB:
AUSTRALIA'S
MOUNT
KOSCIUSZKO,
7,310 FEET

Average numbers of climbers
per year: 10,000

April 5, 2007, age 10

CHAPTER 10

The following April we flew into Sydney and then took a flight to Canberra, the closest airport to Kosciuszko. We met up with Jorge Elage, a Brazilian friend of ours and a fellow adventure racer who wanted to climb with us. I'd known Jorge for years. He was like a brother to me.

We entered Kosciuszko National Park at night under a full moon so bright that we didn't need headlamps. We were planning a full-moon night summit, which was totally cool, but we had camping gear and enough food to spend the night on the mountain if we needed to.

Aboriginals were probably the first to climb Kosciuszko. The first white man to record seeing the mountain was back in 1824. Sixteen years later a Polish explorer reached Australia's highest summit and named it after a famous countryman, Tadeusz Kosciuszko, who helped the Americans defeat the British in the American Revolution.

We had hiked up the summit trail, which was also a service road, to just above the tree line. Then fog, rain, and cold wind rolled in.

After a little while I was pretty miserable. "Let's go back to the hotel and try again tomorrow," I suggested.

Jorge covered his head with his jacket. "I'm with you. Let's get out of here."

We were just about to turn around when out of the mist appeared an unbelievable hut, like something from a fairy tale. It had stone walls, windows on each side, and a red roof made of flat metal sheets. Dad shone a light on a sign next to the front door:

Seaman's Hut. For day use and emergency overnight shelter only.

He looked at me. "Suppose this is an emergency?"

Technically it wasn't, but we all wanted out of the wind and the rain. We'd never expected such awful weather on what should have been an easy summit.

Dad grinned and opened the door. The place had two small rooms, a foyer filled with firewood, and a cast-iron stove. I was so happy to see it.

"Jordan, change into dry clothes while I get the fire going," Dad said.

I was happy to get out of my wet clothes. Jorge did the

same. The fire wasn't really throwing any heat yet, but we already felt better.

There were some emergency supplies of dried food, but we had brought our own and left those for someone who would need it more than we did.

Karen filled tortillas with turkey and cheese and laid them on top of the stove to melt. Nothing had ever tasted so good. We topped them off with fruit while she read about the hut.

"'In Memory of W. Laurie Seaman, who with Evan Hayes perished in a blizzard August 1928,'" she said, reading from a plaque.

Apparently, Seaman died nearby waiting for Hayes, unaware that he had already frozen to death. Seaman's body was discovered on September 9. Hayes, who died above Lake Cootapatamba, a glacial lake 2,600 feet from the summit, wasn't found until 1930. Seaman's family built the hut in the hope that no one else would die in the same way. Shelter makes all the difference in a storm.

Wrapped in my down sleeping bag, I felt lucky to be warm and toasty inside, where the thick stone walls kept out the cold wind.

The next morning Dad wiggled my foot. "Time to get up."

I pulled the sleeping bag over my head and buried myself like a desert frog. "It's too cold out there. I'm staying here until it's warmer."

"It could get worse," Karen said. "And we don't have that many days in Australia. You want to see Steve Irwin's zoo, right?"

Australia Zoo is also called "Home of the Crocodile Hunter." Steve Irwin dedicated himself to making it one of the best wildlife conservation facilities in the world. Perhaps especially now that he was no longer alive, I wanted to see what he'd helped build.

The idea of finishing the climb so we'd have time to go to the zoo got me motivated. I unzipped my sleeping bag and sat up, but I kept it wrapped around me while I ate some oatmeal Karen had brought.

We headed out after breakfast through freezing rain and wind so strong it almost blew me over. After the longest two hours ever, we reached the top of Kosciuszko.

It wasn't exactly what I'd expected.

I'd dreamed of gazing hundreds and hundreds of miles across Australia from that peak, but we were in the middle of a thick fog soup and couldn't see much of anything.

Even though I was a little underwhelmed by the view, I was proud to have reached my second summit. There was a stone pillar about five feet tall, shaped like a pyramid but flat on top. I climbed up and Karen snapped a picture of me leaning into a wind so strong it held me up.

Once all our pictures were taken, Dad suggested we head back to town for a hot meal. We took a different route down, just for a change of scenery. This time we had to cross the Snowy River.

"Take my hand," Dad said.

"I can do it," I insisted. I jumped from slippery rock to slippery rock, something I had done many times on rivers and streams in California. This time I landed in a cold splash. So much for being able to cross it myself.

I raced to the car and climbed in. I changed my wet clothes, and we drove to a nearby town for pizza and hot soup. By the time we finished, it had stopped raining, so we checked out the town and—of course—stopped in the local climbing/ski shop.

"Hey, I know you," said the owner. "You're the kid that climbed Kilimanjaro."

"Huh?" How was it possible that someone halfway around the world knew who I was?

He laughed. "C'mon, I own an outdoor shop. You were big news in climbing magazines."

I guess I shouldn't have been surprised. I had gotten all kinds of press and publicity after I'd climbed Kilimanjaro. But having a total stranger from the other side of the world recognize me was a whole new experience.

The next day we took a train to the Australia Zoo and I raced to the elephant exhibit. You could actually feed an elephant here! The zookeeper showed me how to hold a banana out.

The elephant's trunk stretched toward my palm, and I could hear her breathing in the scent. Then she quickly took the banana with her trunk, curled her trunk into her mouth, and swallowed the banana, skin and all.

Next we went to where kangaroos were just hanging out on the grass. They weren't even in an enclosure.

"Remember, they said not to surround a roo," Karen reminded me. "If they can't hop backward to escape, they feel trapped."

I knelt next to one and gently patted its neck. Then I rubbed behind its big ears. The hair was so soft, and the roo had the longest eyelashes I had ever seen.

There were koalas nearby too, snoozing in a tree. Just like me, they can sleep anywhere—except they sleep almost twenty hours a day. Even I can't sleep that much.

After we'd seen all we could at the zoo, we headed out. On our way I spotted a painting on the wall by the gift shop with a life-size photo of Steve Irwin leaping straight up into the air. The caption read *Crikey! How high can you go?*

I had two summits down and six to go. So I guess I'd have to see.

THE SKI MOUNTAIN:
EUROPE'S
MOUNT ELBRUS,
18,510 FEET

AVERAGE NUMBERS OF CLIMBERS
PER YEAR: 500

JULY 11, 2007, AGE 10

WORLD RECORD

CHAPTER 11

Two weeks after we summited Kosciuszko, Dad and Karen came in from a fifty-mile mountain bike ride, and instead of grabbing a sports drink or a shower, Dad grabbed the world atlas and slapped it down on the counter next to where I was doing homework.

"Okaaay, I don't think you're ready for Denali, Aconcagua, or Everest yet," he said, opening to a map of the world. "Antarctica and New Guinea are too expensive right now."

"What about Elbrus?" I asked. "It's one of the easiest."

Mount Elbrus, in the Caucasus Mountains, is in the southernmost part of Russia, near the border of the country of Georgia. Like Kili, it's a dormant volcano. An Imperial Russian Army scientific expedition reached the lower of Elbrus's two summits in 1829, but no one climbed to the highest peak for another forty-five years, until an English expedition made it to the summit in 1874.

Mountaineering became a popular sport in the years when Russia was part of the Soviet Union. The Soviets even built a cable car system to take visitors as high as 11,500 feet. But after that you had to climb.

I opened my laptop and searched for a picture of Elbrus. I knew that it had nasty, unpredictable weather, but it didn't look all that difficult. "Looks like an oversize ski hill to me. Not much of a climb."

"Exactly," Dad said. "It's an easy number three if you still want to do this. Up to you."

I didn't have to think twice. "Of course I do. You know I don't give up on things."

"Then how about on summer break, Super K?" Dad asked.

She nodded. "Okay. I'll start designing a new T-shirt."

I don't know how much cash we raised selling the T-shirts Karen designed, but we certainly lifted spirits around town. People were excited to hear about my next summit attempt. Rick Herrick, the owner of the local radio station and the former mayor of Big Bear, bought a few, as well as people from local ski shops, the gym, and restaurants—and of course lots of good friends.

Elbrus wasn't a mountain that required you to hire porters and guides like Kilimanjaro, and Dad and Karen had tons of experience in leading themselves in adventure races all over the world. So Karen booked our flights and first night in Moscow and we planned to wing it from there. She was confident we could handle all the details on our own. "It's worked in the past," she said.

We continued our training for the next four or five months—there was no way Dad and Karen were going to let up on that. We ran, hiked, and biked. And since we were heading to Elbrus, I also worked on using crampons and my ice axe. We were so busy that the time flew by. The next thing I knew, we were getting ready to fly to Russia, and I was going to be there for my eleventh birthday. What a present!

Our first challenge, after a long flight to Moscow, was catching a small plane to Mineralnye Vody, the nearest airport to Elbrus.

We asked directions until we found the right airline counter and bought tickets. Crossing the tarmac to the very small, very old plane, I wondered about our safety.

The metal stairs creaked and wobbled under my feet. "How will this thing get off the ground?" I whispered. "I think it's held together by duct tape."

Dad and Karen shared my concerns, but this was the only way to Elbrus.

Most of the seats were broken. The flight attendant didn't speak any English, but I figured she was describing the usual safety procedures as we got ready for takeoff. No one who could understand paid her any attention. Passengers walked in the aisles during takeoff, and the overhead bins kept flying open. When we did finally land in Mineralnye Vody, the air brakes were so loud they sounded like a rocket blast. It was a good thing I didn't have a fear of flying, or I would have been terrified the whole time.

The tarmac in this small town was filled with worn-out, old planes like ours. A broken-down school bus towed by a tractor took us to a cinder-block warehouse with nothing but a luggage belt. The arrival and departure boards didn't work, and it was cold, even inside.

While Karen waited for the luggage, Dad said, "Come on, Jordan, let's find a car to take us to Nalchik for our permits."

Nalchik was about sixty miles away from where we currently were, and it is the access point for Mount Elbrus.

I looked around me in confusion at all the Russian signs. No one on our plane had seemed to speak English, and I didn't have high hopes for the people of Mineralnye Vody knowing the language either. "How? We don't speak Russian," I said.

Dad rested his arm on my shoulder. "Don't be afraid to ask questions just because you don't speak the language. People always try to help."

I followed him outside. I felt like we were lost in the middle of nowhere, but Dad didn't hesitate. Flashing a confident smile, he walked right up to a Russian man standing by the door and used body language to communicate we needed a taxi.

The guy called someone on a cell phone, then smiled and nodded. I guess that meant a car was on its way.

We had no choice but to wait and hope. Dad paced in front of the building. He wasn't nervous. He was just always on the move. Karen flipped through a Russian phrasebook, trying to figure out how to say a few words, and I listened to my iPod and people watched. A taxi arrived forty minutes later.

Dad pointed to Nalchik on a map. The driver smiled and nodded, and we piled into the backseat. Soon after leaving the airport, Dad used his own version of sign language to let the guy know we wanted to stop for lunch and invited him to join us.

The restaurant was filled with cigarette smoke. A group of men sat at a table, talking and laughing. Dad went to the bathroom and returned shaking his head.

"You won't believe what's lying in the hall. I had to walk around a bloody cow's head just to get to the bathroom." He sat back down. "I think I'm going vegetarian, at least in this restaurant."

We all went vegetarian after hearing that. Then we drove through the countryside, passing lots of cattle that seemed to be roaming free, and large deserted-looking concrete-block buildings.

There were several police checkpoints along the way. Our driver seemed a little nervous, especially when the police-men at one of the stops pulled all our gear out of the car and searched every item thoroughly.

My stomach tightened. "What're they looking for?"

"Don't know," Dad said.

Then they hauled Dad inside one of those concrete-block buildings. Through the window I could hear shouted questions in Russian and the low rumble of Dad's calm voice. I couldn't hear his words, but I know he was trying to tell them that we were tourists, planning to climb Elbrus.

The Russians kept yelling.

My hands started to shake and I broke out into a sweat. I flinched every time I saw one of those Russian police officers shout a new question at Dad. "What do they want?" I asked Karen. I wanted to sound as calm as Dad, but my voice was high and shrill.

"Don't worry," Karen said, taking a deep breath. "Everything's fine."

From the backseat of the car I could see the Russians banging our passports on the table like something was horribly wrong.

Karen explained that security was on high alert because Russia had been in a war with a nearby country, Chechnya.

"But that doesn't have anything to do with us," I said. "We're just here for Elbrus."

"I know, but the Russian police are suspicious of everyone right now," she explained.

I wrapped my arms across my stomach to keep it from hurting and slid down in the seat, waiting for my dad.

Finally he opened the car door and climbed inside.

"What did they want?" Karen asked when he got settled.

"No clue. I didn't understand a word," he said with a shrug.

"Why were they slamming our passports down like that?" I asked.

"Still no clue," Dad answered. "I guess they finally decided we were so pathetic that they let me go."

Intimidation never works on Dad. He looks fear in the eye, climbs over it, and moves on. I wanted to be that way too, but still I held my breath every time we came to another police checkpoint.

Finally we reached Nalchik. Our driver took us to the permit building and agreed to wait.

There were a bunch of people inside.

"Does anyone speak English?" Karen asked.

A pretty girl in her twenties came to our rescue. "Yes, a little."

"How do we take care of all the paperwork?"

"Each of you needs to fill out six documents, but the office closes in five minutes," she explained.

"We have to do it tonight," Dad said with that wide grin. "Will you please help us?"

"I'm a guide and must take care of my clients first. Didn't your tour leader do all of this for you?"

"We're here on our own," Karen said.

She raised her eyebrows. "Really? Hardly anyone does that, especially with such a young boy. He's not climbing Elbrus, is he?"

Dad put on a calm face even though I knew questions like that irritated him. "He'll be fine."

She smiled. "I will do my best."

I watched her walk to a back room and speak in Russian to a man who worked there. He peered around the doorway at us and nodded.

The woman returned a couple of minutes later. "He will stay after closing to process your papers. In the meantime, fill out all of these forms."

When all was taken care of, it was about dinnertime. It had been a long, exhausting afternoon. We thanked the woman on our way out of the permit office and climbed back into our taxi.

"See," said my dad, turning to me, "we didn't need to know Russian. Believe that things will work out, and they do. Most people are kind if given half a chance."

Our taxi driver drove through many small villages and farm towns on our way up the valley to the country town at the foot of Mount Elbrus. Along the way we passed many of the gray, deserted cement buildings we'd come to expect in Russia. There was dead silence, and there were no lights anywhere. I dozed off and slept until the car pulled to a stop in front of a hotel at the base of the ski area.

"Looks like there are only a couple of hotels in town," Dad said.

"The girl at the permit office warned us that there wouldn't be any rooms," Karen added.

"Won't hurt to try," Dad said, ever the optimist. "Everybody out!"

All I wanted was something to eat and a warm bed. I dragged myself into the small lobby, which was paneled with pinewood and had giant stuffed animal heads mounted above the fireplace. They all had horns—deer, moose, elk, and ibex—and they seemed to be staring down at us. It was kind of spooky.

The taxi driver helped us bring our things inside and spoke to the woman at the front desk, but she looked right past him and addressed us in English. After having heard nothing but Russian except for the girl at the permit office, we were surprised.

She leaned over the counter and looked down at me. "Hi, my name is Sweetie. And what would you like?"

"We've been traveling all day," Karen said, "and desperately need a room."

Sweetie smiled at me. She was very pretty. "I happen to have one left just for you."

I was so thankful for our luck. Dad gave our taxi driver a good tip for being so nice, and we said good-bye and headed for our room. I couldn't wait to crawl into bed.

The room was cold and drafty and smelled of mothballs. The floor creaked every time you stepped on it. But I was just happy to have a bed. The blankets were so tiny we had to use our sleeping bags, and Dad's feet hung off the end of the mattress. Still, I crashed as soon as I hit the pillow.

When daylight came, we explored the town. We needed time to organize our gear and buy water before we could begin our climb, so we'd be spending at least one more night at the hotel.

Sweetie took an interest in me once she found out that I was there to climb Elbrus and that it was part of a quest to climb the Seven Summits.

"Jordan, if you can have whatever food you want to celebrate climbing Elbrus, what will it be?" she asked at dinner on our second night.

That was easy. "Spaghetti."

Sweetie promised to have it ready for me after my climb, and I was already looking forward to a plate piled high with warm noodles, tomato sauce, and cheese.

Before I could get too excited, though, Karen and I both noticed that Dad was holding his head in his hands.

"What's wrong?" Karen asked.

"It feels like my sinuses are about to explode."

Hearing my dad complain was not something that happened often, so I started to get worried.

Karen moved next to him. "When did this start?"

"Two days ago. I thought it would go away, but it's getting worse. I feel like crap," he admitted.

For a minute I thought we might have to forego the climb altogether, but I should have known my dad would never give up that easily.

"Let's reconsider our strategy," he said.

"It's not a really long mountain," Karen said. "Let's take it easy and go at your pace. Then we'll see how you feel and decide what to do."

Dad nodded, but I could see that he was in a lot of pain. "Do you really think you can summit feeling like this?" I asked.

"Let's push on," Dad said. "And see how it goes."

We worked as a team—always. I knew that if Dad couldn't make the summit, none of us would.

CHAPTER 12

I went to bed that night worried about Dad and worried that he wouldn't be able to make the climb we'd traveled all this way for. But when I woke up the next morning, Dad was peering out the window of our hotel room. He must've heard me wrestling with my sleeping bag.

"Hey, Little J," he said, sounding surprisingly chipper. "Want to climb today?"

I was so happy that he was feeling better, and that all our hard work to get here hadn't been for nothing, I practically jumped out of bed. "I am *so* ready."

Karen was already up, too. "But Paul, how do you feel?"

He waved off her concerns about his sinuses. "The weather's good, but that can change fast. We need to go now."

I knew that Dad was doing this for me. But I trusted him when he said he felt good enough to climb. So I pulled on my thermal underwear and then the rest of my gear.

After a Russian breakfast of bread, cheese, scrambled eggs, oatmeal, and tea, we headed for Elbrus. At its base there was an old Soviet-style ski resort with a dilapidated tram to get skiers and snowboarders up to the slopes.

We boarded the tram and rode from 7,700 feet to 11,500 feet. No one walked this hill, and it was the norm for climbers to start from the top of the tram.

When we got off, Karen looked at the map. "It's a twelve-hundred foot climb to Barrels Camp from here." Barrels was the base camp from where we'd start our climb to the summit. Base camp is exactly that—a base of operations.

"There's the chairlift," Dad said, pointing.

Most of the people who were on the tram with us headed straight for the lift. But they were either sightseers or skiers. Climbers skipped the chairlift and started hiking from the top of the tram.

My insides were doing handsprings as I put on crampons and made sure my ice axe was handy for an emergency.

Karen chuckled at me. "You probably don't need those yet."

"I am not going to be one of those *unprepared* guys."

Dad waved me forward. "Then lead on."

About an hour and a half later we reached the Barrels Camp. I thought Barrels was a pretty funny name for a base camp until I saw it. The camp was literally made of barrels—old metal fuel barrels painted red and lying on their sides, converted into buildings. Each building was a little longer than a boxcar, with the ceiling maybe ten feet tall in the center.

"Hey, check this out." I stepped inside one. It had windows, six bunk beds with mattresses and pillows, an electric heater, outlets, and lights.

We could have paid to stay in one of the barrel buildings ourselves that night, but we had planned to save the money and set up camp ourselves. Plus we weren't nearly ready to stop for the day.

As we hiked past, I saw a bunch of kids getting off the chairlift, carrying snowboards, and then climbing into snowcats—truck-size vehicles that could carry ten or twelve people and were meant to drive on snow.

"Must be some kind of summer camp, I guess," Karen said. "Elbrus is a year-round ski area."

The thought of screaming down the mountain jumped into my head. "I could *so* ski that. Why didn't we bring our skis?" I asked.

"You know the deal," Dad said. "We came to climb a mountain, not ski. We travel light and fast."

"We could've slept in the Barrels and carried skis instead of hauling camping gear," I answered.

"Sorry, Jordan. Maybe on another mountain," he answered.

"Which one? Everest? That would be totally cool!" I said. "I read about one guy who skied down it." I was getting crazy excited. "Or maybe Vinson in Antarctica—there's plenty of snow there—or Denali in Alaska."

Karen interrupted. "Easy. Let's just get up this mountain first."

I dropped it then. Plus I could tell Dad still felt lousy: His smile had disappeared, and there were circles below his eyes. But he was never one to give up easily.

We moved on. I was the leader again. There was no way I could get us lost on Elbrus. It was a big, open, snowy mountain. There was no scrambling through jungles, like at the beginning of Kilimanjaro. The top of Elbrus was almost one thousand feet lower in elevation than Kili, but more challenging because of all the snowfall it received. The weather could get seriously nasty.

As the lead, my job was to set a steady pace. I climbed hard and fast. I was a little short of breath from the altitude, but I'd come for an adventure. Then I spotted something reflecting sunlight on the side of the mountain.

I zeroed in on the metal roof of a two-story building. As we got closer, I saw that it was another camp. The place could easily sleep thirty or forty people, and it looked to have a kitchen inside too.

We paused to try to figure out what to do next. We could spend the night there, but we had the energy to go farther. Dad checked out the map.

"It looks like a lot of climbers summit from the Pastukhova Rocks," he said. "Let's camp there."

The Pastukhova Rocks are the highest rocky outcrop on

a lava ridge running down the mountain, and a landmark for climbers.

Karen's fingers traced the route upward. "They're at fifteen thousand feet. We're only at twelve thousand five hundred feet now. We should acclimatize first, especially with the way you feel."

The altitude was putting extra pressure on Dad's sinuses, and one of his molars had started to hurt too.

"I'll get by. We're running out of daylight. I'm game for going to the rocks and seeing how we feel," he said.

I took two steps forward. "I'm not breathing too hard. Let's go."

"No headache or nausea?" Karen asked me.

"None."

Karen frowned, not completely convinced Dad was up for it. "Okay. We can keep going, but only on the condition that we come back down if anyone has altitude problems. Agreed?"

Dad and I nodded and we set off.

He set the pace now because he was moving slower than usual. We stopped to rest often so he could gather himself.

We took a long switchback to the right a few hundred yards, to the left several hundred more, then to the right again. It was exhausting for me. I couldn't imagine how my dad was handling it when he was in such pain. So I was relieved, for his sake more than mine, to see a line of boulders strewn across the mountain as if they'd spilled out of a giant's pocket—the Pastukhova Rocks.

Dad sat down on a flat rock, his elbows on his knees as he cradled his head in his hands once more. I removed his pack one arm at a time and got out his water bottle.

He looked up at me as I handed it to him. "Thanks, J Man."

He'd called me J Man instead of Little J, my usual nickname. I hoped that meant he saw that I was growing up.

"You can rest," I told him, the new nickname giving me a sudden sense of responsibility. "Karen and I will make camp and fix something to eat."

Karen and I found a small dirt clearing, so we didn't have to set up on rocks or snow. I was excited to try out my new tent from Martha Stewart. As soon as it was ready, I inflated dad's Therm-a-rest pad and rolled a jacket into a pillow. He crawled in to lie down, and I spread his sleeping bag over him. It was kind of nice taking care of him for once instead of being the one everyone else took care of. Karen made some hot tea, soup, and sandwiches.

As soon as the sun went down, the cold bit right through my jacket. I crawled into my down bag, zipped it all the way to my chin, and pulled the hood over my head. I'd camped in snow back home, but not at fifteen thousand feet. I had learned that the higher you go and the lower the air pressure, the colder it gets. For every thousand feet of elevation, the temperature drops about five and a half degrees. But somehow, even with the biting cold seeping through our tent, I managed to fall asleep. Karen prepared everything for the morning so our packs would be ready to go.

Until three a.m., that is. The deafening noise of an engine sounded like it was coming straight through our tent.

Dad pulled himself out of the tent. "Hey, what are you doing?"

I peered through the tent flap and watched a group of ten or so Japanese climbers get out of a snowcat and begin to put on crampons. They let Dad know that they were going to climb to the summit.

Dad crawled back into the tent. "Well, is everyone awake now?"

"Oh, yes," Karen answered.

I nodded, yawning.

"Then we might as well get up," Dad said.

"How's your tooth?" Karen asked him.

"I'll live."

I dressed as best I could without getting out of my cozy bag, but it was hard moving fast with cold hands. Our water had frozen too, so Karen had to melt it on the camp stove to make hot cocoa and oatmeal. I wrapped my fingers around the cup to warm them.

When we were ready to start climbing, we switched on our headlamps and headed for the summit. It was four a.m.

• • •

The temperature was about zero, and the snow was frozen solid. I had to fight to sink my crampons into it to get a good foothold and avoid slipping on the rock-hard ice.

We had been charging full steam ahead for a couple of hours when suddenly my dad stopped and leaned forward, putting his weight onto his climbing poles. "My head's killing me," he said.

Dad never complained. Hearing him say that made me worry. I shone the light from my headlamp on his face. "Will you be okay?"

"I'll survive," he said. "I just need to rest a minute."

We were so close that I hated the thought of turning back now. Even so, I'd do it in a heartbeat if that was what my dad needed.

"We came this far," Karen added. "I know you'll make it. We'll go at your pace. We've got plenty of time."

Just ahead of us I watched climbers wind up the hill. "Is that the Japanese team?" I asked.

"Yes, and they left an hour before we did," Karen added.

"They're not exactly setting speed records." Dad sipped from the bottle carried inside his down jacket to keep it from freezing and started out again, seeming a little stronger.

The first rays of morning light had changed the colors on the horizon ever so slightly. Moments later the sun burst over the mountains, casting the shadow of Elbrus across the entire landscape. The scenery was incredible, total white everywhere we looked.

Colored markers indicated the best route for the monoto-nous switchbacks. We trudged on and on. The higher we went, the farther away the summit looked. Then, when we were within fifty yards of the Japanese group, we reached the saddle, or gap, between Elbrus's two summits. We were going for the highest of the two.

"Take a break and drink lots of water," Dad said.

I took a few sips, planning to save the rest for later.

"Do it now. Dehydration can be worse than not having enough oxygen."

Skeptical, I wrinkled my brow. "No way."

He gritted his teeth at me the way he does when he scolds. "Less air pressure means less humidity and more evaporation from your skin and lungs. You've got to drink more water to keep your body working."

"And we need to eat." Karen pulled out three energy bars, three apples, and her famous peanut butter cookies. We always carried them on hikes because they provided protein and sugar for energy, and they were really good.

I lay in the snow absorbing the sun's warmth while munch-ing on an apple. One of the Japanese climbers was headed back down the mountain.

"I'm surprised they let him go alone," Dad said.

"Not a strong team like us," I said through a mouthful of apple.

After our break we continued along a steeper, icier, narrower ridge toward the west summit. As we climbed, the lower air pressure at high altitude really started messing with me. I was breathing hard, trying to get more air to send oxygen to my legs. My feet were like cinder blocks. I lifted one and pushed it forward a few inches, dropped it, and waited a few seconds before repeating with the other.

"Jordan, you're not going to make it taking heavy steps like that," Karen said.

Dad reached for my hand to pull me up. "Come on, J Man. This is serious stuff. Stop moving and the cold will kill you. It's called hypothermia."

"What a horrible thing to say," Karen called to him.

"He needs to understand what he's getting into. This is no kid's game."

"Hey, I can hear what you're saying," I told them.

"You're meant to," Dad answered.

I did my best to pick up the pace. We passed the Japanese team and other people strung out all over the mountain. Some of them looked just like Faiz and Nikki had before they'd given up and turned around on Kili.

Karen came up behind me and spoke quietly. "That is what happens when you don't eat right and don't train as hard as we do."

An hour above the saddle we came upon a Russian team. Each of them was wrapped up in about five layers of clothing. A girl was sitting folded over and holding her head. A man was puking at the side of the trail. It was like a war zone around their leader, who unfortunately was one of the few Russians who spoke English. He got into our faces right away.

"You do not know what you are doing!" he shouted. "The weather can change anytime."

Dad opened his hand palm up, questioning.

"You do not have the right shoes for the mountain. You do not show it proper respect," he said.

I looked at their massive mountaineering boots with heavy crampons. We were in Salomon trail-running shoes and our ultralight Kahtoola crampons. I was a little cold, but my feet felt fine.

"Good luck on the mountain," Dad said with a crooked smile. After we'd walked on past them, he seemed to be feeling better. "At least we're moving. All that weight is slowing them down."

No one traveled as fast and light as we did. But it was still super hard, and every inch of my body was about to revolt. To keep from sitting down and weeping as I'd done on Kilimanjaro, I thought of our guide, Samuel, and his beautiful African voice: *You're going at an unbelievable pace. You have shown great respect for the mountain. It wants you to climb it.* And then of Dad's very California voice: *Time to suck it up and climb, dude.* So I did just that. After six hours of dragging one heavy foot after the other in thinning air, I was completely done in and swore I couldn't take another step. Then I remembered that Dad was doing all this with a major toothache.

Feeling dizzy, I stopped to catch my breath. *Focus. This is it,* I told myself. *Now or never. Pick up your feet and move!*

Another hundred miserable, exhausting yards and I was there. I felt the same wave of emotion I'd felt when I reached the summit of Kili. It was an awesome feeling. I was so happy that I fell to the ground, sobbing. "We did it! We actually did it!"

Dad and Karen knelt and hugged me. "I'm proud of you, J Man," Dad said.

"I am too," Karen said, tears streaming down her cheeks.

It had been ten times harder than I'd expected it to be, but I'd done it! I hadn't given up.

The summit air was brutally cold. No matter which way I turned, gusting winds hit me and almost knocked me down. My hair was blowing wildly from under my hood and getting into my eyes as I held up each of our sponsors' flags while Karen took pictures in front of the summit marker—a three-foot-tall rock with red lines spray-painted on it.

From the roof of Europe, at 18,510 feet, the views were spectacular. We'd come up from the snowy Russian side and could now look over the Caucasus mountain range into the very lush and green country of Georgia. It was a completely different landscape.

Summit moments are brief. They're on the most exposed area of the mountain, and often there are other people nearby waiting to have their own summit experience. I knew there was a lot of work ahead, but thoughts of heading down the mountain—to my plate of spaghetti—rushed into my head, not to mention thoughts of home, family, and friends.

A Spanish guy in his twenties came up carrying a snow-board. He spoke a little bit of English. He had the same question that everyone seemed to ask when they saw me on a mountain: "How old are you?"

"I'll be eleven tomorrow."

He gave me two fist bumps. "Congratulations and happy birthday."

I was jealous when he took off on his snowboard. I could've skied this, but without equipment I'd have to try the next best thing. "I'm going to go down in a glissade," I announced. Glissading is sliding on your feet or your butt to descend faster. I'd practiced it at home with my trusty ice axe, but I'd never done it on a big mountain. If it would get me down this mountain quicker, I was ready to give it a try.

Dad's big hand grabbed my shoulder. "No you don't. Take a look. See that steep wall on the right? Hit that and you're in deep trouble."

"I'll use my ice axe and do a self-arrest."

"Not until you prove you can." He stepped about twenty feet below me and waited in case I screwed up. "Come down a short way and then try one."

I'd practiced self-arrests at home, but this was a steeper, icier hill. I slid a couple of yards, holding my axe with the pick facing the slope. Then I flipped onto my belly, with my feet pointing downhill and my knees apart so I wouldn't roll from side to side. My crampons were in the air so they wouldn't snag and send me cartwheeling. I tucked my arms in, one hand on top of the axe and the other on the shaft as I dug it into the snow. Then I arched my body to put maximum weight on the axe and my knees and slowed to a stop.

It's a dangerous move if you don't know what you're doing. But I did.

"Way to go, Jordan," Karen shouted.

"Very impressive," Dad said.

"Can I glissade now?"

"All right, but not very far, and just watch what you are sliding into." He stayed downhill from me, and Karen stood above to take pictures.

I slid on my butt. The hill was bumpy and it hurt. Good excuse for another self-arrest with my trusty axe. I flipped over in perfect position and slammed the pick into the hill.

"Come on, keep moving," Dad said.

I got back up, slid a few more yards, and did another one. Self-arrests were fun!

"We'll never get to the bottom if you keep that up," Karen called.

I scooted farther on my butt, then asked, "Can I do it now?"

"Yes, Jordan, go ahead," Dad agreed.

Another self-arrest. The sun was out. No longer cold, I was having an awesome time sliding on my butt, laughing, and using my ice axe all the way down. I loved that thing. A couple of hikers passed us and cheered me on.

When we reached our camp at the Pastukhova Rocks again, it was around one o'clock. The last tram left at three. "Most people coming down either spend the night here or at that hut we passed," Karen said. "They're too exhausted to go on."

"Another cold night up here makes no sense. What do you say to a serious run down the mountain to catch the tram?" Dad smiled and shot a sideways glance at me. "There's spaghetti dinner waiting for you at the café."

It sounded way better to me than hunkering down to a freeze-dried dinner in a cold tent. "Let's go for it!" I said.

We packed everything up and started half running, half sliding down the hill. After the climb and all my self-arrests, I was totally wiped out.

Karen kept yelling, "Jordan, you've got to keep the pace or we won't make it!"

I knew not making it meant a two-hour walk down to the village, and my legs were screaming at me to give them a rest.

All I'd eaten since coming off the summit were two of Karen's peanut butter cookies, some trail mix, and an energy bar. I was starving, and visions of that spaghetti kicked me into racing mode. Dad ran ahead and surprised me by hailing a snowcat. He talked to the driver, then looked back at Karen and shook his head. The snowcat wouldn't be able to get us there fast enough.

He took off even faster toward the tram.

Karen and I sprinted after him.

We made it to the tram one second before it left. We thought we'd paid for our return trip when we'd bought tickets to go up the mountain, and there certainly wasn't time to buy any tickets now. The kid working the tram didn't want to let us on. He kept yelling something in Russian.

A girl who spoke a little English leaned out the door. "Just go ahead and get in."

Who were we to argue? We hopped right on. We're still not sure whether we paid or not. That's the cost of not knowing the local language, I guess.

Spaghetti, spaghetti, spaghetti. I couldn't wait to get to the hotel and eat the meal Sweetie had promised me.

"You're back already?" she said when we walked in the door. "You didn't make the summit?"

"Yeah, we did." Karen showed her a picture of me with the marker.

"That's impossible." She eyed me. "You took the snowcat up."

I shook my head. "No, no. We even walked from the tram to the Barrels Camp yesterday."

"And are back here today? I will tell everyone," she said.

"Jordan couldn't wait to get back to your spaghetti," Karen said.

Sweetie smiled. "Then I will have the cook make it for you right now."

I folded my arms on the table for a pillow and laid my head on them. "How's your tooth, Dad?"

He ruffled the back of my long curls. "Think I'll live until we get home."

I could have fallen asleep right there, but I wanted to stay awake for my spaghetti. I pulled up and slumped back against the chair.

I ate a salad while waiting for the much-anticipated spaghetti dinner. Sweetie brought it to the table, and it looked exactly like a steaming plate of spaghetti covered in delicious tomato sauce should look. I couldn't wait to dig in.

I glanced up at Sweetie and smiled. "Thank you so, so much. I've been looking forward to this the entire time."

"That's good, that's good. I really hope you like it."

"I will," I assured her.

Then I took a bite. The noodles were so overcooked it was like eating mush. And the tomato sauce tasted more like tomato juice.

"What do I do with this?" I whispered. "I can't hurt her feelings. She's being so nice."

Karen looked to make sure nobody was watching before

she stuck her fork in and stabbed some mushy pasta. "We'll help you, right, Paul?"

"Sure," Dad answered.

The three of us working, we managed to clean the plate. But I'll never order spaghetti in Russia again.

My face felt really hot all through dinner. Dad's and Karen's faces were a deep shade of red, and their cheeks and lips were swollen. When we got back to our room and I looked in the mirror, I saw the same creature glaring back at me.

Karen dabbed lotion on my cheeks. "Somehow the sunscreen didn't make it into the bag. I don't know why. Too much going on, I guess. Lesson learned. You can't be at this high altitude with the sun reflecting off the snow and avoid getting a humongous sunburn. It won't happen ever again. I promise."

Dad chuckled to lighten things up a bit. His tooth was still bothering him, but reaching a lower altitude had definitely helped with the sinus pain. "We need to find a sunscreen sponsor."

To avoid getting any more sun, I had to wear a scarf over my face and a hat pulled down over my eyes while we hung out there the next two days. We visited another little ski area nearby and some of the quaint restaurants. It was incredibly sad to see people waiting in long lines at a truck for basic food provisions. Times were hard there.

We took a taxi back to Mineralnye Vody and flew to

Moscow on that same rickety plane. Unlike the countryside, Moscow was very international. A lot of people spoke English, but it was still hard finding our way around because most of the Russian alphabet isn't anything like ours.

The Moscow subway terminals were amazing, with vaulted ceilings, artwork, and musicians playing classical piano and cello. The trains had little tables and curtains like in a James Bond movie. Our fellow passengers wore peacoats and light scarves and looked very stoic and tired at the end of the workday.

We visited the Tomb of the Unknown Soldier and watched the changing of the guard. Soldiers marched in unison, swinging their right arms to their chests and lifting their legs parallel to the ground, knees locked. From there we went to the Armory, where we saw thousand-year-old carriages covered with gold, diamonds, and rubies.

Red Square, the central square in Moscow, was enormous. We saw the Kremlin, the famous Russian fortress, along with Saint Basil's Cathedral, which is said to rise like a flame from a bonfire toward the sky. There are eight side churches around the central one, all with those onion-shaped domes that I'd seen in pictures. It has to be one of the most amazing buildings on the planet.

Russia was a fascinating place. I wished we could stay two more weeks, but even being there for a few days was great. I had just turned eleven two days before, and I had already climbed the highest mountains on three continents and seen wildlife in Africa and in Steve Irwin's zoo, and now I'd visited the Red Square. Climbing Elbrus had been the best birthday present ever.

You'd think I'd have been happy with that—and I was— but I was already thinking about climbing my next mountain. I still had five to go.

THE HIGH CLIMB:

SOUTH AMERICA'S

MOUNT

ACONCAGUA,

22,837 FEET

Average numbers of climbers
per year: 5,000

December 30, 2007, age 11

World Record

CHAPTER 13

I was really happy to get home from Russia, but once again I came home to a sick grandparent. This time it was my grandma Mary Lu, on my mom's side. I was her first grandchild, born four days after the death of her oldest son. We had always been close because of that. She had so much knowledge and loved sharing it with me. We read encyclopedias together and she used to sing me to sleep. I almost hadn't gone to Elbrus because she wasn't doing very well, but she'd insisted. She wanted to hear all about my grand adventure when I returned.

When I got home, I sat with her for two hours every morning, telling her about how Elbrus had been my toughest climb so far, and about the people and places in Russia. She was in and out of consciousness, and I didn't know if she fully understood. She died of leukemia two weeks later, at the age of sixty-five. It left a big hole in me that no one could fill. But I had good friends to help raise my spirits.

My first afternoon back, my friend Cameron called. He and his brother Casey were my two best friends. "How was it?" Cameron asked.

"There were snowboarders up there in July," I told him.

"Awesome. Did you make the summit?"

"Yup, and I used my ice axe for self-arrests coming down."

"Cool. Casey and I saw this guy slacklining while you were gone. We've got to try it."

Slacklining is kind of like tightrope walking, only the line isn't rigid and tight like a tightrope—there's some give to it. In other words, it's like walking and bouncing on a long, skinny trampoline. I was definitely up for giving it a try.

With Dad's and Karen's help, Cameron and I anchored a one-inch flat nylon line between two trees twenty-five feet apart in the yard and added a ratchet to adjust the tension. We spent the last days of summer and the fall perfecting our slack-lining technique and riding our mountain bikes up and down the rugged hills around Big Bear. Once ski season opened, we were all over the slopes.

Big Bear provided the perfect outdoor training ground for my next summit—which I knew would be cold and snowy, no matter which one we chose. I hadn't forgotten my dream. Dad and Karen hadn't either.

"Of the five summits left," Dad said before dinner one night, "the ones in Antarctica and in New Guinea are too difficult to reach. That leaves Aconcagua, Denali, and Everest."

Karen slid a chicken into the oven, closed the door, and turned to me. "You're not ready for Everest yet, Jordan."

"I know," I said. Everest would be the toughest challenge of them all. I needed to check off a couple of the other summits before I even thought about that one.

"Weather's a factor too," Dad added. "We need to climb when it's warmest so we don't freeze."

"It's summer in South America during our winter," Karen said. "What about Aconcagua over Christmas break?"

"Looks doable to me," Dad said. "What about you, J Man?"

"If not now, we'd have to wait another whole year until their summertime. Right?"

Dad nodded. "If we're going to do it when you're not in school."

So it looked like I would be spending Christmas in South America's Andes mountains.

The next night Cameron and I had a sleepover in my room, which Dad jokingly called the reptile zoo because I had so many lizards and snakes. "We're doing Aconcagua over Christmas," I said.

"Where's that?"

"Argentina, in the southern hemisphere."

"You'll miss all the good skiing," he said.

"Tell me about it." I let my bearded dragon out and released a cricket so he could chase his dinner. Spending time with Cameron reminded me of all the fun I missed out on when I was off climbing mountains. And skiing was the most fun of all. I knew the rest of the summits would be even more challenging than Elbrus. I was beginning to have some doubts.

"People on Elbrus were getting sick from the altitude, and Aconcagua is forty-three hundred feet higher. It's the tallest mountain outside of the Himalayas. You can die from your lungs filling with fluid or your brain swelling," I said.

"That's messed up," Cameron said.

I took out another cricket. Its feet tickled my palm. "Don't tell anyone, but sometimes I'm not sure why I'm climbing anymore," I admitted.

"Then forget it. You don't have to go," Cameron told me.

I sighed. I wished it were that easy. But Dad and Karen had totally turned their lives upside down to help me accomplish my goal. Sponsors had come on board, and the whole town of Big Bear had gotten behind me. I was worried about disappointing everyone.

"Nobody would think bad of you," Cameron said.

I thought about that for a minute. The people who loved me would understand, of course, but I began to realize that I would be disappointed in myself.

"But *I* would think bad of me for quitting and not accomplishing my goal," I told Cameron. I plopped onto the bed. "I don't know what to do."

The plan to go to Aconcagua over Christmas break met a hurdle—my age. No one under fourteen was allowed on the mountain without special permission, and I was eleven.

I didn't know whether to be relieved or mad.

"We'll get you there," Dad promised, "with every permission and endorsement they could possibly ask for."

One afternoon Karen let us know that she might have found a way. "Look what I found on the Internet. A thirteen-year-old and his father tried to climb Aconcagua without a permit. Rangers chased them out of the park. They had to go get a legal one."

"How did they get a legal one if he was only thirteen?" I asked.

"I already e-mailed the father and got the name of a lawyer in Argentina who was able to get them a special permit," Karen said.

Karen worked with the lawyer, Arturo, for the next few weeks, and it began to look like our trip was a go. The only problem was that I still wasn't sure if I was totally on board. The idea of missing prime ski season in Big Bear was a major bummer.

"I'm going to fly down to Argentina a few days early and meet with him to get all the paperwork ready," she told me one day. "We'll have to make a special presentation to a judge."

One thing we had to present was a release form from my mom. Dad drove me to her house for my week there and asked me to go to my room while they talked. I put my headphones on so I wouldn't hear them. Theirs wasn't exactly the world's friendliest divorce.

I sat across from Mom at dinner that night.

"Jordan, this is the first time I've been asked to sign a paper giving permission for you to climb a mountain," she said.

I stirred my mashed potatoes. "It's not supposed to be a difficult mountain, only high."

"I just looked at a dozen websites. Aconcagua is only eighty miles from the Pacific. It's bombarded with extremely high winds and storms. Temperatures to minus eighty degrees with the windchill."

I shuddered. Man, that sounded cold.

"*El viento blanco*—'the white wind'—has blown climbers to their deaths. So just being in great shape isn't good enough." She leaned across the table and touched my arm. "This will be a very long, demanding expedition. The coldest, highest, steepest, and windiest climb you've ever done." She had a sad look in her eyes. "It's been a hard summer with my mom dying. I just don't want anything happening to you, too."

"Dad and Karen will make sure I'm ready," I told her. Mom was going to give me permission to go, though it crossed my mind that maybe I could use her concerns as an excuse not to climb. But that didn't seem right, and it would only make trouble between her and Dad. I wasn't sure about doing this anymore, but I didn't want to worry her either.

I was still wondering what to do when Karen's little nephew, Britton, mailed a Flat Stanley to me and asked me to take his picture on the top of Mount Aconcagua. Flat Stanley is a character in a book who gets flattened by his bulletin board;

one of the pluses of being flat is that he can travel through the mail. Kids are supposed to color their own Flat Stanley and send him to grandmas, uncles, cousins—anyone they wanted. Then those people take pictures of Flat Stanley wherever they are and return him to his owner. I couldn't let Britton down. We laminated Flat Stanley so he would survive the long haul up a mountain.

The day Karen announced she'd booked our tickets, I thought, *Okay, here we go*. A friend lent us two special tents, called hypoxic tents, to help us acclimatize to high altitude before we left.

For about a month before our departure, I slept in the sealed tent with plastic windows. A generator pumped low-oxygen air to simulate a high-altitude environment so my body would create more red blood cells. During the day I trained in the oxygen-rich, thicker air. The generator's motor was kind of noisy, but I could sleep just about anywhere. Karen slowly adjusted the altitude meter until I was acclimatized to fifteen thousand feet, about as high as those tents can go.

Dad laid a notebook on the breakfast bar a few days before departure and called me over. "You'll be in charge of filling this out for all of us twice a day. It's a big job, and I'm trusting you to take care of it."

I sat on the stool next to him and leaned on the counter, chin in my hands, as he explained the Lake Louise self-report for the diagnosis of acute mountain sickness.

"It's extremely important that we monitor ourselves all the way to the summit," Dad said. "Acute mountain sickness can be deadly."

The survey included five categories: headache, nausea/vomiting, fatigue/weakness, dizziness/light-headedness, and difficulty sleeping. Each category had a rating scale from zero (not bothered at all) to three (really bad).

"Make sense?" Dad asked.

I nodded. "So how do I know if we're in trouble?"

"When the scores from each category are added up, a total score of three to five means mild mountain sickness. A score of six or more can be deadly."

Wow, this was getting serious. After hearing what Mom had said about people being blown off the mountain and after reading more about the fatalities on Aconcagua, I was pretty scared. Still, I kept my fears from Dad and Karen.

They had considered using a guide to help us climb the mountain, but after some research they'd decided we could do it ourselves. They did hire a friend, Pablo, to set up the logistics. Pablo lived in Buenos Aires and had helped them before on adventure races in South America. He had also climbed Aconcagua. He agreed to arrange for mules to carry our gear to base camp, to make sure we had a good place for a tent, and to have a couple of hot meals ready when we arrived.

We had raised money selling Karen's Aconcagua T-shirts and showing a Warren Miller ski film at the local performing arts center in Big Bear. Warren Miller makes amazing movies about skiing and snowboarding, so we had a good turnout. More sponsors joined us too. I don't know what we would've done without them. Most donated the equipment we needed. In exchange they wanted a video of the climb and pictures of me using their products or wearing their clothing. It was a good trade, and we only worked with sponsors whose products we believed in.

When school closed for Christmas break, Dad and I were heading to Los Angeles airport, LAX, for a flight to South America.

Dad and I arrived in Mendoza, Argentina, five days after Karen did. Mendoza was a cool city—kind of a hippie, artistic, sunny place with several universities. We all agreed it would be worth visiting again.

Our first order of business was getting the permit I needed to climb the mountain. Arturo met us at the courthouse and we walked in together. Karen carried a manila file crammed with all the paperwork that she and Arturo had worked on and collected over the last couple of days along with all the paperwork she had gathered back home: two doctors' approvals, a release from my mom, and character references and endorsements from their adventure-racing teammates and family friends. The folder also contained health records, passport forms, and reams of paper documenting Dad's and Karen's expertise as world-class adventure racers and Dad's as a helicopter paramedic.

"If this doesn't get us a permit, nothing will," Dad said.

Inside the courthouse Karen and Arturo presented our documents to a clerk, who ordered us to go to the medical examination room before she'd even look at anything.

Dad rolled his eyes as we walked down the hall. "Jordan's healthier than ninety percent of the population."

A doctor took my pulse, looked inside my ears, tapped my knees, and examined my tongue. "I find no problems."

Next stop: the chambers of Honorable Elsa Lidia Galera. She sat behind a large oak desk under a slowly rotating ceiling fan, waiting to hear not from the lawyer but from me personally. I'd practiced my speech over and over all the way down there so I wouldn't mess up.

"My dad and Karen climbed Kilimanjaro and Elbrus and Kosciuszko with me. We're a team and always watch out for each other. We saw a lot of other people getting really sick and having to go back down, but none of that ever happened to us. We just moved up the mountain at our own pace and celebrated when we got safely back to base camp after reaching every summit."

She leaned across her desk and studied my face. "Jordan, tell me why you want to do this."

I knew what I said next could make or break the deal. My heart started to beat faster, and I was breathing much too fast. I glanced at Karen, who gave me the go-ahead nod, so I pulled myself together, took a deep breath, and answered the question.

"When I was nine, I saw a mural at my school of the Seven Summits and wanted to stand on the top of each one to look out across the world. It's been my dream ever since, and I've worked really hard to get here. Aconcagua will be my fourth mountain. I really hope you'll understand my dream and be kind enough to give me permission to go after it."

The judge watched me quietly for a moment, making my heart race again. Tiny drops of sweat formed on my upper lip. We'd come too far to be turned down now. She rose, walked around her desk, and gave me a giant hug like I was her own grandchild.

Then she looked directly into my eyes, holding both my hands. "You must promise to cherish our new friendship and not do anything that would hurt yourself. Climb slowly, drink plenty of water, and go down if you feel at all sick." Her lips spread in a warm smile. "And you must also send me a signed photo of you on the summit. Will you do that for me, Jordan?"

"Yes, I promise."

She gave me another big grandmotherly hug. "Then I am pleased to give you special permission to climb Aconcagua. And I wish all of you the best of luck in reaching the summit."

I was a whirlwind of excitement inside but tried to walk calmly and steadily through the door. Once outside, Dad, Karen, and I were jumping up and down, congratulating one another and thanking Arturo. Then we left for the permit office, feeling higher than Mount Everest.

When we arrived to pick up my permit, the ranger greeted us with a sour expression.

"We've been expecting you," he said flatly. "But we're not awarding you a permit. We are not subject to the courts and will not allow anyone under fourteen years of age to climb Aconcagua."

How could they do that after we got the judge's permission? Dad pleaded our case in his best Spanish but got nowhere. Karen called Arturo, and he came to the permit office as quickly as he could. But even he couldn't sway the head ranger.

Soon the lawyer for the national park arrived, wearing a stiff, official-looking park uniform and a huge mustache that was way too big for his face. He was just as determined to shut us down as the ranger. He and Arturo went at it like they had some long-standing feud. Finally both lawyers and Dad disappeared behind closed doors. I could still hear them arguing, and my stomach was in turmoil. I put on my iPod to block them out.

An hour later the park lawyer called Karen and me into the room. Our papers were spread all over the desk. "I will give you the permit, but only on the condition that you sign a release saying you hold the park harmless in case of any injury," he said.

We agreed, and he and Arturo, who'd been at each other's throats only minutes before, shook hands like nothing had happened.

"What was that all about?" I asked when we loaded our gear into Pablo's van. "There are some things I just don't understand."

"You're not alone," Dad agreed.

I was relieved when we were finally on the road heading to Aconcagua Provincial Park. I was afraid the ranger and the lawyer would change their minds and snatch our permit away.

The park was near the border of Chile. After a beautiful three-hour drive we arrived at a dusty parking lot between the yellow rock walls of a canyon that formed a natural gate. All climbers had to present their permits to the park rangers before continuing on the trailhead. The entrance to the trail itself was a stone structure as hard and cold as the ranger who eyed me, my permit, and then me again.

"We heard you were coming," he said. "This permit is not valid. You are too young to proceed."

The veins in Dad's forehead pulsed. He called Arturo, who then called the park service in Mendoza. After a lot of arguing over the phone, the ranger announced, "You cannot continue until the park-sanctioned doctor examines Jordan."

"When will that be?" Dad asked, his voice rising a few octaves.

"He will be here in three hours from Mendoza."

"We've already lost at least half a day and are supposed to meet up with the rest of our team," Dad said calmly, even though I knew he wanted to strangle the guy.

And Dad was telling the truth about our team. Not only were Pablo and his girlfriend, Ali, joining us, but so were three of Dad and Karen's adventure-racing friends: Ryan, Claire, and Mike. An official photographer, John Griber, who'd been provided by our SOLE footwear sponsor to document the expedition, was also joining us. He'd just returned from filming on Everest and was eager to come along because of two failed attempts at Aconcagua.

After doing Elbrus with only Dad and Karen, I was happy to be part of a nine-member team—that is, if the ranger would finally let me go.

I tried to be patient, but this permit thing was really getting old. It was all a bad sign. Doubts whirled in my head about continuing. But after all the trouble Dad and Karen had gone through, I tamped my worries down.

We sat on our backpacks, leaning against the wall, until the doctor arrived at three thirty in the afternoon. He seemed irritated about having been called all the way there. He took me into a room and asked me to get up on the examination table. He tapped me on the back, took my pulse, and asked me to cough.

"I see nothing wrong here," he said. "Go ahead, but you must check in at every camp on the way." He signed the permit, then shot a look at the ranger that said *Get over it.*

The ranger gave each of us a numbered trash bag and noted them on our permits. During the climb we were supposed to put all our trash in them, and on the way off the mountain we were to return them to verify we'd removed all our rubbish, including special poop bags containing kitty litter. At least there wouldn't be trash on the mountain.

Dad checked his watch. "Four o'clock. Unbelievable. Let's get out of here before our friends give up and go on without us."

To enter the park we crossed a bridge next to a wooden sign: DO NOT TRESPASS WITHOUT YOUR TICKET.

Really? You think?

We hiked a beautiful trail along rivers and through canyons with the amazing peaks of the Andes surrounding us. I'd read up on what animals I might spot and hoped to see a red fox or guanaco. Guanacos are wild llamas, and you don't often see them in zoos.

We reached Camp Confluencia at just over eleven thousand feet in a couple of hours. It was even less of a wilderness experience than the Barrels Camp on Elbrus. Colorful tents were scattered among the barren dirt and rocks. There were all kinds of services, including toilets, medical care, mules, and food.

Pablo and his girlfriend, Ali, rushed up to us.

"I think you not come," Pablo said in his best English.

"A little permit problem," Karen explained.

Ryan, Claire, and Mike, who had come a day earlier to take short hikes and acclimatize, soon joined us, along with

John. Now that we were all together, I was getting excited.

John was taking team photos when a ranger approached. He was all business. "You must bring your permit to the medical tent."

My shoulders slumped, afraid that they would try to come up with another way to keep me off the mountain.

"This is really irritating," I groaned to Karen.

"I hear you," she said.

One notch down on the excitement meter, we followed the ranger to his station, where a doctor checked my oxygen level and listened to my heart.

"Drink plenty of water," he said.

I nodded and he waved me on.

My legs were tired after our hike to the Confluencia Camp. Catching z's was my specialty and I wanted to do just that.

The next day we got up early and hiked seven hours to base camp at Plaza de Mulas, or Mule Place. The animals hoofed past us every so often, piled high with gear and kicking up dust. Pablo said mules worked one day and got two days off. It was mandatory. I about fell over laughing when I saw a stray mule rolling around in the dirt, not caring one bit about the duffels on its back. At least they got to have fun on the job, I thought.

Base camp was on a flat, barren area at fourteen thousand feet. John said it was the second largest base camp in the world after Everest. There were hundreds of tents in every size, shape, and color, plus outhouses, a satellite dish, Internet, phone, and even hot showers. Beer, pizza, and wine were available if you had the cash. A Coke cost six dollars and a phone call was two dollars a minute. Argentines moved there during climbing season to sell their services. And business was booming, especially the mule trade.

Pablo and Ali retrieved our gear and set up camp while we reported to the medical tent, where all climbers had to register and be screened to make sure they were fit enough to continue the climb.

Veronica, the head nurse, was grumpy and downright mean. She read our blood pressure, took our pulse, measured the oxygen content in our blood, and listened to our lungs for any infection. "Why are all of you doing this climb?" she asked with a scowl. "I see no point to it."

Dad just smiled. "Are we good to go?"

"Yes." She seemed upset that I'd passed all her tests better than most adults.

We walked out of the tent with grins on our faces. Karen gave me a high five. "Hey, we just made it through twenty-four hours without your permit being confiscated."

When we made our way to our tents, Pablo showed us where we could rent beds rather than sleep on the hard ground. Karen shook her head. "Not for me. I'll skip the bedbugs."

Ryan, Claire, and Mike opted for the beds but paid heavily, not in pesos but in hundreds of extremely itchy red welts all over their bodies. Poor Claire in particular was covered with the bedbug bites.

Base camp was super busy and pretty cool. There were so many people coming and going, and the mules could bring in almost anything. There was even a foosball table in the middle of the camp for anyone to use.

But for me the biggest entertainment came from a slackline. I watched several people flailing their arms trying to keep their balance only to fall on their butts. I couldn't help smiling. One guy picked himself up, brushed the dirt off, and challenged me to do better.

I got on, walked to the middle with barely a wobble, and stopped to do five high bounces before I walked *backward* to the beginning. The crowd that had gathered cheered and whistled for me. Even my challenger gave me a big approving nod.

After having slept in hypoxic tents for ten nights, Dad, Karen, and I were comfortable up to fifteen thousand feet, but the other six members of our team planned to acclimatize by climbing higher into thin air and then sleeping lower in thicker air to recover. That wasn't our style. In Dad's and Karen's world, every minute you lingered meant you risked losing the race. We were ready to climb.

CHAPTER 14

I had proved to Dad and Karen both that I was ready to take on more responsibilities during this climb. I was no longer just a climber. I was a full member of the team, with jobs like keeping track of our elevation, setting alarms for waking up in the morning, and getting weather reports on the radio.

My most important responsibility was taking the Lake Louise survey. High scores were a signal that a climber was facing a life-or-death situation. I paid attention to the details and looked for the warning signs. Before we left base camp on the second morning, I totaled our scores. Everyone was safe to move on, but Ryan, Claire, and Mike weren't feeling all that hot.

The mules didn't climb above Plaza de Mulas, so we had to carry our heavy packs as we climbed to Camp Canada, at 16,568 feet, on Christmas Eve. Earlier we had only hiked up a valley, the Valle de las Vacas, but when we left Plaza de Mulas we were now actually *on* the mountain. The trail was steep, loose, and rocky.

Arriving at camp, the first thing we had to do was check in at the ranger station. The doctor wasn't as uptight as Nurse Veronica.

"Your son's doing fine," he told Dad. "You can check his vital signs yourself from now on and report them to base camp by radio."

I saw the relief on Dad's face. One less thing to deal with.

John returned to Plaza de Mulas to acclimatize while the eight of us packed into Dad's, Karen's, and my three-man tent to celebrate Christmas Eve. Even at 16,568 feet there was no getting cold with all that body heat and our headlamps beaming. We were crammed shoulder to shoulder, with Karen in Dad's lap and Ali in Pablo's.

It was time for some light holiday cheer. We'd shared the rules ahead of time for a white-elephant gift exchange. You couldn't spend more than twenty dollars and your gift couldn't weigh more than half a pound. Dad passed around a bowl with numbered pieces of paper. I got number four.

Ali had number one and chose a box wrapped in silver. She opened it and found a Rubik's Cube. Her face twisted in confusion. "What is this thing?" she asked.

Even after explanations and demonstrations, she didn't see the need for a Rubik's Cube on a mountain.

Ryan, with number two, had the option of taking her

Rubik's Cube or picking another gift. It was fair to say that the Rubik's Cube was safe. He opened a green box containing a down camping pillow.

"Cool," Claire said, with paper number three. "I'll just take that pillow, thank you."

My turn next. Ali wiggled her gift in my face, trying to tempt me. "Jordan, take my Rubik's Cube. Take my beautiful cube."

"No thanks. I'll try this purple box." Maybe I should've gone for the toy instead. I opened an ultralight towel set, but it was way too cold outside for a major wash and dry.

John got the knife I'd brought.

We laughed for hours, drinking hot cocoa and eating Karen's peanut butter cookies. It might have been unusual by some people's standards, but for me this was the second best Christmas ever, next only to the one two years earlier when I'd gotten my ice axe.

Christmas Day, six of us chilled in Camp Canada while Dad took a trip back to Plaza de Mulas for more gear. Karen took a solo trip and shuttled supplies up to Camp Nido—short for Nido de Condores, or Nest of the Condors—and returned that afternoon just as Dad and John came back up from Plaza de Mulas.

When we left Camp Canada behind on December 26, our first obstacle was finding a way through the Penitentes, a field of upside-down icicles that were almost as tall as Dad. It would've been cool to break one off and pretend it was a Jedi sword, but I'd never damage the environment like that.

It took four hours of climbing to reach snowy Camp Nido. There'd been mules at Mulas, so I hoped to see condors here. No such luck. The camp sat on a wide plateau surrounded by rocky peaks of unusual shapes. I got my first full view of the summit and the surrounding glacial peaks. I could see most of the trail to the top and actually spotted the tiny moving dots of five climbers heading across a long traverse. That would be me in a few days.

The air was very thin at eighteen thousand feet, with still a massive distance up to the summit. Maybe it was that, or finally encountering snow on this mountain, or the responsibilities I had for keeping the team healthy and on track, but, for the first time on Aconcagua, I felt like a real mountaineer.

John, Pablo, and Ali arrived half an hour after Dad, Karen, and me, followed by Ryan, Claire, and Mike another thirty minutes after them. The trio of adventure racers dropped their packs and sank to the ground, breathing heavily. Ryan was holding his head, eyes closed.

"Jordan," Karen whispered. "Your survey."

I got out my chart and started questioning them about headaches, nausea, and dizziness.

Ryan waved me off. "No need for that. I've had it. I'm going back down."

"Rest a few days at Camp Canada and do some smaller

hikes," Dad suggested. "You'll feel better and can try again."

Ryan shook his head. "I'm an endurance racer, not an altitude guy. This is killing me."

"I'm with him," Mike said.

Claire's knees were drawn to her chest, and she was resting her forehead on her arms. "Me too," she said. "It's been great, honestly. I never would've seen Aconcagua otherwise." She stood up and put her pack back on.

"Me too," John said. "I'm returning to Plaza de Mulas to acclimatize but will be back to summit with you."

We hugged everybody good-bye, and I watched them leave, wondering what I, a kid barely five feet tall, was doing up here when strong, fit athletes like them had to give up. And what about Everest? It was almost seven thousand feet higher than Aconcagua. I heard somebody from another team puking not ten feet away, and my stomach started to heave. This was insane.

To make matters worse, one of the rangers who patrolled the high camps shook our door flap. "Is this the tent of Jordan Romero?"

"Yes," Dad said. He smiled, but I could tell he was expecting another challenge.

The ranger asked if I'd been eating and drinking well and insisted on checking the percentage of oxygen my blood was carrying. Before we left home, mine had been 100 percent. As people climb to higher elevations and breathe thinner air, their number gets lower.

He clipped an oxygen sensor on my fingertip. "We will not allow you to continue unless your blood oxygen is at least eighty percent."

Mine was eighty-five.

He seemed a little angry that I wasn't suffering more. When he radioed the results to base camp, the doctors below accused him of lying. No one believed that a kid like me could be such a strong mountain climber.

Dad placed the oxygen sensor back on my finger and took a photo of the gauge. "Send that to base camp."

We learned later that someone in another party on Nido had gotten seriously ill that morning with HAPE (high-altitude pulmonary edema), meaning his lungs had filled with fluid and he couldn't breathe. Left untreated, he would die, so they'd rushed him down the mountain. I guess that was why they were being extra cautious with me.

Meanwhile all this heaving and leaving was getting to me. I missed my mom and Makaela. I'd never been this far from them at Christmas before. One of our sponsors, Network Innovations, had lent us a BGAN device that could connect to a satellite for making phone calls and using the Internet. The thing was pretty complicated to set up, but I told Karen I wanted to talk to my mom and she got it going for me.

As soon as I put the receiver to my ear and knew my mom was on the other end, I felt instantly happier. "Hi, Mom, it's me calling you from 18,208 feet on Aconcagua."

"Oh, Jordan, Jordan, are you okay? You're not sick?"

I have to admit, my eyes watered just hearing her voice. I took a deep breath and pulled myself together. "No, I'm good, better than people twice my size and age." Our connection wasn't the greatest, so I cupped my hands around the mouthpiece to be sure she heard what I said next. "I miss you so much."

"I miss you too, sweetheart. Everyone does."

The static got worse then, but I pressed on anyway. "I'll be home pretty soon. We're supposed to summit in three days. Mom, Mom? Can you hear me? I'm okay."

A long silence followed, then one more sentence from her: "Promise you'll be careful and call me when you're down safely." The reception was breaking up, but I think I heard "love you" before we lost the connection.

With a big empty hole inside I gave the phone back to Karen to shut off properly. Her smile let me know she understood how I was feeling. I was lucky to have so much love and support around me.

The following day was one of those un-fun times when it was miserably cold and there was nothing to do but sit around waiting for our bodies to get used to the higher elevation. I kept my eye on the mountain, and I felt like it was challenging me to climb higher than I'd ever been. A storm cloud slowly formed around its peak, and I thought, *Oh man, this can't be good.* An hour later the sky turned dark, as killer winds swept down the face of Aconcagua and rolled toward us, stirring up a whirlwind of gray dust so thick it obscured the mountain. A gust picked up a neighboring tent and tossed it. It looked like a big red paper bag bouncing along the sidewalk. Where were the occupants? I remembered Mom's words: *El viento blanco has blown climbers to their deaths.* Would the wind coming in with this storm send *me* bouncing off the mountain like a paper bag?

Dad and Karen were having tea with some new friends at a nearby tent. It seemed safer to dive into our own tent than walk a few yards to find them. I zipped the door shut and sat in the middle of the tent, my knees drawn to my chest. The wind howled and bombarded the sides. I just hoped I was heavy enough to keep the wind from blowing the tent away.

Finally the flap opened and Dad and Karen scrambled inside.

"Damn, that's nasty," Dad said. "You okay, buddy?"

I nodded.

He gave a reassuring smile. "The weight of the three of us will hold the tent down."

Soon we were in the middle of a blizzard so loud it seemed like a helicopter was permanently landing next to us. I crawled into my sleeping bag and pulled the hood over my head. The wind howled all night long, piling snow on our tent until the side caved in against my back. Dad went out to shake the snow loose, and I held my breath until he was back inside safely. The condensation of our breath formed tiny icicles that dropped from the ceiling in frozen rain. Even I, who could sleep anywhere, had a rough time trying to get some sleep.

I guess we all dropped off, because we woke up to a beautiful winter-wonderland day. There were two feet of fresh snow on the ground and drifts of four feet or more.

"We need to make a break for it and get to Camp Berlin before the weather ambushes us again," Dad said. He called to Pablo and Ali in the next tent, and they crawled out, wide-eyed, and it was just too tempting. I bent over and formed a snowball.

"Oh no you don't!" Pablo said. He quickly did the same and fired the first shot. He missed me, but snow splattered across Karen's jacket.

"Jordan, reinforcements!" she shouted.

Soon we were in the middle of a full-on snowball fight. Missiles flew in every direction. At one point I leaned over to gather ammunition, and a big wet snowball hit me right in the butt. *Splat.* I did a major face-plant.

At 18,200 feet, we only had enough energy for a short battle. Making and throwing snowballs, dodging, falling, laughing—all that left us out of breath. But it was a blast.

We'd put on quite a show for climbers from Britain, Poland, and Italy, who'd all crawled out of their tents at the noise. They gave us a round of applause but didn't offer to help break the trail, or lead the way through the snow, to the next camp, Camp Berlin. Needless to say, the trail was covered with snow.

"Okaaay, team, are we ready to move on to Berlin?" Dad asked.

Weather on Aconcagua was unpredictable, but we knew there was a series of storms coming with short climbing windows in between. It was important that we get going when we could.

The combination of altitude and fresh, deep snow was too big an obstacle for Pablo and Ali. "We're going to stay here for a couple of days to see how we feel," Pablo said.

Wow, two more team members down. It was discouraging. Most expedition groups we met had eight to ten members in them, but it seemed like Dad, Karen, and I were destined to remain a team of three. Nobody could keep our pace. It seemed that most climbers needed more time to acclimatize than we did.

We stuffed everything in heavy packs, and the three of us set out. Dad was in the lead. With each step he sank almost to his knees in the snow. He did his best to drag his legs across the snow and plant them deep, creating a series of holes for Karen and me to maneuver in. His legs were so much longer than ours that we had to ask him to take smaller steps.

It must have been exhausting for him, but he kept a steady rhythm, stopping only to check on me. Each time, he gave me one of those big smiles. I was beginning to realize that my

Dad's cheerful determination was rare in this world.

Climbing was cold and *hard*. I paused for a short rest, leaning on my poles.

Karen called to me, "Jordan, what elevation?"

I checked my altimeter. "We're at 18,500."

"Just think, Jordan. Less than a thousand feet and you'd be on top of Kilimanjaro."

But this wasn't Kili. It was Aconcagua, almost three thousand feet taller. The snow was deep, and the wind felt like it was about to send me bouncing down the mountain like that red tent. My pack was super heavy, and Karen and I had to work twice as hard as Dad to climb in and out of his steps. I dropped to my knees, totally spent. This was it—I couldn't go any farther.

Karen pushed through the snow to get to me and took her mitts off to open a small pack of string cheese. "Eat this and an energy bar. You have to eat. Now. You'll feel better."

She was right. I needed fuel. I bit into the cheese and pretended I was home, eating a big hot pizza with gooey mozzarella.

"You can do it, Jordan," Karen urged. "Don't give up."

After a ten-minute rest and two imaginary pizzas, I got up and plodded on again. I kept telling myself that nothing was easy; just keep going. I climbed another half hour, putting one foot in front of the other. I was feeling light-headed. What number would I give myself on the dizzy scale? Or for a headache?

I was totally exhausted and having trouble moving. For the first time, my Everest steps were real. I planted my foot and stopped cold, not able to lift it.

Karen gave me some M&M's and that helped. It was so cold that they definitely melted in my mouth and not in my hands. Both hands were numb with cold. I continued up the long, steep switchbacks for another hour until the sugar rush ran out. My legs felt as mushy as that Russian spaghetti, and I staggered.

"Jordan," Karen yelled. "You okay?"

I looked back at her with icy tears streaming down my face.

Dad stopped immediately and came back toward me, while Karen pushed through the snow to reach my side. They made a huddle around me, and then Dad sat cross-legged in the snow and pulled me into his lap.

"What's wrong, little buddy?" he asked.

"Why am I doing this?" I cried.

Dad held me tighter. "You're following your dream."

I could hardly push the words out. "I can't do this anymore. I hurt all over and I'm so tired." Tears flowed down my face and froze on my cheeks. "I'm scared and I miss my grandma and Mom. I want to go home."

Dad whispered, "It's all right, J Man. Use the memory of your grandma to help you. She loved you so much."

I inhaled a long, shaky breath. Dad had called me J Man instead of Little J again, and that brought more tears to my eyes—happy ones. His arms felt warm and safe. I knew my dad loved me and would never let anything hurt me. I removed a mitt and rubbed the back of my hand over my eyes, but the tears kept flowing. I couldn't stop them.

"It's okay to have doubts," Karen said quietly. "We all do. There are times when I've stopped and asked myself, 'What in the world did I sign up for here? Why am I doing this race?'"

I sniffed, trying to clear my nose, and looked at her.

"Honestly. So many times. The answer's always the same," she said.

I sniffed even harder, trying to breathe. "And that is?"

"That it feels good to keep going. The best part of the journey is when you overcome the pain and grow stronger." She brushed tears from my cheeks before they could freeze. "You did that on your very first mountain. And I know you can do it here, too. We'll help you."

Then I imagined Samuel saying, *It's okay to be afraid. That shows your great respect for the mountain. It wants you to climb it.*

Karen unzipped my jacket to get my water bottle. "Drink some of this and have another energy bar."

Dad was still holding me. "It's your call. We can go up or down, but the quicker we move, the sooner we'll reach camp and get warm."

I lifted my head and had to decide between climbing higher and giving up, between altitude and attitude.

I chose to push on. Aconcagua was a big summit, second only to Everest in elevation. It would help me get stronger for that climb.

I tried to clear my nose and swallowed the last of my tears. "Let's go. I'm ready," I said.

We had just started back up when an Australian passed us coming down from Camp Berlin. Wind had destroyed his tent during the night and had flattened one that belonged to a Spanish team. They'd been able to repair theirs, but his was gone.

The image of that red tent bouncing on the mountain came back to me, but I blocked it out and kept going. I couldn't allow fear to get in my way. We leaned into the storm for another hour and a half and finally dragged ourselves, exhausted, into Camp Berlin, the last stop before the summit.

I thought I was hallucinating due to lack of oxygen when climbers from Polish, Italian, and Spanish teams clapped and cheered as we entered the camp. They showered me with questions like how old was I, where was I from, and why did I want to climb Aconcagua?

I didn't have much of a voice and let my dad answer. He had the widest grin I'd ever seen on his face.

"They must've heard about you being on the mountain, J Man," he said. "Word spread about a strong young boy following his dream."

His words fed my spirit. Suddenly I knew I could make it to the summit now.

"Can I take a picture with you?" asked a very thin Polish climber. At high altitude you often don't feel like eating and find it hard to sleep. She and her team had been on the mountain for almost three weeks and were about to make their third attempt at the summit. That's what I called perseverance. I smiled to myself. I had it too.

Even the ranger at Camp Berlin greeted me with a smile.

"I think the rangers are pulling for you now," Karen whispered.

After the welcoming committee returned to their tents, Dad and Karen tucked me into my sleeping bag. I was so dead tired that I didn't trust myself to be awake for the weather report. I set my alarm for seven p.m., and when I woke up we all listened to the forecast together.

It wasn't good. The park service recommended that no one attempt to summit the next day. We were going to have deteriorating conditions for about twenty-four hours before the weather would improve midday on December 30. Disappointed, Dad and Karen radioed John and Pablo that we wouldn't be summiting until then.

CHAPTER 15

I was grateful for the foul weather on Aconcagua. It meant a day of relaxing in the tent, listening to tunes, and drinking hot cocoa. Karen and I played a miniature Monopoly game while Dad took a nap. There wasn't room for the game and for Dad, so we spread the board and the tiny money on top of him. Every time he turned over, he totally messed up our game. Then Karen cooked a freeze-dried dinner of pasta Bolognese on our Jetboil stove. It was designed for climbers like us who liked to go fast and light.

Pablo and Ali joined us in the morning from Camp Nido. John arrived much later in the afternoon, looking totally wiped out.

"I thought you went down to Plaza de Mulas to acclimatize," Dad said.

He nodded. "I left this morning when I heard you were going for the summit as soon as the weather clears. Didn't want to miss that."

After helping them make camp, we headed into our tents to escape the wind.

The weather report called for clearing in the late morning the next day, and we decided to make a summit attempt. So did the other teams we talked to.

Dad shouted to the Polish, Italian, and Spanish teams through the nylon walls several times that evening, "Still leaving for the summit before dawn tomorrow?"

"Yes," John answered.

"*Sí*" from the Spanish camp.

"*Sì*" from the Italians.

"*Tak*," yelled the tough-minded Poles.

"Yes," said Pablo and Ali.

Our united assault was good to go.

It was impossible to sleep with the sides of the tent flapping against my head. I burrowed deep in my bag like a hibernating chipmunk and whispered to my grandma Mary Lu, "Am I supposed to be here? Is this how it's supposed to be, or should I turn back? Please help me."

On the morning of December 30, my alarm went off at four a.m. Outside, a gale was blowing sixty miles per hour. The temperature was minus 40 degrees, and another twelve inches of snow had fallen. I put on two layers of polypro, two layers of fleece, then wind gear, double socks, mitten liners, and my big down jacket.

Karen poured a cup of hot cocoa. I inhaled the steam, trying to blow smoke rings with my breath. After stuffing food into stomachs that didn't feel like eating, we filled our bottles with hot water and tucked them into our jackets to keep them from freezing. I put my gloves, balaclava face mask, and goggles in place, and crawled out into darkness.

After all the friendly discussion and big plans made the night before, no other teams showed their faces. Dad shook their tent flaps. One by one the Spaniards, the Italians, and the Poles told us they had no intention of coming out into the freezing wind. They'd wait for the weather to clear a bit. Pablo and Ali decided to wait at least one more day.

John appeared, clapping his hands together for warmth. "Just the four of us?"

Dad nodded. "Yep."

"So why are you going when nobody else will?" he asked.

"It's the tail end of the storm," Karen said optimistically. "It'll clear up."

"We can always come back down if things get too tough," Dad added. "And with no other teams in the way, we'll make faster time."

John's lips were tight. I could tell he wanted to crawl right back into his tent. He didn't seem exactly thrilled that we were going ahead on our own. "I'll get a video of you starting out."

Carrying only the essentials now, we left our snow-covered tent at five a.m. in a complete whiteout of piercing cold and howling wind. Terrified butterflies were careening off the walls of my stomach, but I told myself that that was normal. I trusted the decisions of Karen and Dad.

Our map was almost impossible to read in the whiteout, and snow had covered most of the little flags marking the trail. John attempted to film us as we wound around some rock formations and then zigzagged up the mountain on incredibly steep switchbacks. I was traversing a huge stretch of ice when suddenly I slipped. Instinctively I threw myself against the hill, but I could have just as easily taken a huge fall. What was going on?

"What happened, Jordan?" Karen asked.

"Don't know," I answered.

She made her way up to me and checked my boot. "You lost your crampon."

"Huh?" I looked down at my boot and saw that the crampon had come right off. That was strange. I'd put them on correctly and Karen had even double-checked. At least it was right there in the snow and could be put back on.

She called to Dad and they both knelt just downhill in case I slid.

Karen examined the crampon. "Don't know, little buddy. Maybe too much weight on the upper boot made the crampon come loose. Just sit back and relax. I'm having trouble getting it back on with these thick mitts."

Dad pulled string cheese from his pack. "Meanwhile, eat and drink."

Sitting on ice and snow made the cold creep into our bones. As soon as Karen had my crampon back on my boot, we started out again. We trudged through three-foot snowdrifts for what seemed like hundreds of hours. The wind was ferocious. I pictured this giant monster head with scowling eyes and cheeks all puffed out, blowing icy wind straight at me. It was relentless. At times I had to plant my poles and anchor myself to remain standing in a sudden gust. Karen was always right behind me and often grabbed my jacket to keep us both from blowing away.

We'd been hiking for six hours when the remains of a little A-frame wooden hut came into view. I had read about this place: the Independence Refuge, at 20,931 feet. It was too small to stand in but would serve as a shelter in an emergency. We stopped for badly needed hydration and each ate another energy bar, but we couldn't stay long. We had to keep our bodies moving and make time.

I was nearly fifteen hundred feet higher than I'd ever been.

We reached the saddle where the normal route, the one we were climbing, meets the Polish Glacier Route. I thought I was hallucinating from oxygen deprivation when I saw a team of five climbers coming *down* toward us. How could that be? No one had passed us going up.

They yelled over the roaring wind, "Came from the Polish Glacier. Heavy wind and snow. Couldn't make the top. Had to turn around."

"Good luck," Dad called as they retreated down the mountain.

We found a scrap of shelter behind a boulder. John straggled up behind us, filming the whole time. I could tell that our pace was too fast for him. He was breathing much harder than we were.

Karen studied the map. "The hardest part of the climb is straight ahead at twenty-one thousand eight hundred feet. There's a deep gully called Canaleta filled with scree and sand. And it's really, really steep. It'll be tough. You heard those guys we passed. They had to turn around, and they definitely weren't amateurs. They were all decked out in sponsors' clothing."

Dad and Karen were discussing whether or not we should turn around too. I knew what John would vote for—he didn't think we should have started out in the first place. I think I might have voted with him, but then I saw a small slice of blue in the gray sky.

I grabbed Dad's sleeve and pointed. "Look!"

"Unbelievable," he said. "The sun's trying to break out."

Karen folded the map. "How about going a little farther and seeing how it is."

"Sounds okay." Dad looked at me.

The night before I had asked Grandma Mary Lu if I was meant to be on the mountain, and now the sun was shining through the clouds just when we needed it. I was absolutely certain this was Grandma's way of answering my question. She wanted me to reach my goal. "Let's go on," I said.

"John?" Karen asked.

"I'm with you."

Each time we stopped to check, the weather was improving just like the forecast had predicted. The wind calmed a bit and the sky started to clear.

We reached the base of the Canaleta and discovered that the snow had done us a favor: We were able to climb in our crampons rather than scramble over loose rocks. Every step was still an enormous effort, though. John kept falling behind.

We stopped to wait for him. "What do you think's going on with him?" Karen asked.

Dad leaned on his poles. "Don't know. Just walking really slow, I guess."

John caught up to us but didn't say much. We waited while he caught his breath and hydrated, then moved on again.

I didn't have an altitude headache or feel nauseous, but the thin air was definitely messing with me. I felt sluggish. Even the smallest movement was in slow motion. When John fell behind again and we waited, I welcomed the rest.

A Canadian team came up behind us, breathing really hard. One of the younger guys, maybe in his twenties, asked, "How old are you?"

"Eleven."

"And you're this close to the top?"

My dad's pride jumped in. "Jordan's climbing the Seven Summits, and this is his fourth."

"Will you pose for a photo? Nobody will ever believe it otherwise," another guy said.

I was happy to as long as it didn't take too long. I was getting cold just standing there.

After John caught up again, we met two more teams who were trying to reach the summit, one from the Ukraine and one from the States. They'd come up the Polish Glacier Route and had already heard about me. They also wanted photos. I wasn't used to all this attention from strangers, but it felt good to know that I had the support of the climbing community.

I was posing with a member of the last team when John said, "I can't go on any longer."

"But we're only an hour from the summit," Karen said.

"Take my camera if you want. I'll give you a quick lesson on how to use it," he said.

"You're sure?" she asked.

He nodded. "I'm done."

My heart sank. Six out of nine gone. I'd pictured us standing on the roof of South America together. All my friends had gotten sick on the climb. My chin quivered.

"It's okay," Dad said. "He'll be all right as soon as he goes lower. I think he just pushed too hard and fast yesterday, coming from base camp to Camp Berlin in one day."

"See you later, John," I said. "Please feel better."

We plodded on, reaching the top of Canaleta forty minutes later, and then made a steep left hook for my first glimpse of the summit. I was going to make it! As I stood there, my heart beating wildly, blue reached across the sky as if it had opened just for me. All the scary scenes I had watched in mountaineering videos and all the thoughts of people getting sick and dying slipped away. Just like on Kilimanjaro the best part of the climb was the race to the finish. I threw my shoulders back and took a deep breath.

"I can do this!" I shouted. I was in my comfort zone now. Nothing could keep me from the top of that giant mountain. I surged on. My head popped over the ridge at three fifteen p.m., and climbers rose from the snow and greeted me with a standing ovation, clapping and cheering. I got high fives from an international crowd.

I was beginning to realize just how big my accomplishment was—not just reaching the top of Aconcagua, but reaching the tops of *four* of the Seven Summits. Everyone wanted a picture with me in front of the small aluminum cross that marked the summit.

The Canadian guy said, "I had to work really hard not to get passed by an eleven-year-old. Dude, you're awesome."

Every doubt, every agonizing step, every wind gust that had tried to blow me off the mountain disappeared from my mind. All the months of hard training were worth it because the view was spectacular. This was the most beautiful mountain range

I'd seen so far. I looked across peaks and valleys all the way to the Pacific.

We were probably the highest people on earth at that moment because nobody tries to summit the Himalayas when it's winter there. Karen used John's camera to snap photos of me with an American flag.

"Now let's get one of you with Flat Stanley. Britton's going to love this," she said.

I thought about what an awesome story I'd have to tell when my teachers asked my classes what each one of us had done during winter break. But the person I wanted to tell most about my adventure wouldn't be there.

I decided to dedicate this climb to my grandmother Mary Lu Drake. I knew she'd been responsible for brushing the clouds away so perfectly and clearing the way for me to make it to the top. In fact, as soon as we started back down the Canaleta, the skies closed in behind us once more.

Thanks, Grandma, I thought.

Most climbers return to Camp Berlin to spend the night. Then they carry some gear down to the next camp, go back up for the rest, and then go down again to sleep. They repeat that cycle all the way down the mountain.

We'd never gone back down to acclimatize. Our plan had always been to keep moving up. So we didn't intend to follow a cycle going up and down on the descent to haul all of our gear.

I'd already climbed the mountain once, and Karen had two or three times running up and down shooting videos. We loaded everything into massive packs on our backs, clipped and tied things to the outside of our packs when they became too full, and carried everything else. We looked more like gypsies now than mountaineers. The trail was extremely steep, and below Camp Nido there was no snow. It was like walking straight down on loose rock. All that heavy stuff kept throwing me onto my back like a turtle, and I'd have to pull myself up again.

At each camp the rangers who'd stopped us earlier to check on me were now yelling, "Wait, wait. We want a picture with Jordan." Of course I happily obliged.

After a grueling sixteen-hour day we reached Plaza de Mulas at dusk. John, Pablo, and Ali were among the crowd cheering for me, and I discovered that I'd set another world record. That felt good, but more important was the fact that that Dad, Karen, and I had made it up and back together—and safe.

"So, J Man," Dad said, "all the people who criticized us and didn't want you on the mountain are celebrating that you made it."

I was grinning ear to ear. The climb hadn't been as scary as I'd imagined. It had had its bad moments, but I hadn't struggled as much as I'd thought I would. I'd stuck it out and moved one summit closer to my dream.

The next day we hiked all the way out with mules carrying

our equipment. We passed climbers starting up the valley toward their own encounter with the mountain. "I wonder if they have any idea what's ahead of them," I said.

Karen shrugged. "It all depends on the weather."

We climbed into Pablo's van and headed back toward Mendoza, where we planned to meet the rest of our friends for pizza and a New Year's celebration. I thought of almost nothing else on the ride, but there was something we needed to take care of before we went out in public—our body odor. On the mountain you don't notice smells so much. Sweat kind of freezes, and everyone's got the same problem. But we didn't want to show up at the restaurant smelling like we did.

Pablo drove us to our hotel for showers. "We're in serious need of clean clothes," Dad told him. "Everything we have is filthy."

We drove all over town searching for *anything* clean to wear, but it was New Year's Eve and no stores were open. I ended up wearing one of Karen's tops that she insisted didn't look girly on me.

John had the video camera rolling when we entered a garden restaurant to applause and whistles. I was so relieved to see that Ryan, Mike, and Claire were all happy and feeling good again.

Ryan held up the *Buenos Aires Herald*. "Look at this, man. You made the front page, and we even saw you on the international news on TV."

What? That was mind-boggling. I hadn't done anything truly important in the scheme of things. Maybe the world was looking for good news, and a floppy-haired kid on the top of a mountain could make the headlines. I had to admit it was totally cool being on the front page of newspapers all over the world. And even though my summit wasn't going to change the world, it was still a huge accomplishment: Only about 60 percent of the climbers who try to summit on Aconcagua actually make it all the way to the top, and I was one of them.

Before leaving Mendoza, Karen got a color print made of me standing on the summit. I signed it and took it to the Honorable Elsa Lidia Galera's chambers as promised. Unfortunately, she was away for the holiday, and I didn't get to see her in person. I hoped she was proud.

And then it was time to go home—time to see my mom and my friends, and start thinking about my next mountain.

THE STORMY CLIMB:
NORTH AMERICA'S DENALI,
20,320 FEET

AVERAGE NUMBERS OF CLIMBERS
PER YEAR: 1200

JUNE 21, 2008, AGE 11

FOUR MONTHS SHORT OF THE
WORLD RECORD

CHAPTER 16

After Aconcagua I was stoked to continue the Seven Summits. It had been a tough mountain, but I had done it. Denali was 2,517 feet lower, but that didn't make it an easier mountain. It would be another tough climb. It would also be more technical than our previous ones: The snow and ice combined with the steep slopes meant we'd need to use ropes and climbing harnesses.

Denali, also known as Mount McKinley, is one giant, moody, frozen bear. It's just a few degrees south of the Arctic Circle, and like Aconcagua it's close to the Pacific Ocean. That means it has some of the fiercest weather in the world — fiercer than Aconcagua. It wasn't a matter of *if* we'd run into a storm on Denali but *when*.

In addition, the atmosphere is even thinner than usual at that latitude, so you feel two thousand to three thousand feet higher than you really are.

It's also the tallest climb in the world when you measure

from base to peak. Denali rises eighteen thousand feet above the Alaskan tundra. Everest rises twelve thousand feet from the Tibetan plateau, so you start out higher on Everest.

Denali would be the most difficult climb yet.

Serious German and British mountain climbing expeditions had been the first to reach the summits of the other mountains, but Denali's first climbers had been total amateurs. Reading about them was pretty hilarious.

In 1910 four Alaskan locals known as the Sourdough Expedition attempted to summit wearing homemade crampons, overalls, and parkas. They were trying to win a bet with a bar owner. Two of them made it to the north summit, the lower of Denali's two summits. They were carrying bags of doughnuts, flasks of hot cocoa, and a fourteen-foot pole with an American flag to plant near the top. Nobody believed these guys had really made it until members of the first documented ascent in 1913 found the pole.

That was a cool story, but I also knew that the mountain had taken more than a hundred lives over the years and that only 58 percent of the climbers who tried to summit were successful—a lower percentage than on Aconcagua.

The three of us hadn't talked much about Denali, but a few weeks after we got home from South America, Karen called me outside one day after school.

"Jordan, come out in trail shoes and bring your crampons. I want to show you something."

Why did I need those?

"Time for a lesson," she said. "On Denali we'll be using ropes, carabiners, and a climbing harness. You need to know how to use them and be able to react quickly and instinctively."

I checked out the carabiners, metal loops that would keep us attached to the ropes on the mountain. Hard to believe that our lives could depend on something so small.

Karen had tied a rope from the front door to the garage, then up the side of the hill to our neighbor's garage. It was threaded through cars, off the decks of both houses, around trees, and back to the front door again.

"Wow, nice job, Karen. What the heck is it?"

Karen put a harness around my waist with straps that fastened over the tops of both thighs. Then she attached two nylon slings to my harness with carabiners.

"These are autolocking carabiners. They are a little harder to unlock than a regular carabiner, but if you are tired and forget to lock your carabiner, these will lock automatically," she explained.

I had seen all this equipment around the house — Dad and Karen had raced with it several times — but I'd never used any of it. "What's all this for?" I asked.

"On the steep parts of Denali there will be ropes anchored in place to help us climb and descend without falling. You'll have to connect yourself to the rope on your own. Dad and I won't be able to do it for you. This is a practice course."

I looked at the ropes strung all over the place, "Are you serious?"

"Oh, yes I am. Your life and mine will depend on being attached to that fixed rope. It's your lifeline," she said. "Click each carabiner open, hook it around the rope, and let it snap closed to secure yourself."

There were eight inches of snow on the ground. Wearing my spiked crampons, I slid the carabiners easily along the rope. What was the big deal? Then I came to where Karen had attached the rope to the garage-door handle.

"How do I slide around that?" I asked.

"You don't. When you come to an anchor, yell 'clipping' to let us know that you're stopping to move around an anchor," Karen explained. "Unhook one carabiner and move it past the anchor while you're still attached to the rope with the other. Once the first one is securely in place, unclip the second one to do the same thing. When you're safely past the anchor, yell 'clear' to let us know you're done."

We went through this routine for hours—up, down, and around, first with bare hands, then wearing gloves. It was hard in the beginning to open and close the carabiners with my gloves on, but I got the hang of it.

"Now let's see how fast you can do it." She set the timer on her watch. "Ready, set, go!"

After that day, I practiced until I got faster and faster. I never knew when I would come home from school and find a new course winding around the front yard. I loved the challenge, and it became second nature to clip and unclip the carabiners. I could even do it with one hand.

"Perfect," she said one afternoon as she timed me. "Challenge your dad to a race and I'd put money on you."

Knowing how to use a carabiner on a fixed rope raised my confidence, but I was still nervous about climbing Denali. Then one afternoon a huge problem jumped out at me. "On a really steep slope what's to keep the carabiner from just sliding down the rope?" I asked.

Karen grinned. "I was waiting to see if you'd ask. That's the next lesson. You'll use an ascender along with your carabiners," she said.

I raised my eyebrows, still confused.

She went inside the house to get one and showed it to me. It had a metal handle I could grip.

"It does just what the name implies. It helps you *ascend*, or *climb*, a rope," she said, attaching it to my harness with another nylon sling and then clipping it onto the rope. "Slide it up the line a ways, then pull down."

I tried to do what she asked, but once I slid the ascender up the rope and pulled, nothing happened. "It locked."

"Exactly. The teeth grab onto the rope to keep it from sliding back. There's no way you can slide down the mountain if you're locked in with this. You can only go up. Slide it up the rope, use the handle to pull yourself forward, and then slide it up again."

"Cool."

In the spring Dad and Karen talked about the expedition one night over dinner. We had all done more research on the mountain and the best routes to the summit. When we climbed Denali we'd be totally self-sustained, meaning no porters like on Kilimanjaro or mules like on Aconcagua. We had to transport everything ourselves to multiple camps. Expecting the worst weather on earth, we had to be prepared for anything that might come up. Not only would I be carrying a heavy pack, I'd also be hauling a sled up a glacier.

I had gotten really good at Karen's ropes courses, but that didn't mean I was prepared to tow a heavy sled. "How do I train for that?" I asked.

Ask a question around Karen and the next thing you know she has a plan all worked out. One day after school she brought out an eight-foot rope attached to an SUV tire.

"What's this for?" I asked.

"Endurance and strength. Put on your climbing harness and clip yourself to the rope."

Snap. Done.

"Now run to the bottom of the hill," she said.

"Pulling this tire? It'll run me over."

"Come on, J. Keep it flat on the ground and it won't roll."

"Okaaay," I stretched the word out the way Dad does.

Hauling that tire, I stomped to the bottom of the hill and bent over, panting. That had been incredibly hard. "Are we done now?"

She wrinkled her brow. "The real test is going back up."

She had to be kidding. Dragging a heavy tire four hundred yards up a steep, bumpy dirt road? I glared at her.

"You can do it," she said.

I clenched my jaw and decided I'd show her. I leaned in to the hill and planted one foot after the other, up, up, up. By the time I reached the house, my heart was pounding so hard I thought it would break a rib.

"You're doing great!" Karen shouted.

Yeah, right.

It took us a while to figure out the tire thing. At first Karen tied the rope all the way around it. But after a few laps the rope would wear through. Sometimes the tire would bounce on its side and roll past me down the hill, forcing me to run to keep up with it.

Once we had it worked out, I'd walk up the hill from the bus stop after school, grab my iPod, and run eight or ten rounds with the tire before heading out to race mountain bikes or hang out at the lake with Cameron and Casey.

As soon as I got used to the weight of the tire, Karen and Dad took my training to a higher level by adding twenty pounds of canned food and bottles of water to my pack to carry at the same time. *No freaking way,* I thought. I was so frustrated, and

I wanted to tell them to back off, but instead I rolled my eyes and looked away. *Come on, Jordan, you can do it. One step at a time,* I told myself. I made it all the way to the top on my first try.

"Awesome, J Man, give me five!" Dad shouted.

I lifted my arm as far as the heavy pack would allow me and met his hand. That crazy big smile of his spread across his face.

The training for Denali could be exhausting. I constantly tried to bargain for fewer trips up and down the hill. But I did get stronger and stronger. Dad's pushing forced me to recognize just what I was capable of. And I'd need every little bit of strength I could muster to be ready for Denali.

I was working on my strength, and we had all the necessary gear, but we needed sleds to haul it all up the mountain. A friend we called King Richard was always volunteering to help. He was a big strong guy with pale skin and a ginger-colored goatee. He had been to Denali twice already, and even though he'd never made it to the top, he had some creative ideas.

"I'll make you the same sleds I did for my team," he said, a note of pride in his voice. "The guides thought they were brilliant. Instead of ropes I used PVC to keep the sleds behind us, especially on slanted terrain."

"That probably kept them a good distance from you too," Karen said, "instead of chasing you downhill and running into your legs."

"My sleds are the best," he said.

With King Richard's sleds, it was as if we had put the last puzzle piece in place. Before I knew it, sixth grade was coming to an end and we were packing to go. Ready or not, I was going to climb Denali.

CHAPTER 17

Some things about climbing Denali were definitely less hassle than on Aconcagua, like registering for the climb. We just had register at least sixty days in advance to get a spot because they limited the number of people on the mountain every year. The climbing season was late April through July. June was prime time. I skipped the last day of sixth grade and off we went.

We flew into Anchorage and met up with an old friend, Jacques. He was an adventure racer who'd done the Argentina Eco-Challenge with Karen and Dad. He had also climbed Denali and gave us a lot of tips during the three days we stayed with him.

After spending a few days and learning all we could from him, Jacques drove us three hours to the ranger station in Talkeetna, where everyone was required to check in before starting their climb.

A ranger greeted us as soon as we entered. "Welcome, Jordan."

"How does he know who I am?" I whispered to Karen.

"From our registration, I guess. Probably don't get too many eleven-year-olds up here," she said.

The ranger came from behind the counter and shook Dad's hand. "We're thrilled to see a family doing something together. Normally I'd be cautious, filling you with all kinds of warnings, but I see from your registration that you've already done Kilimanjaro, Elbrus, and Aconcagua." He looked directly at me. "But this *is* a bigger and much more aggressive mountain. Think you can handle it?"

It was the same question I'd been asking myself for months, but I couldn't tell him that. We were here. I was as ready as I was going to be. And anyway, it was too late to turn back. I filled him in on all the training I'd done.

"Okay." He kept one eye on me while he went over all the safety precautions and discussed high-altitude medical information with all three of us. Then we had to watch a video about litter control and what to expect on the mountain. We each received trash bags and a canister for our solid human waste, to be flown out by airplane when we finished our climb. Much like Aconcagua, Alaska was taking care of its environment.

Karen had looked into climbing with an expedition, but we didn't want to alter our pace by going with a group of strangers.

We'd already learned that other climbers didn't adapt well to our fast and light style. We raised a lot of eyebrows wherever we went. *You're doing what and how fast?*

Denali's base camp is about sixty miles over rugged tundra away from the nearest road. To get there, you have to take a small plane that's equipped to land on the glacier. Karen had booked us a four-person plane, with one of those seats reserved for the pilot. It was the oldest and most well-known flight service to Denali and also the cheapest. Our pilot, also named Jacques, was a grumpy old man who didn't seem at all happy to see us.

"What's his problem?" Dad mumbled under his breath.

Karen gave him a hip check. "Don't even go there. He's all we've got."

The rangers had made us feel welcome, but this skinny, bearded guy in his old flannel shirt was the worst. We helped him weigh our bags, and then we hauled all the gear to the plane ourselves while he sipped a hot cup of coffee. Then he gave us a very cold safety briefing before we boarded the plane. I put my iPod on in anticipation of a turbulent plane ride over the rough mountain air.

I would have listened to my music for the entire ride, but Karen signaled me to take off my headphones. When I did, I realized that our scruffy, grouchy pilot had suddenly turned into an amazing tour guide. During the flight he gave us an excellent hour-long description of the sights below. He told us the history of the formation of the Alaska Range. He pointed out the rivers and forests and the colored rocks with white and black stripes, and told us about the wildlife. He even pointed out a bear and a moose walking in the river below.

The views of the tundra and the rest of the Alaska Range were awesome. The mountains got bigger as we flew closer to the jagged, rocky peaks. I held my breath when we went through passes with only about a ten-foot clearance on the side of each wing.

As we went to land on the glacier, Jacques lowered the plane's skis to glide onto the surface; wheels wouldn't gain the traction needed for a smooth landing. The Denali base camp, at 7,200 feet, was a crazy international scene. About a dozen tents were pitched parallel to the runway. Climbers were busy sorting their gear and preparing to head up the mountain. They barely looked up when we landed.

I grinned. Like all the climbers on Denali, we'd done the first 7,200 feet of that eighteen-thousand-foot climb by air. Yeah!

Karen pulled out the map. "We can stay here tonight or push ahead five and a half miles to the camp at Ski Hill. Votes?"

"Move on," Dad said.

"Same here," I added. Hanging at base camp didn't sound as fun as heading out.

We dug a deep hole and cached a few days' worth of food

and fuel in case weather prevented our return flight out. The place was swarming with big black ravens. If you left any food out, they went crazy for it. One of the rangers told me that people used to mark their caches with a flag, but ravens had quickly discovered that the flags meant there was food below. They'd peck and claw their way under to retrieve the food. So climbers started using three flags in a triangle around their caches instead of right on top of them. So far the ravens hadn't figured out the triangular markers. Their math skills were even worse than mine.

We rigged our King Richard–modified sleds with the rest of our supplies and gear. Dad helped me get everything tied down on my sled and attached it to my mountaineering pack with a couple of carabiners. He made sure the weight of the sled fell onto my hips, not my back, for easier climbing. He also adjusted the distance of the sled from my body, keeping it as short as possible but far enough away that it wouldn't bump into my snowshoes, which we needed to pull the sleds.

Dad, Karen, and I were ready to go. Together the three of us were transporting about three hundred seventy pounds of gear. Including the cache we buried at base camp, we'd brought enough food to last a month in case we were trapped by storms. I thought that would be the worst thing that could happen to us on this trip.

We were on our way out of base camp when we heard a thunderous roar—like a jet was landing right on top of us.

I looked around, waiting for some kind of disaster to strike, but the people in base camp were totally unfazed.

"What was that?" I asked.

"Avalanche on Mount Hunter," someone said.

I knew that Mount Hunter was about eight miles away. If an avalanche was that loud from that far away, I couldn't imagine what it would be like to experience one first hand.

"Get used to that sound," Dad said. "Avalanches are a pretty common thing in these mountains."

Nearly forty climbers had died in avalanches in Denali National Park since the forest service started keeping records in 1976, but reading about that on the Internet had never felt real to me. Now, even eight miles away, hearing colossal amounts of snow and ice crashing down the mountain was staggering.

Still, worrying about avalanches the whole time would take all the joy out of the climb, so I put them out of my mind. I was on a glacier thousands of miles from home and the road I'd trained on. Dragging that tire had really sucked at the time, but in my heart I'd known it was preparing my mind and body so I'd be able to take in what nature had to offer. We had landed in a frozen paradise, and I was about to haul all my personal supplies up the mountain. It was real. It was massive.

"Time to rope up," Dad said. "There are giant, man-eating crevasses along the entire glacier."

He wasn't kidding. Fall into one of those deep chasms in

the glacier and you'd never be seen again. We'd be dodging death from the start of our climb. On the bottom of the mountain we roped to one another. On steeper sections, when there were fixed lines, we would clip in to those.

Dad tied a rope to his harness, then tied it to a carabiner on my harness. Finally Karen tied the other end to her harness. If one of us slipped, the others would be able to stop a bad fall. The trick was to keep the rope almost tight, but not so much that you were pulling on the person in front of you. We were close enough to communicate, but not so close that we'd all be in a dangerous spot at the same time.

We'd practiced this dozens of times at home, but that wasn't the same as knowing you could actually fall in a crevasse and need to be rescued. It felt like things were getting super serious, super fast.

From base camp we actually had to follow a trail down Heartbreak Hill before we could begin to climb up the mountain. "I think it's called that because it breaks your heart to have to go *down* when you really want to go *up* a mountain," I told Dad and Karen.

Dad laughed and nodded. "Happens that way, J Man."

From the bottom of the hill we had to swing out wide onto the main Kahiltna Glacier to avoid the large flag-marked crevasses on both sides. Ahead there was nothing but snow. The beautiful mountains towering around us were awe-inspiring, but they made me feel very small at the same time, especially when avalanches came screaming down on all sides. The route took us safely through the middle of a glacier, so I knew that we didn't have to worry about an avalanche hitting us directly, but that eerie sound was going to be hard to get used to.

It was a tough climbing day. We couldn't see the summit from where we were, which was a major bummer. Seeing the summit always helped me push on. I also had to constantly adjust the weight of the pack and sled. I was glad I had trained as hard as I had, or this would have been torture.

"Next time I'm hiring a yeti or abominable snowman to be my beast of burden," I yelled.

Karen laughed. "Let me know how that goes." She was her amazing Super K self—rock steady, cheerful, and strong. She always helped my whole attitude, and made me appreciate the smaller details on the climb. She was always pausing to point out special moments and ask, "What do you think of that?"

Dad was more like an adventure novel, spouting lifesaving health tips while living on the edge. "Just be glad we have sleds," he said. "Otherwise we'd be shuttling all of this stuff up the mountain on our backs. Think about how many trips that would take."

We climbed for about seven hours with no real drama to distract me before reaching the base of Ski Hill around seven p.m. It was only six hundred feet higher than the landing field and a thousand feet higher than Big Bear. It seemed like a long haul for such a small gain in elevation.

After setting up camp, Dad buried supplies and planted three flags with my name on them.

By ten o'clock I was wiped out and ready to crash, but it was still light outside. The sun never really set the whole time we were on Denali. It moved down onto the horizon a little after midnight and just hovered there before crawling back into the sky around two a.m.

Since it never got really dark, we weren't in any rush to break camp the next morning. We decided to wait for the sun to rise above us where it belonged and warm things up a bit. I tried to remember exactly how Dad had rigged my sled the day before so that I could get it situated by myself. I hooked the rope to my carabiner, and then asked Dad and Karen to check it. They were pretty impressed that I had figured out the rigging on my own.

We set out, and the climb got steeper and steeper. I had trained for this, though, and my sled stayed behind me where it belonged.

Karen pointed to some guys just ahead of us. They were climbing the same slippery slope as we were, but they didn't have our PVC stabilizers. Their sleds, attached with ropes, were pulling them off-balance and sideways on the hill.

Thank you, King Richard, for building us such amazing sleds, I thought. But I was bummed a couple of minutes later when four skiers swished past us. And me without my skis again!

We climbed past the guys with the sliding sleds and made it

to the base of Denali's Motorcycle Hill in less than four hours. I dumped my pack and flopped onto my back, exhausted.

The hill, a particularly steep section of the mountain, was incredibly windy, and avalanches threatened to come roaring off the ridges north of us. Climbers had carved big blocks of snow to build protective walls around their camps. With all those colored tents surrounded by huge ice cubes, it was a pretty weird scene. It looked like an Eskimo city.

We were like birds claiming an unused nest as we set up camp inside a vacant igloo wall. Dad and Karen used a snow saw to cut more blocks of ice and fortify our shelter.

The guys with the swervy sleds arrived in camp about forty-five minutes after we did.

One of them removed his goggles and studied me closely. "How old are you?"

"Eleven." I was used to answering that question on climbs by now.

"You charged right past us," he said.

"Just because of your sleds," I told him.

He nodded. "Yeah, yours are pretty impressive." His face was badly sunburned, and the goggles gave him raccoon eyes. We'd learned our lesson on Elbrus about sun, snow, and high altitude and wouldn't make that mistake again.

Soon after he left with his team, a guy in his early thirties came through wearing a Buff headwear from one of Dad and Karen's adventure races.

"Did you do that race?" Karen asked.

"I was just there filming and taking photographs. I'm more of a mountain climber than racer," he said.

Dad leaned on an eighteen-inch block he had just added to our wall. "They require a whole different set of skills," he said. "In racing it's all about speed. Here you have to slow down."

"And racing's mostly about physical endurance," Karen added. "Here the mental game is just as important. It's about making good decisions."

"Yeah," he said, "and some of those can be life-altering."

I'd noticed his right hand was a prosthetic. I was curious but would never say anything or ask a question that might embarrass him.

"Good luck on the mountain," he said. "Nice talking to you."

We said good-bye and then Dad turned to me. "Know who that was?" he asked.

I shook my head.

"Aron Ralston," he said.

I still had no clue.

"Remember the guy who was hiking in Utah when his right arm got pinned beneath an eight-hundred-pound boulder?" he asked.

"Not really."

"It was five years ago," Karen said. "Jordan was probably too young to remember."

I didn't remember, but now I wanted to know. "What happened to his arm?"

"He tried every possible way to free it but it wouldn't budge. By the fifth day his water had run out and he had to drink his own urine."

I made a face. "Ewww, gross."

"It was that or die. Your body can't store water. You have to replace it," Dad said.

I shuddered just thinking about that.

"You heard him mention a life-altering decision," Karen said.

I nodded, suspecting I wasn't going to like this. The guy had no hand.

"His only chance for survival was to cut off his own arm. He used a pocket knife to cut through it."

"Oh my God!" I said. "Are you serious? I can't imagine the pain."

Dad nodded. "I've endured some pretty brutal stuff, but nothing that even comes close to what he experienced. He had to climb out of there and walk five miles before some other hikers spotted him."

"I recognized him from TV interviews," Karen said, "but didn't want to say anything. I'm sure he's tired of reliving it."

I'd read about animals chewing off legs to escape traps, but I wondered if I'd have had the courage to do what Aron did. His story also reminded me that a split-second error in judgment could put you in a situation in which you'd be forced to make a desperate choice. A minute ago I had been about to complain about blisters.

I wasn't going to complain, but I couldn't ignore them either. Neglecting them would be a bad decision. So after dinner I let Dad know that I needed help.

Dad was a master at caring for foot problems after all those years of endurance races. Sometimes he'd come home looking like his feet had been through a meat grinder. Just like he'd done so many times for his own feet, he rummaged through his first-aid kit for a sterilized needle, popped my blisters, and pressed the fluids out.

"You need to tighten your boots better," he said as he wrapped tape around my feet, "or you won't make it to the top."

I felt like I'd screwed up with my boots, and I wanted to prove I was responsible. So I immediately tended to my nightly jobs to compensate. First I took the Lake Louise survey. Then at 7:05 p.m. I turned on the radio to be ready for the 7:10 p.m. weather forecast. It sounded pretty good for tomorrow.

Someone shook the tent flap. "You the kid going after my record?" a voice asked.

Huh?

Dad peered out, then held the flap open so we could go out and greet what looked like a father-son team.

"Jordan, this is Johnny Strange," Dad said, introducing me

Age 9, with the mural that inspired me to climb the Seven Summits

In front of Kilimanjaro, at the last camp at the bottom, after our descent

Striking a pose atop a marker at the summit of Kosciuszko,
with Karen (left) and my dad, Paul (right)

Camping out on the way up Elbrus

With a mule on the route up Aconcagua

On one of the knife ridges leading up the West Buttress route of Denali

Midway up Carstensz Pyramid

Karen, me, and Dad on a day hike during an
acclimatization stop on the way to Everest Base Camp

Me, Karen, and Dad at a pit stop on the drive to Everest Base Camp, somewhere on the Tibetan Plateau. Tibetan prayer flags cover the archway over the road.

Taking a break on the way to Everest's Advanced Base Camp as a yak train carrying gear passes by

At Base Camp on Everest's north side, we held a Buddhist ceremony known as Puja, in which mountaineers ask permission to climb Everest.

Me, Dad, and Karen with the Chinese team on Everest. They had just recorded an interview with me about my mission, climbs, and experiences.

Left to right: Dad, me, and Karen at the summit of Everest

Karen (left) and me, messing around on my skis and looking for
jumps to do tricks off of, at Union Glacier in Antarctica

Left to right: Dad, Scott, Karen, and me heading up to mid camp on Vinson, towing sleds filled with gear for our trip

Negotiating the rope section below high camp on Vinson

to the younger of the two men. "We've known his dad and mom for years."

Johnny looked like he was about five years older than me.

"Johnny's out to break the record for youngest person to do the Seven Summits, set by Samantha Larson, who did it at eighteen," Dad said.

I wasn't after anyone's record—it wasn't something I had given much thought to—but I was interested in the fact that he had the same goal as me: climbing the Seven Summits.

"How many have you done?" I asked.

"Denali's my fourth. I did Vinson when I was twelve, then Kilimanjaro, then Aconcagua."

"This is my fifth," I told him. "I guess we're both holding off on Everest."

"Not me. I'll knock off Elbrus this year and Everest next spring. Maybe Kosciuszko two weeks after that."

"So how old will you be when you finish?" I asked.

"Seventeen."

I nodded. His self-assurance amazed me. "Impressive. I wish you luck."

Like everyone else he was surprised that we were climbing without a guide. "Scott Woolums is guiding us," Johnny's father, Brian, said, "and he's the best."

Johnny and I compared climbing notes awhile, and we got to meet Scott. After Johnny, Scott, and Johnny's dad left, Karen made us some more some more cocoa, and I sat back with a steaming cup. "He didn't mention Carstensz. I want to do that one next," I said.

"Let's climb this mountain first, J Man," Dad said, "and then worry about the rest."

He was right, of course. It was time to get some sleep so that we could tackle the next phase of this mountain in the morning.

We had a team conference the next morning on whether to rest a day or go up to Advanced Base Camp at 14,200 feet.

Dad stirred his tea. "We're already acclimatized to fifteen thousand feet. The weather's too unpredictable here. Why stay longer and risk getting hammered by wind and snow? We did that on Aconcagua and it wasn't fun."

We were all feeling good enough to move on. Because the hill was so steep, it was going to take two trips to reach Advanced Base Camp with all our gear. I hung out just below Motorcycle Hill to let my blisters air out while Dad and Karen took a load of gear up.

I felt totally safe and liked having a break just to chill by myself. I lay in the tent listening to some hip-hop and reggae until I was roasting from the sun beating in on the side of the tent. My watch thermometer read 80 degrees F. I tried calling my mom but had no luck. We hadn't brought the BGAN we'd used on Aconcagua because we'd been told we'd have some cell phone coverage, but ours didn't work. Bummer. I really wanted to let her know I was okay.

Dad and Karen returned with empty sleds around six thirty p.m. They rested awhile and had dinner, and then they started packing for the trip to Advanced Base Camp.

"But it's nine o'clock," I said.

"And still daylight," Dad pointed out.

He was right about that: Alaska has nearly twenty-four hours of daylight in the summer. But it still seemed strange to begin the climb now. "Yeah, but . . ."

"You've been lounging around all day. We already made a trip up there," Karen said.

I couldn't argue with that, so we roped up and climbed Motorcycle Hill. I wasn't exactly in high gear; it was more like a duck walk as I dragged myself up the steep hill. My heels hurt every time I set my foot down. I was totally miserable and kept stopping.

"Pick up the pace, J Man," Dad said, "or we'll never get there."

Karen caught up to me. "You're doing great." She gave me some water and trail mix to spike my energy. "Just a few more feet to the top. I know you can do it."

I didn't ask how many feet she meant by "a few." I just let her encouraging words help me follow Dad to the top of the hill, and then we began a long traverse toward Windy Corner. Karen kept grabbing my jacket to keep me from blowing away like that red tent in South America.

From Windy Corner the route opened into a basin filled

with huge crevasses—more man-eaters. Dad moved slowly, constantly testing the ground with his hiking pole and planting warning flags. I imagined the ground opening up and swallowing me whole.

Just before Advanced Base Camp, Karen and Dad collected the gear they'd stashed earlier. Dragging even heavier loads made the rest of the hike nearly impossible. At two a.m. we finally reached Advanced Base Camp, or ABC, at 14,200 feet.

I was completely wiped out, and my mouth was raw from breathing cold, dry air. All I wanted to do was sleep. I dropped everything, including me, and just lay there wasted while they set up camp.

Karen made some hot water and cooked a couple of dehydrated meals. It was hard to force ourselves to stay awake long enough to eat, but we had to keep our strength up. Then we crashed.

The next morning when we turned on the radio, we heard a lot of activity on the common channel.

"That's a Swedish voice," Karen said, "and he sounds frantic."

We held the radio close to our ears and listened. The man speaking over the radio had dropped his gear at sixteen thousand feet and was coming down the most dangerous section of the mountain, the West Buttress headwall, when he discovered a sole Russian climber going in and out of consciousness and completely unable to descend by himself. The Swedish man was requesting that rangers come help, but conditions were too dangerous; the weather had turned vicious.

"They're only two thousand feet higher than us," I said. "Should we go? He'll die if nobody helps him."

"We're not ready for that altitude," Dad said. "We'd create three more victims and turn this into an even greater catastrophe. Even the national park rangers aren't going because of the danger."

"But—"

Dad looked me sternly in the eye. "Jordan, it's really important at moments like this for you to assess the situation and make the right decision. A simple split-second mistake and you could end up without a limb like Aron."

I couldn't help worrying about a similar thing happening to me—or worse, to Dad and Karen. My goal of climbing the Seven Summits had brought the three of us here. Suddenly the fact that one of us could die on this climb felt very, very real.

CHAPTER 18

Advanced Base Camp was on a big plateau where rangers had set up what looked like a small village. There was a large medical tent, a ranger station that broadcast weather reports and could offer emergency help, and a landing pad for a rescue helicopter. In the dead center were holes for toilets surrounded by snow walls for privacy.

Rumors and stories about the Russian man swirled around camp. He had been quite sick high up on the mountain. The Swedish team worked for hours and risked their own lives to get him to safety. We were there when they arrived in camp. The Russian felt better almost immediately, just being at a lower altitude. He planned to spend the night at ABC before continuing down to a lower altitude. He'd never reach the summit—not on that trip anyway.

His experience brought home all those safety lectures I had gotten from Dad and Karen. Not only was the guy out there all alone—not a good idea—but he had obviously tried to climb too high without being ready for the altitude. That wasn't a mistake I planned on making.

After the drama, hanging out at ABC was pretty cool. Climbers from all over the world gathered there, and it was fun being around them. Dad and Karen needed a day to rest after their double climb anyway.

I found them studying the map and asked how long they thought it would take us to summit.

Karen folded the map. "Depends on the weather and how we're doing."

On the second day the weather was clear and sunny. "Looks good for moving to High Camp," Dad said. "Jordan, get your stuff together."

I gathered my crampons, harness, ascender, and carabiners. Then a sudden panic slammed me in the head. My ice axe. Where was my ice axe? Had I dropped it on the trail coming up? Left it in the lower camp? I didn't want to tell Dad and Karen that I had lost it.

"Okay, J Man," Dad said. "Let's go."

I let out a long shaky breath. The axe wasn't on Dad's list of gear. Maybe I didn't need it. Should I not say anything? This was a moment of decision, and I couldn't risk making the wrong one.

"Ready in a minute. Need to find my ice axe," I admitted.

"Where is it?" Karen asked.

"Don't know."

"Better find it," she said. "You'll need it."

My heart raced into overdrive as I ran from one ice shelter to the next. "Did you guys see a blue ice axe?"

"Sorry, no," they answered.

"Anybody here find a blue ice axe?"

"Nope, but we'll let you know if we do."

At the sixth tent I spotted what looked like my axe being used to anchor some prayer flags to a wall made of ice blocks. I quietly approached the climber sitting in front of it with his morning coffee. "Excuse me, is that your ice axe? It looks kind of like mine."

He immediately got up and retrieved it for me. "We found it lying in the snow and asked all around. Here you go."

My heart slowed to a normal rhythm again. "Thank you so much."

When I returned to our camp, Dad and Karen were ready for a stern talk about me keeping track of my gear.

"I guess I was so tired I dropped it," I explained.

"It's up to you to keep *all* of your gear accounted for at *all* times," Dad said. "Being without your axe could mean the difference between life and death."

"That could have been the end of our attempt to reach the summit," Karen added.

I knew they were right. Being tired was no excuse. I'd messed up big time. Another lesson learned: Keep track of everything.

We couldn't take our sleds any farther, so we buried them in the snow along with a cache of food and the gear that we wouldn't need at High Camp or in our push to the summit. Then we took our tent down, but we also noticed that no one else was budging.

We walked over to the ranger station to see what was going on.

"Why's no one going up?" Dad asked.

"The wind on the ridge is about eighty miles per hour," the ranger told us. "It's too dangerous. The trail's only a foot wide, with two-thousand-to-three-thousand-foot drops on either side. If you get blown off there, you'll never be seen again."

"What's the latest forecast?" Dad asked.

"Even more wind," he answered.

We asked other teams what they were thinking of doing. Everyone was staying put until the wind died down.

"Okaaay, looks like we're not going anywhere either," Dad said.

We put the tent back up and Karen made some tea. Three guides were tossing a football around and asked us to join them.

One of the men threw to Dad. "How long have you been on the mountain?"

He caught it and heaved it back. "This is our fourth day."

The guy clasped the ball in both hands, paused, and gave him a funny look. "You're joking, right? We've been on Denali for ten days and thought we were doing well."

"I don't like being exposed to storms any longer than necessary," Dad said.

The guide still seemed a little incredulous. "So when are you planning to summit?"

"Soon as the weather clears," Dad answered.

The guide threw the ball again. "Don't count on it. Some of us have been waiting here a week. We even built a snow statue to the gods." He laughed. "But the wind god blew it down."

A few other climbers joined us, and soon we had enough people for a game of touch football. I hit the line of scrimmage and went long in a picture-perfect slow-motion hook to the left as a frozen football skyrocketed toward me. I caught it with fingers so cold I thought they'd chip off. After two fumbles I benched myself on a snow seat and decided it best not to count on an NFL career.

I relaxed while keeping one eye on the ridge. About three p.m. the wind seemed to be dying down. Dad noticed it too and talked to the other teams. "Things seem pretty calm up there now."

"Looks quieter than it has in days," said the Australian guide. "I'd like to get my team up there, but twelve people can't break camp and get organized fast enough. Hopefully the weather will hold a while longer."

Score one for the small team. We were way more mobile than those big groups. In twenty minutes our tent was folded, everything was packed, and we were ready to head out to the

High Camp. We carried only what we needed, along with extra food in case a storm blew in and we had to spend an extra day.

Dad waited for me at the base of the eight-hundred-foot vertical face of the West Buttress headwall. My eyes walked up, up, up the wall and around every anchor holding the fixed rope in place. Until now Dad, Karen, and I had been roped to one another, but not to the mountain. This would be my first time using an ascender to climb a fixed rope. I was excited to use the skills I had developed on all those ropes courses in Big Bear.

"Clip in," Dad said. "Stay focused and do exactly as you practiced."

I took a deep breath and replayed my training in my head, going through all the steps to make sure I didn't miss anything. I attached my ascender to my harness with a sling. Then I clipped my carabiner onto the fixed rope, followed by the ascender. It locked, just like it was supposed to. Then I waited for Dad to move up a proper distance before I followed.

When it was time, I pulled myself up and shifted my weight onto the next step. Then I moved the ascender and repeated the process.

"Way to go!" Karen yelled from below.

I moved right up that wall to the first anchor. I remembered that I had to let the climbers around me know that I was moving around the anchor. "Clipping!" I shouted.

The wall was steep and it was hard, but everything was

going great. I was doing it! Dad and Karen encouraged me the whole way up.

I came to the last anchor. I unfastened my carabiner and moved it past the anchor, making sure it was clipped on before I unhooked my ascender. But when I tried to attach it on the other side of the anchor, I couldn't get it to clip into place.

"J, you okay?" Karen asked.

Focus. Focus, I told myself. My hands felt awkward in my thick mittens. I took a deep breath and tried again. This time the ascender locked in place.

I took another step. My crampon couldn't sink into the hard ice, and for a moment my feet slipped out from under me. My heart rate shot through the roof, but my ascender held me as I tried to get my feet back underneath me.

It had been easy at home, but this was real. Now I understood how important my harness and every other piece of equipment were. There was no room for mistakes on the mountain. I was proud and happy when I took those last few steps and reached the top of the wall.

Dad waited for me with a huge grin on his face. We slapped a high five with our thick gloves. The sound echoed and made me laugh. I was flying high now. I'd done it, really done it.

"I'm Spider-Man on ice," I said.

"That you are, J Man."

I looked down on the camp we'd just come from. It was so

tiny. The tents looked like the footprints of baby mice in snow. It was a magical moment.

As we moved along the crest of the buttress, the views were incredible. There was a huge glacier to the north, across the tundra, and dozens of other peaks in the Alaska Range to the south.

The dreaded ridge above the West Buttress headwall wasn't all that steep, but it was razor sharp, and less than a foot wide in some places. That was no big deal on level ground, but the steep, icy slopes on either side plunged down thousands of feet. We couldn't see the bottom. If you fell, there was no chance of stopping yourself.

Now I knew why no one had gone up when the winds were high. One fierce gust would send you down the side of the mountain like a twig. There were no fixed ropes here because there was nothing to anchor them to. Instead the three of us were roped together, ready to lean to one side or the other if someone slipped.

I swallowed hard to keep my heart in place. I needed it in my chest where it belonged, working for me, pumping away. Even leaning only slightly could mean instant death. Every move had to be thought out like a serious game of chess. I declared checkmate in the dim polar light at one a.m. when we arrived in High Camp at 17,200 feet. We quickly set up camp protected from the wind on the lee side of an abandoned half igloo, had some food and tea, and crawled into our bags.

I was asleep against the tent wall when the wind unleashed

its fury on us, flapping the side of the tent like the wings of a giant pterodactyl. It was a wild and crazy night. None of us could sleep. Dad propped himself on one elbow and held the wall back with his other arm to keep it from suffocating me. It was at times like this that he amazed me the most. He has an endurance no one can match, but seeing that big grin he always wears, nobody would guess it.

By morning the wind had died down, and we decided to go for the summit during the break in the weather. Karen made sure I had lots of sunscreen on my face, and Dad attached a sun guard to my glasses. It hung down over my nose like a beak. The air was super cold, definitely below zero, but we had all the right gear and were pretty warm. Still, within half an hour ice had frozen on the curls sticking out from beneath my red parka hood.

We were roped up to a fixed line again and had to cross a steep diagonal traverse that was called the Autobahn because of how quickly a German team had slid down and lost their lives from there. The park service had put up ice anchors and metal pickets with carabiners on them where we could attach our team rope as we moved across the traverse. One misplaced step and you were gone, down a thousand feet into the jaws of a crevasse.

"Clip in and walk with your ice axe," Dad said.

The slope was steep and endless, and we were far ahead of the other teams still back in High Camp. I heard only howling winds and the squeak of crampons biting the snow. I plodded on and on. My down jacket and layers of Polartec fleece kept me warm.

I leaned in to the hill to rest a moment and thought of my friends and family. I was climbing for them, too. I moved the axe forward, using it like a cane to help me walk. The tip hit a hollow spot and sank only an inch or two, but that was enough to throw me off-balance. Having practiced on Elbrus, I instinctively rolled onto my stomach, feet downhill, and slid to a self-arrest.

Karen caught up to me. "Jordan, what's up?"

I was worn out and frustrated. Tears flooded my eyes.

Karen helped me up. "Take your time; take some deep breaths. This is really hard work, J, and you're doing great." She brushed the snow and ice off my jacket and hair. "Let's just try to go at a slower pace for a little while and see how that feels, okay?"

Karen's voice warmed me. I nodded and continued on to a corner where we found shelter behind a rock to take a break and regroup. She fed me trail mix, cheese, and water to keep my energy high enough for another hour.

We reached a high, flat plateau at 19,389 feet called the Football Field. When we arrived, I let myself crash to the ground, and I lay staring at the enormous expanse of snow ahead of us. My only thought was *All right, here we go.*

We were just under a thousand feet from the summit, but

in front of the Football Field stood a long open face—a field of ice and snow—going straight up to the summit ridge.

Dad led the way, I was behind him, and Karen was in the back, somehow managing the rope, filming, and constantly encouraging me.

I kept thinking we were there, but the climb was deceiving and took much longer than I thought. We finally hit the summit ridge, where the climb became extremely treacherous and exposed. Dad had to do a bit of crazy free climbing to reach anchors or place new ones. I watched him skillfully maneuver with the rope and his ice axe to add additional anchors, making the route safe for me. My heart was pounding, but Karen's careful words of encouragement behind me calmed me down again.

Just before the summit we stopped for a minute. Karen ran ahead with the video camera to film me reaching the top. Seeing the summit gave me the push I needed. I went for it with everything I had. As they had on other summits, my mind and body teamed up to give me something more when the peak was within reach. A natural high took me up, up, and up. When there was no more up and I reached the summit, I threw myself on the ground, sobbing out of control.

"Oh my God! Oh my God, I did it!"

Dad was right behind me. He dropped to the ground too, holding me, tears pouring down his face. "I love you. Love you so much."

"I love you too."

"No other boy in the world could have done this. You're so brave."

Tears were flying everywhere, Karen's too as she filmed us.

I can't describe the feeling I had when I reached the top of a mountain. It was like nothing else. Suddenly all the pain and heartache it had taken to get there was forgotten when I found myself standing on the top of the world. I'd put so much into getting up Denali. It was the coldest, most physically demanding thing I'd ever set out to do.

The mountain was tough, but that day I was even tougher. Even better, I had conquered my fear and my doubt.

This was the most amazing moment in my life so far.

I stood up to look around and take in the view. I threw both arms in the air, my axe in one hand, and let out a hoot of excitement. Karen snapped a picture to remember the moment forever and to prove we'd made it. A plane of tourists circled several times overhead, and I wondered if somewhere in a photo album there would be a picture of us standing on the summit.

We were at 20,320 feet in perfect weather—bluebird skies and barely a breeze. Another team was heading toward the summit, but for the moment we had the place to ourselves. I was standing on a big snow-covered mountain looking over an ocean of clouds with peaks poking through like islands in a white sea.

After turning a full 360 degrees, I went to a calmer center

inside me. My dad's brother had died recently. "I'd like to dedicate this climb to my uncle Tony," I told Dad and Karen. "I will miss him and wish I'd had longer to know him better."

Dad nodded. I knew he missed Tony too. "We need to head back now."

I took one last look around and we set off.

We were moving quickly, and our mood shifted. From the emotional high of the summit we were hitting a low of exhaustion, and we got angry and short with one another. On the fixed rope my lines got so tangled that I couldn't unhook to get around an anchor. Karen had to fix everything.

"Think about what you're doing, Jordan," she said.

I knew that most accidents occurred on the way down when climbers were exhausted, but still the tone of her voice cut through me. I swore to never make that mistake again.

After crossing the Football Field and making it down that long traverse we picked up our tent at the High Camp and booked it to Advanced Base Camp by six p.m. Since my cell didn't get reception, the first thing I did was borrow someone's phone and call Mom to tell her I'd made the summit and was safe. It was great hearing her voice.

After a much-deserved sleep at Advanced Base Camp, we broke camp and headed on down through Windy Corner, past the campsite at the base of Motorcycle Hill, and back up Heartbreak Hill to the landing strip. The snow had melted on the cache we'd buried the first day, leaving our stuff completely exposed. Fortunately, we were smarter than your average raven and had packed everything in a duffel bag so the birds couldn't get to it.

We were ready to go, but we had to wait a whole day for the weather to clear enough to fly out.

Hudson Air arrived to take us out at ten p.m. the next day. It still seemed weird having daylight so late at night. In Talkeetna we had to check in again at the ranger station and let them know we'd reached the summit.

While waiting, I met a teacher who explained her method of showing kids how cold it was. "I take a cup of boiling water outside and toss it in the air. If it's minus 50 degrees or colder, the water freezes in midair."

I wanted to try it out myself, but it wasn't cold enough.

The rangers kept notes on who summited, reasons for failure, and accidents, injuries, and illnesses. Thank goodness we had none of those to report. They let us know that an eleven-year-old boy from Talkeetna had climbed Denali when he was a few months younger than me. So no world record for me, not this time. That was cool. Reaching the summit with Dad and Karen and coming back safely was what mattered—not a world record.

I also realized that I had turned a corner. The awesome feeling I'd had in reaching the summit of Denali had been like nothing I'd ever experienced before. All my doubts and fears about my goal of climbing the Seven Summits melted away.

THE ROCK CLIMB:

AUSTRALIA'S

CARSTENSZ

PYRAMID,

16,024 FEET

AVERAGE NUMBER OF CLIMBERS
PER YEAR: 500

SEPTEMBER 2, 2009, AGE 13

WORLD RECORD

CHAPTER 19

When I got back to my mom's after Denali, she brushed the curls from my forehead and looked into my eyes.

"Something's changed," she said. "There's a light shining in you that wasn't there before. I think the mountain brought out some of the man in you."

Her words made me feel good. I was glad that someone else could see the change in me.

"You've done so many mountains so fast, like a hamster running on a wheel," she said, putting her arms around me. "I wish you'd stay home for a while and just be a kid."

I needed that also. I was heading to seventh grade and wanted to feel part of something. It had to be healthy, active, and outdoors. That summer Dad and Karen and I had joined hundreds of students at Big Bear Middle School to run around the track as part of a send-off for Ryan Hall, a local marathon runner leaving for the Beijing Olympics. He had run around

Big Bear Lake when he was thirteen. I was now twelve. Could I do the same run? I'd ridden my bike around the lake hundreds of times.

Dad and Karen ran around the lake with me, but it was *not* fun. At the end I was torched—happy that I had tried, but it had taken me the same amount of time to run sixteen miles as it took most people to run a full marathon. Apparently I hadn't inherited my dad's speed genes, but I had gotten his burning desire to always improve.

I signed up for the cross-country team when school started, but not with the intention of competing in races. I hated the pressure and, even worse, I hated to lose. I joined to be part of a team sport for the first time, and I wanted to be a better runner.

There were fifty kids on the team. I was one of the slowest runners, but I kept working to run a faster mile. With Dad's help I moved toward the front of the pack, but I was never the fastest.

I'd learned a lot about the importance of a healthy diet from Dad and Karen. Being on the team gave me a chance to crusade against junk food and sodas in school. Our coach, Tracy Tokunaga, said I inspired her to work for school lunch reform.

Even though I got caught up in middle school and cross-country, I hadn't lost sight of my dream. Mom was right about Denali having changed me. It made me more secure in myself. I no longer feared the unknown.

I thought about my conversation with Johnny Strange on Denali and his quest to climb all Seven Summits. He hadn't included the Carstensz Pyramid on his list, but that was the mountain I wanted to climb next.

I talked it over with Dad one morning.

"Everest is the most challenging and Vinson's the most difficult to get to. We should do Carstensz next," I said.

He grinned. "Really? Then better start researching."

"I already have. It's a pile of rocks rising right out of the jungle on the island of New Guinea. It's the most technical of all the summits."

"You'll have to learn to rappel," he said.

I knew what rappelling was—a descent down a rock wall using a rope. I hadn't done it before, but I was looking forward to trying.

No surprise, by the end of the day Dad and Karen had come up with a new training regimen. Instead of hauling a tire up and down the mountain to build strength and endurance, I now had to master true rock-climbing skills and build upper-body strength.

Instead of crampons for snow, I wore special climbing shoes made by Five Ten that had Stealth rubber soles to give me a more sure-footed grip on the rocks. I had loved scrambling up those rocks on Kilimanjaro and could hardly wait to test myself on Carstensz.

Karen looked into the logistics. "The true adventure here

isn't getting to the summit. It's getting to the mountain itself. The whole area was sealed off for ten years. It only reopened in 2005."

Carstensz Pyramid, also known as Puncak Jaya, is on the island of New Guinea, which is part of Indonesia. The country is made up of more than seventeen thousand islands. Separatist movements by islands that want to form their own countries, as well as Islamic militants, have led to political unrest and even terrorist attacks. Sometimes entire areas of the country are sealed off with no warning.

Karen pointed to a map on her computer to show me another reason for local trouble. "Carstensz is located near the Grasberg mine—the world's largest gold mine."

"Seriously? In the middle of a jungle?"

"Yep. It's so big it can even be seen from space. An American company owns ninety percent of the mine. No one's allowed to use the road that goes into the area. It's heavily guarded."

"So if we can't use the road, how do we get there?" I asked.

"We could hire a helicopter to fly over the mine or hike around it through thick muddy rain forests and bogs." Karen leaned back and crossed her arms.

Muddy rain forests and bogs? Seemed to me that a helicopter was the way to go, but I wouldn't be surprised if Dad and Karen wanted to hike. They were all about the experience.

"We'll be facing a time crunch. So we're thinking helicopter," Karen said.

Inside I thought, *Whew!* But I knew there were other considerations. "That has to be more expensive."

"True, but hiking is expensive too. Local tribes can be a problem: They each want to be paid for permits to hike through their territory. It would be impossible without hiring a company and negotiating with each tribe."

Continuing my dream wasn't cheap. Dad and Karen never complained about the expense, but I helped with fund-raising whenever I could. Big Bear was completely behind us. Three local restaurants—Sonora Cantina, BLT's, and Azteca Grill—held taco nights to raise funds. They gave all the proceeds from the one-dollar tacos to us, and they kept the profits from their other food sales. Bad Bear Sportswear printed Karen's T-shirts at a good price and helped by mailing them to people who ordered online. We showed more Warren Miller ski films, and Karen applied for the Polartec Challenge grant and we were awarded five thousand dollars.

All of that helped, but I still heard whispers from Dad and Karen's bedroom and learned that they had maxed out their credit cards.

Somehow we had come up with enough to make the trip.

Karen hired Adventure Indonesia, based in Bali, to coordinate our travel and arrange for all the permits we needed. Even then it was a ton of work for her. She had to gather multiple copies of the papers they needed to make everything happen.

We were finally ready to go and had booked a flight to

Jakarta, Indonesia. The day we were going to leave, there was a horrible terrorist bombing of several major hotels in Jakarta. The US State Department issued a travel advisory warning US citizens against going there.

"So after all your work, Super K, we're stuck with these extremely expensive, nonrefundable tickets," Dad said.

"Maybe not. I've been reading the fine print," Karen said. "An 'act of terrorism' is an exception."

Dad sat at the breakfast counter, thrumming his fingers. "I'd say this qualifies. So we can get our money back and reschedule when we know what's happening there?"

"Looks like it," Karen said.

The next morning Dad was cooking one of his favorite healthy breakfasts of paper-thin sweet potatoes stir-fried with red bell peppers and lots of spices. I loved the aroma coming from the skillet. "Okay, so I called this guy in Jakarta last night, and he thinks things will cool down in about two weeks."

Karen thought about that for a minute. "We're only going to pass through, not spend time in Jakarta. We might be able to avoid it altogether by flying from LA to Hong Kong to Bali."

I was totally bummed about having to wait while Karen tried to put this new itinerary together. Then something happened that made me realize just how lucky I was. My most favorite place to eat was a Himalayan restaurant owned by the Bhandari family, who had become good friends of ours. Just before we left for Indonesia, Mrs. Bhandari and her two children, ages five and eleven, were struck by a hit-and-run driver while they were crossing the street. Five-year-old Kushan was killed. Mrs. Bhandari and eleven-year-old Kushal were injured, but would recover.

The whole town rallied behind the family. Karen even helped them with a variety of state victim-assistance forms to get financial aid for medical bills and to help pay for the funeral.

My grandma and uncle had died recently, but Kushan was only five. I thought of Dad's motto on the front of our house: GO FAST. TAKE CHANCES. You could die just crossing a street holding your mom's hand. I cut an article about Kushan out of the paper and got an eight-by-ten photo so I could dedicate my next mountain to him. He'd never have a chance to climb one.

I hoped that carrying his memory with me would help me reach the summit. Carstensz is one of the more demanding climbs, not because of weather or elevation, but because of the extreme rock climbing required. I'd been training with Dad and Karen, and had really built up my upper-body strength. Still, I was just thirteen.

Would I be able to tackle the tallest mountain in Indonesia?

CHAPTER 20

It took Karen just a few days to put a new travel plan together. Instead of flying to Jakarta, on the island of Java, we flew to Bali, another Indonesian island, to pick up our permits and to relax for a few days before heading to the island of New Guinea for our climb. Bali was amazing, with plants and flowers everywhere making the air smell sweet. We visited a couple of the usual tourist places, and my favorites were, of course, animal sanctuaries.

At the Bali Bird Park, a docent had me hold my hands out, palms facing up. She placed a large blue-and-gold macaw on them and said, "Play dead." The bird rolled over and lay on its back, claws up. It didn't move a feather until the docent gave a signal. I wanted one of those for a pet.

Next stop was the Hindu monkey temple. Signs at the entrance warned everyone to watch out for the monkeys and remove glasses and all jewelry. I slipped my shades into my pants pocket. Only Hindus were allowed inside the temple, but the grounds were pretty cool until a monkey grabbed a man's glasses, scampered up the rock wall, and disappeared over the top.

A Balinese man rushed up to him. "Oh, so sorry. You wait here. I try get back, kind sir." Then he disappeared.

The man was shaking all over. "They're prescription. I can't see a thing without them."

A few minutes later the Balinese man returned with the guy's glasses. The man threw his head back and clasped his hands together as if praising the gods. "Thank you, thank you so much."

Dad said, "Here it comes."

The Balinese man negotiated for a reward. The last bid I heard was fifty dollars. I wondered what the monkeys got out of it.

The next day we took a four-hour flight from Bali to the island of New Guinea. I had a window seat as we flew over untamed, remote rain forest. It was awesome seeing smoke rising from island volcanoes.

We landed in Timika, West Papua, on a hot, humid day. I loved all the colors and smells. It reminded me of Tanzania: Women dressed in brightly colored clothes sat on the ground selling fruits and vegetables.

We met Patrick, a local liaison with Adventure Indonesia,

the company that would provide our guide and other logistics. Patrick was a clean-cut, chubby guy with a nonstop smile. The top of his head barely reached my chin, but then at thirteen I was already five feet nine. Patrick introduced us to our two guides. Meldy was a young long-haired guy from Java who was all smiles. His English was great and he was totally outgoing. Poxy looked like a rocker too, but he was a lot quieter. He didn't say much, but his dark eyes showed his quiet confidence.

Patrick had arranged for our afternoon flight to Nabire, a small fishing village on the Pacific with a population of less than a thousand. Nabire definitely felt like a remote corner of the world, but amazingly, it had Internet. Our hotel was U-shaped, with rooms opening onto a courtyard full of beautiful plants and trees. I had my own room across from Dad and Karen's, with a little patio facing the courtyard. Every morning I came out to find bread, jam, and a warm cup of tea. It was nice to be able to chill and have my own breakfast.

We had to wait for a helicopter to the Carstensz base camp. The helicopters were big, but they could only take five carefully weighed passengers along with their gear. There was a group ahead of us. They had already been waiting for a week at the hotel. One of them was a famous guy from Austria named Andy Holzer, who'd been blind from birth and was climbing the Seven Summits.

"How can you climb without being able to see?" I asked him.

He touched the arm of the man next to him and introduced

him as Andreas Unterkreuter. "My very good friend here is with me every inch of the way. He tells me exactly where to place my hands and feet." He laughed. "Sometimes it's a good thing not being able to see how far I could fall."

Every day we got another excuse about why the helicopter hadn't come. The first day they said it was broken. The second day it was due to bad weather.

Rain was an almost daily occurrence. The island was one huge rain forest.

When the helicopter finally arrived days later, Andy, Andreas, their guide, and Meldy left for Carstensz. We'd have to wait for them to climb and come back before we could catch a ride. We were starting to wonder if we should hike through the jungle instead of waiting, but Patrick confirmed what Karen had read. He'd worked for climbers who had chosen the trek through the rain forest.

"Local tribes are very isolated. But they figured out that if you want to pass through their land, you must pay the price," he explained.

"Did they try to stop you?" I asked.

"There was a roadblock at every village. One had placed logs across the trail. We were greeted with bows and arrows at another. At one village a tribesman wore a wild headdress and carried a spear. Big curved bones stuck out of his nostrils, and he'd painted his face with bloodred lines. He thumped his spear into the ground to warn us not to pass. Some tribes were wary of strangers, but others wanted to scare us into paying huge sums to pass through."

"What would happen if you just went around the road-blocks?" Karen asked.

Patrick shuddered. "They threatened to chop us with machetes. Two weeks after my trip, the natives took a group of climbers hostage and held them for two weeks."

"Okaaay," Dad said, leaning back and stretching his arms over his head. "We'll keep waiting for the helicopter."

Everyone who took care of us at the hotel and the local restaurants was super nice, but the people in the village wouldn't give us a smile. And that seemed weird, because at every other beach community we'd ever been to, the people had been relaxed and friendly. Peacefulness seemed to go along with sunshine and water.

"There's an overall angry feeling around here," Dad said.

Karen nodded. "Probably because of what happened to the mine workers. I heard that the week before we got here, some of them were on a bus when protesters opened fire and killed seven of them."

I knew the mine was unpopular—it damaged the environment and took advantage of its workers—but that was no reason to shoot at the people who couldn't find work anywhere else.

Still, Nabire was beautiful. Metal shacks with palm-leaf roofs lined an incredibly wide beach. The water was as warm as could be, but we were the only ones going swimming. The natives stared at us like we were crazy, but the kids were great as always. They came up with creative ways to have fun. They rolled a wad of trash up into a ball, wrapped string around it, and kicked it around. When the ball landed near me, I tossed it back and actually won a smile.

Despite their poverty, they were like children anywhere else in the world. When we gathered for pictures, they all wanted to be in them with me. They were fascinated by my long curls. I was probably the first white kid they'd seen. The only other outsiders they encountered were climbers, and none of them were as young as me.

Carstensz was the last of the Seven Summits to be climbed. No one even tried before World War II because of dense jungle, lack of maps, no real information, and head-hunting and cannibalistic tribes. In 1962 the first white men went up the mountain; one of them was an Austrian, Heinrich Harrer, who wrote a bestseller about it, *I Come from the Stone Age*. He encountered some of the most primitive tribes on the planet deep in the jungle.

CHAPTER 21

Finally the helicopter returned, and it was our turn to fly to base camp. Patrick stayed in Nabire and Poxy flew with us. Meldy was already at base camp, waiting.

The trip was a long one. We flew over jungle as far as you could see. At one point we flew into a canyon between solid rock walls that shot straight up out of the jungle. I swore the blades were going to hit the rocks or stir up the waterfalls spilling down their faces.

The helicopter had to carry extra fuel to drop off along the way so that the pilots could refuel on the return trip. Suddenly, in the middle of the dense jungle, a helipad appeared on the ground next to a small hut made of bamboo and palm leaves. The helicopter landed but kept the engine running. I don't know how the hut stood up against the fierce winds coming off the blades. When the pilot opened the door to roll out a barrel of fuel, kids ran out to help. He exchanged packages with them and we were off again.

"How'd you like to live there," Karen asked, "where your only contact with civilization is through helicopter?"

"With no skiing? No way," I answered.

As soon as we left the hut, a heavy fog rolled in. The pilots didn't speak everyday English, but it's the universal language of aviation, so Karen was able to understand some of what they said when she listened in on a headset. The fog was so heavy they couldn't see, and they needed to fly higher to avoid hitting the mountains. Dad kept an eye on his altimeter with a bit of a worried look on his face. Karen and I checked ours and verified we were flying at twenty thousand feet—way higher than a helicopter normally flies.

The pilots put on oxygen masks but didn't have any for us. We'd gone from sea level to that high altitude in too short a time. I was feeling woozy.

"I've landed in a lot of emergency situations as a flight paramedic," Dad said, "but there's no way we could do that here."

The pilot said something over his shoulder. Poxy translated. "Usually heat from the mine clears the fog around the camp because they're at the same elevation. But today the pilots can't see the landing zone. We have to turn back."

I was disappointed but relieved too. The idea of crashing in the jungle and being surrounded by unfriendly natives was too much like a video game I didn't want to play.

Back in Nabire we had to sit out yet another day due to weather. Meanwhile, poor Andy and Andreas were waiting at the other end to be brought back to the village. When we finally took off again the next day, we had clear blue skies and lush green jungle.

The rain forests in New Guinea and Brazil are the largest triple canopies in the world, meaning that vegetation grows in three main layers, each with different plants and animals adapted for life in that particular area

But the jungle wasn't all we could see from the helicopter.

"Look at the pollution in the rivers," Karen said.

Directly below us, the river coming from the Grasberg mine joined another. It was like cocoa mixing with clear water from the other river. The pollution from the mine had turned the river chocolate brown.

We arrived at base camp, at fourteen thousand feet, about two hours after we took off. The helicopter left the engine running while we hopped out and unloaded our gear. Andy's group was ready to go.

"If you'd come two days earlier, you would've been hiking in a blizzard," he said.

I laughed. "Snowstorm on the equator. That's so sick."

Even though we were so close to the equator, the elevation on the Carstensz Pyramid meant that snow was possible at any time. The summit is free of ice, but there are a few glaciers on the mountain's slopes.

We waved good-bye to Andy's group and checked out base camp.

Meldy and Poxy set up camp in the most spectacular setting I could imagine. We were in the middle of a grassy savanna—there's no rain forest at that high altitude—surrounded by jagged limestone peaks. We were the only climbers at base camp. It was like we had the whole mountain all to ourselves.

Dad, Karen, and I sat on a boulder gazing at Danau Tage, the lake that was only a few yards from us. It was a deep turquoise blue.

"It's so peaceful here," I said, "kind of like we're in our own private world."

Dad laughed. "What do you mean, 'like'? We are in our own private world, buddy."

It was a rare moment on a climb—just the three of us. "I'm really, really grateful for all of this," I said. "I'm getting to experience things most adults can't even dream of."

Dad put his arm around my shoulder. "I'd climb any mountain to make your dream come true," he said.

"Tomorrow's going to be so awesome. I'll be standing on a summit surrounded by jungle at four degrees south of the equator. On Denali we were surrounded by ice and snow and only three degrees south of the Arctic Circle. It's amazing!"

"We're definitely covering the planet," Karen said with a nod.

I looked at that incredibly blue lake and then remembered the rivers we had flown over. "It really upsets me when I see people not taking care of the planet."

"I know. Me too," Dad said.

I was grateful to have this time to talk to Dad and Karen about these things. My goal gave me a lot more time with them than most kids have with their parents. I'm not sure how many kids can handle being stuck in a three-man tent with their parents for days at a time with no one else to talk to, or being roped together on a steep mountain where you could face death any second, but I wouldn't trade a minute of it. And I knew my dad and Karen wouldn't either. We sat there for an hour, just the three of us, and then we joined our guides to talk about the next day's climb.

Preparing for the climb the next morning was a lot easier than preparing on Denali. I didn't need all that puffy clothing, crampons, an ice axe, snowshoes, plastic boots, or a sled for climbing on snow and ice. We carried emergency supplies in case we had to camp, but the plan was to summit and descend in one day. I simply wore a Polartec fleece jacket, a helmet, thin gloves for good handholds, and my new climbing shoes with the grippy soles. I also put on a climbing harness with carabiners, ascender, and ropes attached. We'd be doing some serious rock climbing, and I needed to be ready.

Mental preparation was important too. There were fixed

ropes all the way up, and I didn't want to make any careless clipping mistakes like I had on Denali.

We left camp at nine thirty. Karen went first to film us coming up. I was in the middle followed by Dad, where he could keep a good eye on me to make sure I clipped my carabiners in to the right places and found the right foot- and handholds along the way.

Poxy brought up the rear. Meldy was struggling with altitude sickness and had to stay behind at base camp.

The first section was rock scrambling. I was thankful for good gloves when I discovered how sharp the limestone rock edges were. We gained altitude quickly before hitting some scree. From there the route went straight up a freaking wall. I remembered Dad warning me on Denali to stay focused. I was a year older and had matured a lot since then. I trusted myself, and I knew that Dad and Karen trusted me too.

I was a real rock climber now, intent on every detail, like locating cracks to dig my fingers into and places for my feet. I loved every minute of it. The time went super fast.

It became clear pretty quickly that Poxy couldn't keep up with us. Karen checked on him and then caught up to Dad and me. "He says that the altitude's bothering him but he's fine. Think we should wait?"

Dad shook his head. "There's no chance of getting lost. We've got fixed lines all the way to the top."

"Yeah, but some of them look pretty sketchy," I said.

"That's because they don't take the old ones down when they put new ones up," he said. "I'll test each rope and anchor before we clip in."

So we set out again with Dad in the lead and Karen filming us from behind.

Carstensz was like a giant jungle gym. It was hard in spots, but I was never bored for a second. We reached a beautiful but really exposed knife-edge no wider than my shoe. I was roped in but could still fall a long way before the line stopped me if I slipped. I was hyperaware of how far *down* was and never took my eyes off the path.

Twenty minutes later we came to a spot where the rock edge dropped abruptly, leaving a large gap like a giant missing tooth.

Dad and Karen studied it. "Climbing down and going back up would be too dangerous and take hours," Karen said.

Dad looked at me and arched his brows. "Okaaay, looks like you're about to do your first Tyrolean traverse."

A Tyrolean traverse is a way to use a rope to cross through free space, or empty air, between two points. In other words, I'd be dangling over a thousand feet of nothing except the jagged rocks below, with only a rope to hold me!

The only way across was to clip my harness into a handful of ropes and pull myself hand over hand across the eighty feet to the other side.

Poxy caught up to us while we were waiting for Dad to go first.

"You're moving much faster than most groups," he said. "Great job, Jordan. Don't worry about this. I've done it a thousand times."

I felt more confident now. Dad tested the line and crossed first. I watched his every move so I could do the same. When he reached the other side, he signaled me to come. Karen helped me clip a large locking carabiner through my harness. Then she clipped my safety sling around three or four of the newest ropes. It was really awkward, because I had to get my waist as close to the ropes as possible and rotate so I was facing the sky—all of this while perched on the edge of a cliff.

"Now trust the system," she said, "and lower your weight onto the ropes."

Fear kicked in as soon as I left the ground and the ropes sagged. If they broke, I was dead.

They held.

I remembered how to breathe again, but my stomach was knotted tight as a fist. I was hanging a thousand feet in the air, too terrified to look down.

Karen's calm voice talked me across. "You can't just rely on the rope. You have to pull yourself. Use both hands and get a swinging motion."

I tried doing as she said, but it was hard. My carabiner kept rubbing on the rope, creating friction. My arms and abs ached and were super tired. I focused on putting one hand after the other.

I looked up for a second and discovered that I was nearly halfway across. Dad was waiting for me on the other side, and that gave me the confidence to look around. Over my shoulder I saw nothing but bone-crushing rocks. That got my adrenaline pumping, and I worked twice as hard to move toward the end of the lines.

"Two more pulls and you're here," Dad said.

I had trouble maneuvering the ropes to reach him. But with his help I awkwardly pulled myself onto the rock. I'd made it, my first Tyrolean traverse!

Karen came next, followed by Poxy.

"How far are we from the summit?" I asked him.

"It'll take another hour or two," he answered.

After the Tyrolean, there were two more gaps that looked even more difficult and dangerous than the one from my first traverse. One was several feet across between sheer walls that faced each other and had a large boulder wedged in between. It required a big jump across while tied into the fixed line and then scrambling up rocks that were hard to grip because of weird shapes.

The second gap was even scarier, because I couldn't see the bottom. The only way to descend was by lowering myself down the fixed rope in a rappel. I'd practiced this at home on climbing walls and was pretty good at it. Then I had to jump across a gap and climb up the other side.

The trail to the summit was rocky and steep. We walked

single file and followed several switchbacks. The final thirty feet took us across snow to an amazing mountain peak that rose out of the jungle: the roof of Oceania.

Karen took a picture of me standing on the summit with my backpack, harness, carabiners, and ascender as a memento of my first technical rock climb.

The sky was sunny and clear blue. The view went beyond the gold mine all the way out to the sea. The mine's ugly brown concentric circles grew wider and wider as it chewed its way through the jungle, destroying everything around it, including the canopy. Vast amounts of flora and fauna would be lost forever. No wonder the natives hated it. I did too.

Poxy pulled out a four-foot-wide banner that said THE WORLD RECORD, JORDAN ALEXANDER ROMERO, YOUNGEST CARSTENSZ SUMMITEER. It also had Dad's and Karen's names. It felt good knowing I'd accomplished something no one else my age had even attempted, but the most important thing was standing there together.

I'd carried the article about Kushan and his picture in my backpack all the way up the mountain and across the Tyrolean traverse. When I reached for them to dedicate the climb, the wind whisked both out of my hand and carried them away. At first I was upset, but then I realized that this would be a peaceful place for him. He'd climbed to the heights with me.

On the trip down we clipped and cleared, then clipped again and did some rappels. The Tyrolean traverse seemed easier now. We reached base camp just before dark. All three of us sat on boulders watching the last of the sunset over the turquoise lake. It had been a ten-hour day but the most fun I'd ever had on a mountain — definitely my favorite one so far.

Clear weather the next morning allowed us to get out on time. On the plane from Nabire to Timika, Patrick told us about a four-star hotel run primarily for mining executives. They had an awesome swimming pool with a beautiful deck, and the staff served drinks and snacks while you dried off waiting for your next swim.

"Tell me more about the mine," Karen said. "I read there's lots of controversy."

"The world comes here to take our gold and destroy our land," Patrick said. "The mine is owned by one of the richest companies in the world, but the people here remain poor and uneducated while the mine's profits go elsewhere."

That made me super sad. Meldy said that local tribes were gathering to revolt against the mine's owner, an American company with the support of the Indonesian government. I wondered what chance the natives would have fighting with spears or bows and arrows against military assault rifles.

When I got home, I promised myself that I would talk about the gold mine in Indonesia and tell people about the damage it was doing to the people and the land. Before we even left Timika, news of our ascent spread quickly to the mountaineering community, partly because we gave Patrick my password so he could leave word on my blog—a blog I was terrible at keeping up.

He ended his message with these words to me: *Keep on searching for another summit, and tell the world that there is always a mountain to climb, a great destination to go in life, never waste life for doing nothing.*

THE BIGGEST CLIMB:

ASIA'S
MOUNT
EVEREST,
29,029 FEET

Average number of climbers
per year: 600

May 22, 2010, age 13

World Record

CHAPTER 22

I was back in school after summiting Carstensz, happy to be with my friends again and psyched for ski season to begin. I told Cameron and anyone else who would listen about how cool it had been to climb rocks to a summit in the middle of a jungle. That memory stayed with me all through the fall, but in the back of my mind I kept thinking about what Patrick had written.

I was so close to achieving my dream—only two more mountains to go: Everest, which I had begun to think of as the big one, and Vinson, the cold one. At thirteen I felt much stronger and more mature than when my doubts and fears had haunted me before Aconcagua and Denali. Reaching the top of Denali had been the turning point for me. It had taught me I could survive total exhaustion, bitter cold, ferocious winds, and high altitude. With Dad and Karen behind me, I felt ready for Everest.

I'd done my homework and knew that if we didn't go the following spring, I'd have to wait another year to accomplish my goal. Twice a year the jet stream moves north of the Himalayas, reducing heavy winds and precipitation on the summit, but at the same time draws moisture up from the Bay of Bengal, creating a monsoon.

There is a short seven- to ten-day window between those two events every May. A similar window opens in the fall, but then the days are shorter and storms are more likely. So we began planning for the spring of 2010.

Our next decision was which side of the mountain to climb. Everest sits on the border between Nepal and Tibet. I'd read the history of both first ascents.

After the North and South Poles were explored early in the twentieth century, adventure seekers wanted a new world to conquer. They turned to Everest, which many called the third pole.

The border between Nepal and Tibet runs exactly across the summit of Mount Everest. For a long time, both countries were closed to foreigners. When Tibet began to let outsiders in in 1921, an English mountaineer named George Mallory explored the north side. The next year he tried to reach the summit, using local people, known as Sherpas, as guides. Seven Sherpas died in an avalanche—the first of many deaths of people trying to climb the mountain.

A reporter asked Mallory why he wanted to climb Everest, and he famously answered, "Because it's there."

Mallory tried again in 1924 with another Brit, Andrew Irvine. The two men were last seen about eight hundred vertical feet from the summit before vanishing into the clouds. No one knows if they made the summit. A search party found Mallory's mummified body seventy-five years later, but they didn't find a camera. Irvine is still lost on the mountain.

Nepal opened its borders in 1951 after 134 years of isolation and allowed expeditions to approach the mountain from the south. Two years later Edmund Hillary, a New Zealand beekeeper and explorer, and Tenzing Norgay, a widely respected Sherpa, became the first to reach the roof of the world. Their route is still the most popular but has at least one extremely dangerous section—the Khumbu Icefall, which is full of enormous crevasses and giant towers of ice that are constantly shifting and tumbling down.

Just before we climbed Carstensz, Dad and Karen had made a scouting trip to Nepal to check out the Hillary route. They had a permit to climb Nuptse, which lies next to Everest and uses Hillary's Everest route through the Khumbu Icefall into the Western Cwm, or valley. Above a high camp they discontinued their attempt and turned back. Dad had been in the lead on the descent when he heard Karen calling. When he looked back, her headlamp was gone. Karen had dropped six feet into a hidden crevasse before her two ice axes, one on each hip, somehow jackknifed and dug into the wall, saving her.

They had made it safely through the Khumbu Icefall,

but they decided there was no way they would risk taking me through that treacherous area. We'd have to climb the mountain via another route.

Everest was always on my mind. I dreamed about being on the mountain. Then finally one day Karen said, "Two years ago, I never imagined you'd be ready for Everest this soon. I've always thought sixteen at the youngest."

I was weaving back and forth on the stool at the breakfast bar, about to tip it over with excitement. "So does that mean we're going?"

"Yes, in early April," she answered.

"Excellent!"

"And from the north side," Dad added. "That icefall is no place we ever want to visit again. More people die there than anywhere else on Everest. The north is more our style."

"From Tibet?" I said. "Sweet. It's such a mysterious place."

When I told my mom, she sat without speaking for the longest time. Then her voice cracked. "When I think about you on Everest and all the risks, I can hardly breathe."

"I'll be well trained, and I won't make mistakes," I told her. "If things don't look right, we'll turn back and try another time. I promise."

Her shoulders slumped. "And how long will you be gone?"

"About two months, I guess, to acclimatize to the altitude."

She let out a long sigh. "This is really hard for me." Then

the corner of her mouth turned up in a half smile. "But you really want this, don't you?"

I nodded. "I want to finish my dream."

"Then I want that for you too." She pulled me close, giving me a hug.

A few days later I was skiing when she called me on my cell. "Come to the ski-patrol hut. Steve has something to show you."

"Now?" I asked.

"Yes. It's important," she answered.

Steve is a part-time ski patroller who knew my dad, Karen, and my mom. He'd climbed Everest from the north side in 1995. He had his laptop with him that day so he could show us the photographs from his expedition. The pictures were incredible, and he knew firsthand what it took to make it to the top of that mountain.

"So be honest. You really think I can make it?" I asked.

He gave me a fist bump. "Go for it."

He'd known me all my life. If he believed I could do it, then I did too.

Steve was able to help in another way too. "My father-in-law is in charge of the US military's weather reports and can help you on the mountain," he said.

It felt like things were coming together. Not only would we have access to expert weather reports, but a company called SPOT had signed on to be one of our sponsors. Their

GPS tracking system, combined with a website app that Karen and a friend had created, would allow friends, family, and especially my mom to follow me on the mountain. It was a small device I could carry with me. Mom was relieved, and that helped me feel better too. I knew she'd worry no matter what, but this would make things a little easier for her.

We'd managed all the other climbs during school breaks, but Everest would require too much time. In January I switched to an independent-study program. I did all the regular schoolwork but on my own schedule. I met weekly with Karen and my teacher to review what I'd done. I missed my friends at school, but it was important to do the right training for Everest.

I'd basically been training for Everest my entire life by spending all my time outdoors at a fairly high altitude. Now I trained every day by skiing and hiking on ice and snow.

My regimen shifted from endurance building to strength building. I focused on my core muscles through circuit training, which includes both resistance training and high-intensity aerobics. I felt like I transformed from a strong kid into a strong adult. Mentally I knew this was going to be the hardest thing I'd ever done.

On one of our training hikes up California's highest peak, Mount Whitney, we met a climber named Garry Harrington. He was climbing all of the fourteen-thousand-foot mountains in the US plus the highest point in each of the fifty states.

Garry and I hit it off immediately and talked about how long it was taking him and all the logistics involved.

Meeting Garry started me thinking. I was on my way to achieving a big goal, but what about after that? I knew myself well enough to know that I'd always want to have a goal in front of me.

"I want to do something big again after the summits, and climbing the highest point in each state like Garry seems like a good one," I told Dad and Karen on the way home. "I could talk to kids in every state about staying healthy, about setting goals and achieving them. That's really important to me."

"I like it," Dad said.

"Me too," Karen added. "But let's reach this goal first. We need to raise at least a hundred thirty thousand dollars to climb Everest on a shoestring budget."

As always, the town of Big Bear really came through for us. We relied on our old standbys to raise funds: taco nights at local restaurants, T-shirt sales, and Warren Miller ski films.

News that a thirteen-year-old was going to attempt to summit Everest spread quickly through the media, and at least a dozen new corporate sponsors came on board. Some donated products; others provided much-needed money. In return we did product testing, provided testimonials, and let them use photos and videos of me in advertising and publicity. I'm proud to say that not one of them put pressure on me to make the summit. They all emphasized that my safety and health came first. Even so, I hoped I'd make it for them, because we never could have tackled Everest without their help.

The media attention also brought out a barrage of critics who knew nothing about us or how hard we'd trained. All they saw was my age. We'd hired a Kathmandu outfitter to provide base-camp facilities, food, oxygen, and three climbing Sherpas. Dad's critics ripped into him for not going with a Western commercial expedition, which they believed would be safer.

In interviews Dad always replied in a calm, steady voice, even though I knew the criticism had kept him awake some nights.

"We've poured about every resource we have into preparing for this," Dad told one interviewer. "We hired three experienced, altitude-savvy, professional Sherpa guides from Nepal who have a combined nine summits. They know the weather and the mountain better than any Westerner. I trust them and my team."

Next the critics jumped all over him for planning to take me up the more technical and less popular northern route.

"We've thought this out carefully and weighed every aspect. We're not doing this on a whim," Dad responded. "Yes, the north is a whole lot colder and windier, but Karen and I did a scouting trip on the south and would never risk taking Jordan into the deadly Khumbu Icefall."

Some climbing experts questioned whether my young

lungs could handle the thin air on Everest. Others said that a teenage brain was only 80 percent developed and putting an emotionally inexperienced child on one of the world's most dangerous mountains was irresponsible. Dad explained that he'd researched every bit of published information and could find nothing negative about children and altitude.

Even though we had an answer for every criticism, I knew climbing Everest was dangerous. But so was climbing into your car every day. I couldn't understand how people who didn't even know me had any right to criticize. I'd read everything I could about mountaineering and had trained hard physically and mentally for four years. I was probably better prepared than half the people who'd be on the mountain.

I shrugged the critics off and focused on my goal. I didn't feel like I was rushing. The opportunity to climb Everest just happened to come when I was thirteen.

I decided to use other people's doubts to make me stronger. I'd feed on their negative energy and prove them wrong.

After my experience on Aconcagua, I was relieved to learn that I didn't have to pass any physical exams to climb Everest. Still, Dad and Karen wanted to make sure I was ready. They took me to Sky High Training, a high-altitude training center in Big Bear, for some medical tests. The owner, Bob Antonacci, did a blood profile to measure my iron, minerals, and red and white blood cell count. All my numbers were right on target.

I trained hard all winter, and by the time ski season ended

I was ready to go. Except that I still had to pack. And packing for Everest was an enormous undertaking. We packed thirteen huge bags of gear, medical supplies, freeze-dried food, high-energy supplements, cameras, two satellite phones, a BGAN unit from Network Innovations for satellite communication and Internet connection, plus solar panels to charge it all. I was stoked about being able to call my mom and sister almost every day. I knew I'd feel a lot less homesick if I could hear their voices on a regular basis.

I always carried little things for support when I went climbing. To ensure success on Everest, I packed my lucky rabbit's foot, a cross from my grandfather, a beaded necklace from my friend Doug, and something extra special from a boy named Nigel Holland.

My mom had dated Nigel's dad for a while, so I'd spent a lot of time with Nigel. I was good friends with his brother, Lucas, who was in my grade. Two years earlier Nigel had been just an ordinary eight-year-old, mountain biking, ski racing, jumping on a trampoline, and swimming in the lake. Then out of nowhere he was diagnosed with brain cancer. Doctors removed the tumor, but he couldn't walk or talk after that. He was undergoing chemo and fighting for his life. So while I'd been climbing Aconcagua and Denali, Nigel had been dreaming of being able to walk again. A week before we left for Nepal, I went to see him. Nigel was bald from the chemo and in a wheelchair. He could only talk in broken sentences, but he could laugh and smile. He wanted to know if I'd take a gift to the mountain for him.

"For sure, man," I told him. "I'd do anything for you."

Nigel giggled, looked at his dad, and then handed me a pair of slightly hairy round objects.

They were kind of gross looking, but I smiled just to be polite. Were they for some kind of sport I had never heard of?

Nigel's dad announced in a fake Australian accent, "Kangaroo 'nads will bring ya good fortune when rubbed, mate."

Nigel was totally cracking up, and so was my dad. *What is so funny?*

Finally Dad stopped laughing long enough to explain what 'nads were: "Testicles."

Testicles! I nearly dropped them, but I held on for Nigel. Now I was cracking up too.

"Awesome, Nigel. I promise to protect them all the way to the summit." *Take that, Guinness book. I'll be the first person to take kangaroo testicles all the way to the top of Everest.*

The day before our departure, Ayla Brown of CBS News came to Big Bear to interview us. A man named Terry Torok had been coaching me for the media blitz certain to strike after Everest. He'd helped me to feel more comfortable on camera. I'd discovered that most reporters were friendly and seemed genuinely interested in my story. They all asked pretty much the same questions, so I'd repeated the answers often enough that they came naturally.

Ayla was interested in how I trained, took some footage of the hypoxic tent, and talked to Dad and Karen about the criticism aimed at us.

We watched the interview on TV that night. Ayla concluded her interview by saying that she'd been skeptical when she'd first heard about a thirteen-year-old wanting to climb Everest, but after having met me, she felt I could do it. That made me feel good.

On the way to the airport the next morning we stopped at my mom's office to say good-bye. She immediately broke out in tears.

"Please come home safe," she said.

"I will. Promise. I love you, Mom."

I meant it when I promised her I'd come home safe. Everest was one of the most dangerous summits in the world, but I had every intention of coming home in one piece.

CHAPTER 23

King Richard, who'd built our sleds for Denali, came to Tibet with us. He didn't plan on summiting. He offered to be our support system and build whatever we needed at Chinese Base Camp and Advanced Base Camp. I was glad to have him along because he loved to joke around.

We arrived at Nepal's Tribhuvan International Airport about thirty hours after leaving home.

"This is it," Dad said. "Kathmandu, where every expedition begins and ends. Hillary passed through here."

Kathmandu lies in a valley surrounded by snow-capped peaks. I wanted to experience every sight, sound, and smell. I hung my head out the van window and watched vehicles and pedestrians move around in complete chaos. Horns honked; dogs barked; children cried. The smell of diesel, incense, and curry filled my nostrils. Vegetable, fruit, and spice carts appeared everywhere as we drove down narrow, cobbled streets.

A man on a wobbly bicycle hurtled toward us, a squawking chicken under one arm. In the split second before the bike swerved, the bird and I stared into each other's eyes, and I wasn't sure who was more startled—it or me.

The story of my being in Kathmandu had slowly spread throughout the city. One by one the local and international press arrived, wanting to talk to me. Finally Karen told the next reporter who knocked on our door, "I'm sorry, but we don't have time for any more interviews now. We need to focus on the climb. We'll be happy to talk to you on our return."

The next day we got together with our climbing Sherpas: Ang Pasang, Dawa, and Karma, plus Kumar the cook. The Sherpas had straight black hair, dark eyes, and high round cheekbones. Having read so much about their ability to carry heavy loads at high altitude, I was surprised by how wiry and small they were—probably no more than five feet four to five feet five. I'd had growth spurt and was now five feet ten and a hundred sixty pounds.

Ang Pasang came from a mountain village near Everest and was in charge of all the logistics. Over the next three days he took care of the last details for our climb and tested all our gear.

King Richard bought a bunch of DVDs for a dollar each to bring along.

When all the other details had been taken care of, Ang Pasang had one last task for us. "Now it's time to test out and learn how to use the oxygen masks."

We hadn't needed oxygen for any of our other climbs, but most mountaineers use it for summits in the so-called death zone above twenty-six thousand feet. Only a few of the most rugged (some say crazy) climbers attempt to climb Everest without oxygen. On the summit one breath only gets you about 33 percent of the oxygen that you would get at sea level. That can be deadly.

Even with all the prep work, we took time to explore Kathmandu. Nepal is mostly Hindu and filled with shrines to the religion's many gods and goddesses. We passed women in colorful saris making offerings of marigolds and rice to a god with the body of a man, four arms, a potbelly, and an elephant head.

Karen looked him up in her guidebook. "That's Ganesha, the most popular god in Nepal. He's the lord of success and remover of obstacles. People pray to him to clear the path before starting anything new."

"Can we offer something?"

She rummaged through her pack and handed me an energy bar. I offered it to Ganesha and made a request: "Please remove obstacles to bring all of us back in one piece."

Next we hired bicycle rickshaws beautifully decorated with flowers and brightly painted images of Hindu gods and spirits on their sides, backs, and roofs. Kids no older than me pedaled us around. They reminded me of the porters on Kilimanjaro, working so hard at such a young age to help support their families, and I made sure to tip them well.

We rode down narrow side streets past crumbling brick buildings. Each rooftop terrace had brightly colored saris hanging out to dry like flags fluttering in a gentle breeze. Then we came to a shrine that looked like something out of a horror movie. A statue of a goddess with fiery red eyes and an angry expression stuck her tongue out at us. She wore a necklace of human skulls and a belt of dismembered arms. In one of her own ten arms she held a severed head and in another a skull used as a cup to catch the head's blood. Her foot rested on a man, who appeared to be dead too.

"Oh man," Karen said as she thumbed through the pages in her guidebook. "That's Kali—the goddess of destruction. She sucks the blood of her enemies and then dances on their corpses. That's her dead husband, Lord Shiva, under her foot."

I shivered and hoped the goddess of destruction would stay far away from me and the mountain.

I enjoyed seeing Kathmandu, but I was ready to climb. On our last night we packed and weighed all our gear and headed out to dinner.

The next morning the Sherpas loaded all our gear and food onto a truck, and we climbed into a rented van to begin our journey. From Kathmandu we'd drive to the border and then cross into Tibet.

Communist China took over the country of Tibet in 1950.

Human rights organizations around the world have argued for Tibet's independence ever since, but the Chinese government continues to rule what used to be an self-governing country.

Ang Pasang warned us that the Chinese charged ridiculous permit fees of twenty thousand dollars per satellite phone and ten thousand dollars per professional video camera. They absolutely did not want outsiders communicating or filming anything about their country.

We were worried that some of our gear was going to be a problem. Lots of different media companies wanted to follow our progress on the mountain, and we had agreed to do interviews from the mountain.

"We've scheduled times to do live feeds with CNN and CBS through Skype," Karen told him. We didn't have a professional video camera, but we did have a satellite phone, a computer, and the BGAN unit for a satellite Internet connection.

"Let's not take a chance with having anything confiscated," he said. He carefully wrapped our camera, computer, phone, and the BGAN and packed them carefully deep within the barrels of food and supplies.

I was a little worried about what would happen if we got caught. The Chinese could kick us out or force us to pay a big fine. I was relieved when Ang Pasang assured us we wouldn't get thrown into a Chinese jail.

We headed north out of Kathmandu on a five-hour drive to the Friendship Bridge between Nepal and Tibet. Leaving the city, we drove through a lush canyon. There were white-water rafters on the river, and we passed a lot of small villages.

No vehicles of any kind were allowed to cross the border. Everything had to be unloaded and carried by hand about two hundred yards across the bridge. It was an amazing sight. Before we'd even come to a complete stop, a mob stormed the truck and began unpacking our bags and barrels of gear. Men, women, and children were yelling at one another in a crazy tug-of-war over the bags we'd taken such great care to pack. Our stuff disappeared in the mass confusion, and ours wasn't the only truck being unloaded.

"How will we ever get our things back?" I asked Dad.

"They know what they're doing," he said calmly.

I watched a kid about eight years old hoist a duffel on his back. It had to weigh more than he did. Wearing flip-flops, he trudged across the bridge and added it to our pile of gear, hoping to be paid.

The Chinese guards inspected our bags, but luckily didn't find our phones or camera equipment. They were young, only about twenty, but they looked glum and stoic in their starched uniforms. There was a coldness about them that reminded me of the Russian soldiers at checkpoints near Elbrus. Not one of them smiled or even greeted us.

"Ha! Friendship Bridge," King Richard roared. "These guys are anything but *friendly*."

"Richard," Karen whispered. "Don't attract attention."

Amazingly, all of our gear and food arrived at the same spot instead of being lost in a jumble of other duffels. A driver waited for us on the Chinese side of the bridge. He knew the accepted price to pay and handled that for us. I watched the eight-year-old I had noticed earlier dart back across the bridge hoping to grab another bag. The cost of our trip would probably be enough to feed his village for many years.

The Sherpas had already arranged for our climbing permits, and we picked them up at the border. We and every other climber who climbed from the north side in Tibet were forced to hire a liaison officer whose job it was to make sure we followed all the rules. We had to pay his salary, his room and board, and for his gasoline all the way to base camp. Every time I looked at him he gave me the stink eye—I had the distinct impression he really did *not* want this job.

We climbed into a Toyota Land Cruiser, and our gear, which had been loaded into a truck on the Chinese side of the border, followed behind. The area was humid and almost subtropical, with forests covering the steep hills on either side of the bumpy gravel road to the village of Zhangmu, where we planned to spend the night. Its single narrow, winding street was jammed with trucks and cars, and pedestrians squeezing between the vehicles. Every driver with a working horn seemed to be honking it. Square concrete houses were stacked one after another up the steep hill, clinging to the mountainside.

"We're definitely in Chinese territory now," Dad said. "Every road marker states the number of kilometers from Beijing."

I was checking out the strings of colorful prayer flags draped from roof to roof above the streets. "Why so many of those?"

"They're part of Tibetan Buddhist beliefs," Karen said. "The Chinese government destroyed many of the Buddhist monasteries when they first came into Tibet, but Buddhism is still practiced here."

We left Zhangmu early the next morning and climbed more than five thousand feet on a wicked narrow gravel road barely wide enough for one car until we arrived in the next settlement, at 12,300 feet. Nyalam was another one-street town with faceless concrete buildings.

We stayed in Nyalam for two nights to acclimatize, like everyone else. Everest was a two-month commitment no matter how fit you were. Since I was going to school via independent study, we didn't have to rush back for anything.

On our first full day King Richard wanted to hang out at the hotel, but Dad, Karen, and I decided to try to get our communication up and running. Doing that in town would draw some unwanted attention from the Chinese, so Dad told our driver that we wanted to go for a hike. Our liaison officer was happy to stay behind when he heard we would be hiking. The driver took Dad, Karen, and me about ten miles out of town until we spotted what looked like a good place to position our equipment. He dropped us off and left with a promise to return in a couple of hours.

Dad and Karen tried to find reception while I checked under rocks for lizards, snakes, or any kind of beetle or spider. We had a live interview scheduled with CNN and were trying to connect with them to test out our camera with the BGAN unit.

"Jordan," Karen called. "Quick, we've got a signal. Come say something on the camera."

"Cool." As I shoved a rock back into place, I saw a police car stop right where our driver had left us. My heart shot to the roof of my mouth as I saw myself locked in a Chinese jail before I was even old enough to shave. "Hide. Cops."

"Get up here to the rocks," Dad said.

All three of us crouched behind a boulder and eyed one another nervously.

"Why here?" Karen whispered. "There's no reason to stop in the middle of nowhere in the *exact* spot we were dropped off."

We had been warned about how the Chinese felt about people transmitting information. "Are they going to arrest us?" I asked.

Dad held a finger to my mouth. "Shhh. I don't know."

My heart was thumping so hard I thought for sure the cops could hear it. But then they walked *down* the hill instead of coming up toward us.

The whole thing was totally mysterious. We didn't budge until after the police left. The whole thing was going to be one sick story to tell when I got home.

We headed out again the next day and reached the fourteen-thousand-foot Tibetan plateau. It was amazing how dramatically the landscape changed at that elevation. It was no longer the humid green landscape. There was no sign of vegetation anywhere, just gray desert that spread out in every direction.

I was just starting to doze off when we turned a corner and there it was — Everest. It shimmered in the heat waves rising from the desert.

I took my sunglasses off to get a better view of the mountain. It was right there, that white plume blowing on the summit where it pierced the jet stream. The mountain I had seen in so many pictures. After four years of thinking about this moment and working so hard to get here, I couldn't find the right words to describe my feelings. I was face-to-face with the mountain of my dreams.

We asked the driver to stop, and Dad, Karen, and I got out of the car.

"Just two more days, J Man, and we'll be standing at its base," Dad said.

Being that close changed everything. It was no longer a far-off goal. We were here and this was Everest.

Just standing in the sight of this enormous mountain was a dream come true.

We drove on to Tingri, the last village before base camp. Almost everyone stopped there one or two nights to acclimatize at fourteen thousand feet. There were no trees to supply wood. Buildings were made of mud bricks several feet thick and then whitewashed. The doors were only about five feet tall. I kept forgetting to duck and bumped my head many, many times.

"The doors were built low," Ang Pasang explained, "to keep tall evil spirits from entering."

And here I'd thought it was because Tibetans were short. At six feet two, Dad was particularly challenged and had a welt on his forehead to match mine.

Tingri felt like an old Wild West town. Tibetans rode down the dirt streets not on horses but on strange-looking creatures that I learned were called dzos, a male crossbreed between a yak and cow.

We checked into one of the guesthouses. The mud walls and ceilings of our rooms were draped with pink cloth—to keep down the dust and the odors from yak-dung fires. I also suspected they had a major flea population, judging from the hundreds of wild dogs roaming the streets. I gave Tingri a nickname: Dogtown.

In the evening we went out on the porch to look at Everest and chat with teams from South Africa and Europe.

Dad whispered to me as we approached them, "It's important to remain humble in front of other climbers."

He didn't have to tell me that. I knew I was really lucky having the chance to even be there. As always, the conversation turned to me with the same question.

A German asked, "How old are you?"

"Thirteen."

That took everyone back.

"*Mon dieu*," said a Frenchman. "So young."

"I've got great parents helping me," I told him.

King Richard jumped in. "He's doing the Seven Summits and only has Everest and Vinson left."

I shot a sideward glance. Apparently he hadn't gotten the humility message.

The Frenchman gave me a serious nod of approval. "Then you're a very good, experienced climber. I hope we'll meet many times on the mountain."

A big grin spread across my face. "Me too."

It was cool hanging out with the climbers. Everyone was surprised by my age, but nobody had anything negative to say. I went to bed feeling like I'd been accepted in the international mountaineering community.

Next stop, Chinese Base Camp: seventeen thousand feet.

Beginning tomorrow I'd be tackling the biggest challenge of my life—climbing the tallest mountain in the world.

CHAPTER 24

We packed up and headed out of Dogtown on a gravel road through a landscape of nothing but gray dirt and rocks. Then all of a sudden, in the middle of nowhere, there was a sign with a drawing of Everest and a large arrow pointing south as if to say, *Everest: This Way!*

We were closing in on what would be our home for the next six weeks.

The only color we saw in several hours was the red, blue, and green clothing of two six- or seven-year-old kids who were herding about two hundred goats across the road. I didn't see a single blade of grass anywhere. I knew goats could eat anything, but really? What did they find to eat up here?

The massive north face of Everest was straight ahead, and I couldn't take my eyes off it. When we reached Chinese Base Camp, I just stood there, awestruck. I shivered, not from cold but from being in the presence of the highest mountain in the world. The summit looked close enough that I could put on a fleece, pack a couple of water bottles, and walk on up.

"We made it!" I shouted. "We're here!"

Dad gave me a high five. "One giant step toward your goal."

We stopped at the gate to base camp and went into a tent where we showed the Chinese officials our permits and our passports. They looked everything over carefully and then talked among themselves before stamping our papers. Then we loaded back into the van and drove to the spot where we would set up our base camp.

We were at seventeen thousand feet, in cold, windy, super-dry air. There were no trees, just millions of broken rocks covering every inch of ground. The first priority was getting unpacked and making Chinese Base Camp livable.

We helped Dawa and Karma clear spaces for our tents while Ang Pasang, Kumar, and a kitchen boy they'd hired at base camp unloaded the truck. His name was so hard for us to pronounce that we called him Kevin. Like the others he was cheerful and hardworking.

Even though it looked like we had packed up our entire house and dumped it into the middle of base camp, ours was definitely one of the smallest expeditions. As the critics had been quick to note, we were one of the few teams without a Western guide. It was King Richard, three climbing Sherpas, Kumar, Kevin, and us. Our dining/communications tent was simple and low budget. Most of our gear and food had to be left outside in large plastic barrels, heavy bags, or boxes covered by tarps.

The main tent went up first. We each had our own small sleeping tent, but the main tent was the one we used for Kumar's rock kitchen, a small table and chairs, and the communications equipment. It was where we hung out, played cards, and got to know the other climbers who stopped by. It was also where I did my homework.

Once our tents were raised, Ang Pasang hung a sign that read HEARTY WELCOME TO JORDAN ROMERO MOUNT EVEREST EXPEDITION SPRING 2010.

I pumped both fists in the air and turned around. "Yeah! It's totally official now."

As soon as the BGAN satellite Internet and phone equipment was unpacked, I asked Karen if I could call my mom and let her know that we had arrived.

"I don't have a good signal," she said.

"Can we try somewhere else?"

"Not with that liaison officer hovering over us," she said.

"I've never seen him smile. I don't think he likes me," I said.

She shrugged. "I think he's just collecting his pay and making sure we don't do anything stupid like try to use satellite communication."

I resigned myself to waiting to talk to Mom for at least

another day, or until the liaison officer got busy somewhere else.

My first night at the base of Everest I could hear King Richard coughing and rustling around in his sleeping tent a couple of yards away. He'd never been this high before, and altitude could definitely be a royal pain until you got used to it. Some people had a harder time acclimatizing than others. Partly it had to do with genetics. I had it covered—good genes, living at a high elevation, and sleeping in a hypoxic tent for a month before we left.

Chinese Base Camp was spread out over an enormous gravel valley. Once we were set up, I decided to see who else was here. The largest group of climbers, a Chinese team, was camped in the foothills. Closest to us was a British group about a hundred yards away; South African and Russian teams were two hundred yards away but in opposite directions.

They were major expeditions with separate dining, community, and sleeping tents. The Russians had a giant white dome about twenty feet high and fifty feet across that was just begging to be checked out. I stood in the doorway and poked my head inside. It was totally over the top. They had the luxury of comfy chairs and a television, which was amazing enough at this altitude, but also a Ping-Pong table! I guess you could hire a truck to bring anything up here.

A young Russian man with a mustache came up behind me. *"Dobroye utro!"* he said.

Huh? I managed to squeak out, "Good morning?"

He smiled and waved me into the tent. He handed me a paddle, got one of his own, and served a fast one. We played two games, laughing and chasing after the ball, not understanding a single word the other said. He beat me by five points in both games. But I'd be back for a rematch.

We took two full days to acclimatize and organize our gear and food before planning to join the yak highway that ran through the center of base camp toward the mountain. The constant clanging of their bells, all at different pitches, was the music of Tibet—kind of hypnotic and always in the background at base camp. When the yaks were absent, I noticed the silence.

Yak boys walked with the animals, whistling and hissing and yelling, "Eee-yuk, eee-yuk." The animals grunted and snorted. To maintain speed they hunched their back muscles and thrust themselves forward with their heads lowered. If one of them slowed the train, a yak boy tossed a small rock at its butt. Those kids had arms like major-league pitchers and unreal accuracy from two hundred feet away.

Ang Pasang explained that the Tibetans call Everest *Chomolungma*, Mother Goddess of the World. They won't trespass on her home without a puja ceremony asking for permission to climb and seeking forgiveness for hurting the mountain with ice axes and crampons.

One of the greatest things about traveling to other

countries was experiencing their cultures. I wasn't one of those climbers who thought only of getting to the top. I wanted to know more about the Sherpas and their world. From research back home I knew that they had migrated from Tibet to Nepal almost six hundred years before, bringing their Tibetan Buddhism with them. One thing they did before every summit attempt was raise an altar, and I looked forward to watching the ceremony.

Dad, Karen, King Richard, and I sat quietly while our Sherpas stacked rocks into an altar almost as tall as I was. They draped it with bright yellow cloth and colorful prayer flags that stood out boldly against the barren gray landscape. Dawa and Karma molded intricate sculptures out of yak butter and *tsampa*, which I learned was roasted barley flour.

"The sculptures are called *torma*," Ang Pasang explained, "and are used as offerings to the gods instead of sacrificing animals like in Hindu ceremonies. For a Buddhist to harm any living creature is a sin."

Dawa placed the tormas on a cloth at the base of the altar along with offerings of butter, fruit, a variety of our health bars, and beverages. They asked us to bring out some of our gear—like boots, ice axes, and clothing—to be blessed. I also hung a banner for Team Duke—the John Wayne Cancer Foundation—on the front of the altar to receive a blessing. Kids less fortunate than me who were suffering from cancer had painted colorful pictures and signed it. I wanted to carry their art with me in hopes that it would raise awareness and support for cancer research.

The ceremony began with Dawa and Karma chanting prayers. Occasionally, as part of the prayer ritual, they rang a bell or clacked a small wooden instrument. Ang Pasang passed a plate of rice around for us to toss on the altar at key moments. After half an hour we all stood in a circle and received a handful of dry tsampa. In unison we raised our right arms to the sky and lowered them three times. When Ang Pasang gave the signal, we tossed the barley flour up and let it drift down on us.

"Tsampa in the air means good wishes and happiness for overcoming all obstacles," Ang Pasang explained.

Then the fun began. The Sherpas rubbed tsampa on our faces and in our hair.

Ang Pasang smeared some on my cheeks and into my hair. "This is my wish for you to have a long life and grow old with hair as gray as the tsampa."

I totally got into that and helped make everyone else's hair gray with tsampa too.

Dawa blessed a handful of rice for me to carry to the summit and then passed pieces of our equipment through smoke from juniper branches to protect it. They filled a small cup with beer and we each drank it after it was blessed. When it came to my turn I looked at Karen and Dad to see what I should do. They said it was okay and I drank the small glass of blessed beer.

Immediately after the puja the Sherpas brought out trays of food and drink. A couple of yak boys climbed our hillside to join the party. Everyone was laughing and chatting in Nepali and Tibetan. We didn't understand a word, but it was an incredible afternoon.

Afterward it was time to hire yaks to make our way up to Advanced Base Camp at twenty-one thousand feet. There was way too much gear for us to carry, even in multiple trips. The yak herders sent another Tibetan to negotiate the price of the yaks that would carry our gear from Chinese Base Camp to Advanced Base Camp. With a calculator and notebook he slowly walked among our blue barrels, boxes, heavy plastic bags, and duffels. "You will need fifty yaks."

Dad had done some research before we arrived. He crossed his arms. "We were told thirty yaks before we left home."

The guy shook his head. "You have too much. Yaks are not strong after the cold winter and can only carry forty kilograms."

"A friend came here two years ago and was told sixty kilograms," Dad answered.

The Tibetan was a firm negotiator. "In the fall yaks are stronger and have fattened up during the summer monsoon."

Dad was just as firm. The conversation went back and forth, the price going up and down like the cost of gas in America. It was yak, yak, yak until Karen jumped in and accepted the negotiator's offer.

"Just start loading the yaks," she said. "Let's get moving."

I'd been wondering how they did this. There wasn't exactly a weighing station where you could drive a yak onto a scale and measure its load. Several Tibetans appeared. Two of them placed a bar across their shoulders while a third hung a barrel from a rope in the center and used a balance scale to weigh our goods.

Loading 4,400 pounds of gear and supplies wasn't easy. One guy had to hold a yak by its horn while two others balanced the weight evenly on each side of the animal. I stretched out my arm to pet one, but it gave me an eye that said *Don't even think of coming closer.*

When all of our gear was finally strapped onto forty yaks, we thought we'd come out ahead. But that wasn't the end of it.

"You need ten more. There's very little to eat along the trail. One yak must carry the food for every four animals."

Dad threw his arms in the air and walked away like he was negotiating for a used car.

"We've already spent twice our budget for this," Karen said. "We can't do more."

The Tibetan negotiator just stood there with his calculator and waited, knowing that he had us. We couldn't move two tons of gear up the mountain by ourselves.

Finally they agreed on a price per animal per day—fifty dollars a head. I thought Dad was going to lose it, but he kept his cool by taking a brisk walk around the other camps.

That afternoon I watched fifty animals leave, walking in

single file, decorated with bits of colored ribbons and yarn tied in their hair, bells tinkling. In the morning we'd say good-bye to our liaison officer, who would wait for us to return to Chinese Base Camp, and I would hoist my pack on my back and walk one step closer to my dream. After waiting for four years to get here, I was about to take my first steps on Everest.

Advanced Base Camp was too far to reach in one day. We arrived at Interim Camp at nineteen thousand feet and settled in for the night. It would definitely not make the list of places I wanted to visit again. It was a cold, dusty, windy place. So windy that it took all of us to raise the tent where we would sleep and eat. It was also narrow and filled with yak dung—not to mention yaks.

Ang Pasang had warned me that the creatures were pretty disagreeable, but I'd always had a way with animals. They were smaller than I'd imagined, smaller than cows, but could carry heavy loads at high altitude. They were as incredible as the Sherpas. I approached one slowly, doing a pretty poor imita-tion of a yak-boy whistle. The animal gave me that same look I'd gotten earlier and turned a sharp horn toward me, as if to ask, *Do you really think you can come any closer?*

"Hold this out in your hand, and you'll win him over," Ang Pasang said. He gave me a wad of brown dough. "We carry balls of tsampa for energy. Yaks can't get enough of it."

The animal eyed me a minute before sniffing my hand. "Go on. You'll love it," I whispered.

I felt its warm breath as the yak took the whole treat in one mouthful.

Ang Pasang explained, "In Tibet your wealth is determined by how many yaks you own. Herders use the lean meat, plus dried dung for fuel, hair for clothing and blankets, leather for boots, and fatty milk to make into butter, yogurt, and cheese."

The grizzly was the California state animal. I laughed to myself, imagining a grizzly trying to carry a load up to Advanced Base Camp.

That evening we finally got a connection using our BGAN, and I did a live interview with *Good Morning America*. I'd done enough interviews by then that I wasn't too nervous.

I assured everyone watching the program, "I do feel a bit overwhelmed. I mean, I do respect the boundaries of the mountain. But we take all the precautions. We're going as safe as we can and feel really good about it."

The next morning we hiked a strip of flat stones that split the glacier in two parts. I practiced the yak-boy whistle. It would be a megahit when I got home. I felt great. The altitude wasn't getting to me at all.

King Richard, on the other hand, was feeling lousy. He was kind of out of shape and had been eating all the wrong stuff. He bragged about not eating vegetables and how much he loved cheese, hamburgers, and 7-Eleven burritos. No matter how much we lectured him on the importance of a healthy diet and exercise, he just didn't get it.

We arrived at Advanced Base Camp in four hours. I was only eighteen hundred feet lower than the summit of Aconcagua. We made camp on cold, rough rocks surrounded by snow and ice. We did upgrade, however, to a dining tent that had a separate kitchen area and gave Kumar more space to work and store things.

Advanced Base Camp was much smaller than the Chinese Base Camp down below. There were no Ping-Pong tables here, but there was a great community of international climbers, especially an awesome Chinese team. They were so different from the stiff officials we'd encountered. One spoke good English and was up on current world affairs. He asked what we thought about the US House of Representatives approving the new health-care bill and sending it to President Obama. Dad was a total news junkie and enjoyed a good conversation with him.

We stayed two nights at Advanced Base Camp to acclimatize and to organize gear. King Richard had come as our support staff. He'd never planned to climb above ABC, but he had planned to help out. He was a having such a tough time with the altitude, though, that it wasn't possible. He never left his tent except to eat and then coughed all through his meal. He and Dawa, who was also sick, stayed behind when we left for an acclimatizing hike to Camp 1 on a saddle-shaped ridge called the North Col.

Ang Pasang and Karma were like mini yaks, carrying

seventy pounds each of extra gear and oxygen tanks to stock Camp 1. The trail was rocky and jagged, and sometimes we lost it among the rocks. When that happened we'd search for the next cairn to show us back to the trail. The real climbing began at a place called Crampon Point.

I put on my crampons, feeling so much more certain of myself than I had on Elbrus and Denali. Karen didn't have to zip my jacket, check my boots, or adjust my pack. I was a full-fledged, responsible member of the team—all of us had one another's backs.

We reached Crampon Point, solid ice littered with rocks, and then came to a really steep climb with fixed ropes. There were two fixed lines there, usually one for going up and one for going down, but if no one was coming down you could use the second for going up as well. Groups of Sherpas carrying big loads to Camp 1 passed us on the ropes with amazing speed and dexterity. You could tell they had climbed those ropes many times.

The weather was perfect, blue sky everywhere, and the trail was easy to follow. All you had to do was connect the dots of climbers snaking their way up a hill that steadily gained altitude. On the steep 60-degree vertical climb, the ascender on the fixed ropes was my best bud. I slid it up the line, locked the teeth, and lifted myself with a natural rhythm and strength I had lacked when I was younger.

A large crevasse lay in front of us, too wide to go around

safely. The Chinese Mountaineering Association, which sets the route every year and sets up the fixed lines for everyone to use, had connected two aluminum ladders lengthwise and placed them across what looked like a bottomless cavern of blue ice. They were secured on both sides of the crevasse with anchors driven deep into the snow and ice. There were two ropes tied to each end of the ladders, just long enough that you could hold one in each hand to help you balance as you went across.

Ang Pasang was the first to cross the ladder. Karen went next. I watched carefully. I didn't want to make a mistake.

"Your turn," Dad said. "Clip a carabiner onto one rope, then pick up the second rope with your other hand."

The lines were slack when I gripped them. "Use the ropes to help you balance. Rely on your feet."

"Got it," I said.

"Now take the first step. It's always the hardest," Dad said.

I kept trying to place my foot, but steel spikes and round aluminum rungs weren't remotely compatible. I was never going to get across.

"Try to fit your crampon points on the rungs," Karen called to me.

I slid my hands along the rope as metal met metal. The tips of the crampons on the front of my boot had to hook over one rung while those on the back hooked over another. This was a technical challenge, but I was up for it. I was even excited about my first traverse across a ladder.

"Stay calm and focus on each step," Karen said. "You'll be fine."

I moved forward slowly. One step at a time. I kept my eyes on the ladder, not daring to lose my focus. Before I knew it, I heard the crunch of my crampons on snow when I stepped onto solid ground.

But that wasn't our last challenge of the day. Only minutes later we came to a long, steep traverse beneath two enormous seracs, towers of ice rising above the glacier. Ang Pasang and Karen went first so she could film us coming across. She turned and signaled me to come.

"Move quickly," Dad told me. "I don't have a good feeling about this."

I clipped on to the fixed line and hurried, not because I was convinced that anything would happen, but because Dad had asked me to keep moving. Below us the slope continued steeper and steeper until it spilled over into a bottomless cliff, but we were secure with our safety line and ascenders. I had the rhythm down: Slide, lock, step. Slide, lock, step. Slide, lock, step.

Two members of another team were making their way down from Camp 1. The first was a Spanish guy with this crazy long curly hair poking out of his hat and goggles.

"*Hola, ¿cómo estás?*" He threw his hand out for a high five as he passed me. We swapped places with our carabiners to both stay on the line yet get around each other.

Another climber followed about two hundred feet behind, decked out in a yellow down suit as bright as the sun. He wasn't clipped in and seemed focused on getting back to Advanced Base Camp as fast as possible.

He smiled and said something in a language I later learned was Hungarian.

I smiled and waved. "Hi."

Seconds later a thunderous roar ripped through the air. The earth rumbled beneath my feet. I looked up and saw a ten-story wall of ice and snow break free and explode into an enormous cloud of white! It hurtled down the mountain, building higher and higher as it gained speed, Snow and ice dust billowed everywhere.

A killer wave was coming straight at me.

So big. So fast. What was happening? What to do?

High altitude robbed my mind and body of oxygen. I couldn't think, couldn't react fast enough.

The avalanche slammed into me and sucked my breath away. Everything was white, whirling about me, tossing me around like a toy. I was tumbling out of control and couldn't breathe.

I was completely disoriented and blinded by the cloud of white around me. Where was the sky? The earth?

I kicked desperately, trying to sink my crampons into snow, ice, anything to keep from sliding toward the deadly crevasse.

I thought Karen and Ang Pasang were far enough ahead

that they were safe, but where was Dad? Karma? I tried to scream but no sound left my lips.

I was still clipped in to the fixed line, my one connection to safety. With a jolt that ran through my body, the rope snapped and zipped past my head. My ascender was above the break, still hooked onto the part of the rope that was attached to the mountain. Would the rest hold me in place or yank me away? And what about Dad?

I clung to the lifeline as I waited for the air to clear. "Dad!" I screamed.

The ground finally stopped moving, and once again I heard the cold, whipping wind. Finally, after what seemed like forever, I sank my crampons into solid ice, and I could see the blue sky above. My head spinning and heart racing, I searched for my teammates in the heavy snow cloud. I sucked the burning cold air into my lungs and screamed, "Dad!"

No answer. Only the frozen breath of Everest against my face.

I whipped around, frantically searching in every direction, screaming again and again until the cold shredded my throat.

I finally saw him. Karma was right behind him.

I tried to manage a few words, but Dad beat me to it. "You okay?"

"Yes!" I shouted, my air coming out in steam clouds. I was alive.

Karen was just beyond the reach of the avalanche, with Ang Pasang. "You guys all right?" she shouted.

"Yes," Dad yelled, "but the rope's gone, and we need to get Jordan up to you."

I held my ascender—my connection to safety—in my right hand. It was supposed to be strong enough to tow a truck but now looked like it had been run over by one. It was bent 90 degrees. "My ascender's broken."

"Can't be," Karen called.

"But it is!"

Karma rose from the icy wreck. Moving steadily, he gave me a nod as if to say, *Pull yourself together. Keep going.*

We needed to get off this crumbling slope. Dad was right behind me. "Come on, J Man, just like we've practiced. Walk slowly, make sure your crampons are secure, and head toward Karen."

I focused on Karen and headed up the slope, my heart thumping. Tears clouded my eyes. I didn't know if I wanted to go back home or on to the summit of Everest. These had been the most terrifying minutes of my life. If we had been just a few steps slower, the avalanche would have crushed us or sent us tumbling down thousands of feet off an unknown cliff. Death felt very real and very close at that moment.

When I finally reached Karen, she grabbed me and pulled me close.

"I was so scared," she said, studying my face. "You're all right, nothing broken?"

Dad walked up a few minutes later. He had helped Karma, who had been down the slope a little farther. Together they'd shared an ice axe to get them both to safety. "Jordan was unbelievable," he told Karen. "He got himself together and made it here as well as any man."

I loved hearing those words. I looked up at him and noticed blood seeping through his wool cap and spreading slowly. "Your head, you're bleeding."

He was either unaware or still on such an adrenaline rush. He didn't feel the pain.

Karen gently lifted his beanie and revealed a deep gash on his scalp. His hair was matted with blood. "Don't you feel that?"

"Nah, it's okay," he said.

I realized that my crampons had punctured his flesh while I'd been fighting to get my feet under me. I swallowed hard to hold back tears. I was so, so sorry. I hadn't meant to hurt him.

Blood also dripped from several torn places on the thigh of his pants leg.

That was my dad. Even wounded, he'd propped me up and helped me make my way to safety.

"We need to get you to a camp as soon as possible," Karen said.

"I'll be all right," he said.

"Nonsense. You know things don't heal well up here."

Urgent voices came from below us. "The Spaniard is hanging from a rope on the side of the cliff," Ang Pasang translated. "Sherpas are trying to pull him up."

"Is he alive?" I asked, knowing very well that we could have been right there with him.

"They don't know. He's not moving."

"And the guy in the yellow suit?" I asked.

Ang Pasang yelled to them in Nepali and got a sad reply. "No one can find him. He probably disappeared over the cliff. He wasn't clipped in."

I'd known the dangers, but having just said hi to someone who died minutes later hit me harder than the avalanche. Death wasn't a remote possibility. It was real.

On Everest you couldn't let your mind wander, even for a second. Even if he'd been clipped in, who knows what would've happened? It was like playing Russian roulette. I hoped they'd at least find his body, but I knew that most people who died on Everest remained there forever.

Our plan had been to drop gear at Camp 1 on the North Col and return to Advanced Based Camp the same day, to acclimatize.

"Shall we go on up and try to get help for you," Karen asked Dad, "or go back down?"

"Going to Camp One is the safest now," he answered.

"Then up it is." Karen said.

We were close to twenty-two thousand feet and had to

pass immediately under the second serac. It looked even more precarious than the first. I remembered Dad saying he wasn't comfortable here.

Now I was petrified of being buried alive. I moved as quickly as possible. Karen stayed closer to me than usual, and Dad was holding up okay just behind me. But he definitely needed someone to look at his wounds. Karen took my bent ascender and gave me her good one so I'd be secure on the rope.

At Camp 1 we did an inventory and discovered there weren't enough supplies for an overnight stay. Plus no one there had the first-aid supplies to help Dad. Karen looked at his head again and told him he'd definitely need a stitch or two to close the wound. So we decided to hike back to Advanced Base Camp. That meant moving through the avalanche zone again, underneath that tilting tower of ice.

Before we headed back down, Dad pulled out the satellite phone to call Terry, the man who'd coached me for interviews and become a close friend. "We'd better alert him that we're okay in case the avalanche on the north side has already hit the press," he said.

"Yeah, best if Terry knows we are all okay and can keep rumors from going wild. Let's make sure he calls Jordan's mom," Karen said.

As soon as Dad let Terry know that we were safe and alive, we moved through the same scene but in a different direction and with longer shadows. When we reached the danger zone, we saw that some Sherpas had already crossed the shaky avalanche debris to secure new safety lines and anchors, risking their lives to save ours.

Ang Pasang led and told us to cross the area one at a time for safety. There was some danger of another avalanche.

"No way," Karen told him. "Jordan, you're staying right here with me."

"We can do this," Dad said. "We have to move quickly, but we can do this."

Like drummers playing to the same beat, we unclipped, passed anchors quickly, and clipped in again. The shift in the mountain had created huge piles of snow that we had to walk over and around. My heart was racing as I descended through this chilling scene. I tried hard not to think about the man in the yellow suit but couldn't help pausing for a second and looking where the snow had carried him down the face of the mountain and over the edge of the cliff.

Ang Pasang spoke to the Sherpas who'd rescued the Spaniard and learned he'd dislocated a shoulder, broken several ribs, and bruised the whole left side of his body. But he was alive.

"What about the guy in the yellow suit?" I asked again, holding my breath. "Did they find him?"

He shook his head. "They'll search for another week or so, but I'm sure he's lying thousands of feet below the cliff."

I could still hear the guy saying hi in my head and didn't think I'd ever forget it.

Once we got through the avalanche zone, Karen and I continued at a steady pace. Dad was limping. His face twisted with pain with every step, and he wasn't the kind who winced often. Ang Pasang and Karma stayed right with him all the way to Advanced Base Camp.

King Richard and Dawa had heard about the avalanche and rushed out to meet us, worried that we were hurt.

"Just Paul," Karen told them.

The Chinese camp had a doctor with them to take care of their team. We set out to find our Chinese friend who spoke English.

Karen showed him the big patch of dried blood on the top of Dad's head. "His leg's cut too. Do you think your doctor can take a look at him?"

"Come with me to the dining tent and someone will send for him."

The Chinese doctor placed Dad in a chair and cleaned his wounds. Karen held the instrument tray while he stitched the three punctures on Dad's thigh and the gash on his scalp. Dad stared straight at me and worked up that big smile of his to hide the pain—pain caused by my crampons as I thrashed about wildly in the avalanche. What if I'd killed him? I'd never have been able to live with that.

Climbers in Advanced Base Camp were restless that night. News of the avalanche and the dead climber, who we had learned was Hungarian, had made everyone a little nervous. I lay quietly in my tent and looked out the door at the summit. It seemed so close, but we still had another three-thousand-foot push to the top through the death zone, where your body dies little by little. We'd have to pass the avalanche area several more times while acclimatizing and going for the summit.

I'd hurt my dad today. I didn't want to harm anyone else. I thought about the warm California sun, a hot breakfast, and my friends riding around Big Bear Lake in shorts and T-shirts. Lack of oxygen was already messing with my brain. Part of it told me to go home. I felt so far from everything, especially my dream.

CHAPTER 25

The following morning, team representatives met to dis-
cuss the events of the previous day. As a veteran climber and
a well-known and respected Sherpa, Ang Pasang represented
our team. The remaining serac, that tower of ice, threatened
anyone who passed beneath it. The Chinese Mountaineering
Association was ready to get started fixing ropes on a new route
that would avoid the dangerous second ice tower.

While they planned the new route, Dad rested and gave
his leg a chance to heal. That was vital. For the next four days
we'd have to climb up and down the mountain to stock higher
camps and acclimatize. At sea level breathing requires only
five percent of your energy. On the summit it would require
seventy percent. We had to get our bodies ready.

"The *Today* show and Harry Smith on CBS both want
Skype interviews from Advanced Base Camp," Karen said
when she checked her e-mail. At ABC we'd been able to

connect the BGAN and get Internet, e-mail, and Skype. Our PR person, Rob, was in New York and coordinating interviews.

Dad lightly touched the dressing on his head. "Then let's show everybody we're fine."

Live interviews no longer gave me butterflies, but this was different. I'd witnessed death firsthand and didn't know what to say if they asked how I was feeling. The last thing we needed was more criticism.

When we finally got online, Dad gave me a reassuring thumbs-up from behind the camera. Neither of my interviewers even mentioned the avalanche. Either they didn't know, or they just wanted to check on our progress and wish me luck. I hoped I'd be able to report in a few days that we'd summited.

After two or three rest days we spent the next four days with our Sherpas, stocking the upper camps and acclimatizing to the altitude. There were three camps above Advanced Base Camp: Camp 1 at 23,000 feet, Camp 2 at 24,750 feet, and Camp 3 at 27,390 feet. We made several trips to the first camp so that everything we needed would be there for us. Camp 2, where we would stay for a much shorter amount of time, required just one trip, and the Sherpas made a solo delivery to Camp 3. Everything was in place for our climb to the summit. We just needed to wait for the weather to cooperate.

We returned to Chinese Base Camp to wait for the seven- to ten-day window between winds moving north off the summit and the monsoon arriving from the south. King Richard and Dawa had already gone back there after learning we were safe the day of the avalanche, and it was nice to see them again.

Dad's wounds were healing well, and being at lower altitude helped them even more. Karen checked them every day and made sure that the bandages and the wounds stayed clean and without infection.

I wanted to hang out with King Richard and watch movies, but Karen was pretty strict about my independent-study homework.

"Jordan," she said one day, "you really need to work on your journal for English class."

"What should I write about?"

"Let's go see the stone memorials. You can write about them."

The two of us hiked to the edge of the camp and up a steep hill until the path leveled out to an area filled with cairns, or piles of stones, along with carved boulders, engraved plates, tombstones, and prayer flags in memory of climbers who'd died on the north side of Everest. There were dozens of them—young and old, famous and unnamed. The Mother Goddess of the World didn't care. They were all the same to her.

"Look at this one, Jordan," Karen said. "A woman climbing at twenty-seven thousand feet leaned back on her harness and it wasn't fastened properly. Everybody should come here before starting a climbing career."

We walked among the names and felt the history of

Everest. I was most interested in large gray slab surrounded by rocks. On the front it read IN MEMORY OF GEORGE LEIGH MALLORY & ANDREW IRVINE LAST SEEN ON 8TH JUNE 1924 AND ALL THOSE WHO DIED DURING THE PIONEER BRITISH MT. EVEREST EXPEDITIONS.

Our hike to the memorials gave me lots to write about in my journal, but I dreaded what came next—algebra. Math just isn't my thing. I must have sent some kind of psychic vibes through the camp, because every time I settled down to figure out what x and y stood for, people stopped by our tent. We had the smallest, lowest-budget tent in the camp, but everybody came to us to hang out. So, as I told Karen, it wasn't my fault that I didn't finish my algebra problems. Besides, I was learning a lot just by being around all those climbers from different countries and cultures.

Base camp was a blast. We were a community of climbers who all had the same goal—to climb the mountain. Almost everyone spoke at least some English, and I was surprised that, unlike the rest of the world, none of the climbers criticized me for being on the mountain at the age of thirteen. Instead they were all rooting for me.

The big teams had trucked in a lot of equipment including generators and solar power. Both the British and the South Africans invited me for movie nights. I got to watch *The Matrix* on a big plasma TV in the South African camp. They had comfy couches and a barrel filled with things to drink.

The Russians had built a rec center at their base camp and were totally cool about letting everybody use it. In addition to the Ping-Pong table, they had a flat-screen TV and a DVD player. I hung out there for a little while every day. They were wicked Ping-Pong players, but I won once in a while, or at least they let me think I did.

The hardest part was being away from my mom and sister for so long. I was super homesick. But I was able to use the satellite phone to call them at least every other day. One night the Russians had a big party with music, food, drinks, and dancing. I told Mom about it the next day.

"Sounds like tough times there, buddy," she said with a chuckle.

"And you wouldn't believe the food our Sherpas are making for us. It's definitely gourmet, and they're using rocks for a kitchen. You know, if I had to turn around and come back home without setting another foot on the mountain, I'd be one hundred percent satisfied. I'm here. I've seen Everest with my own two eyes. I'm so lucky."

"I just want you back here in one piece. I'm watching every move on the SPOT tracker on your website. All of us in Big Bear are. Let me know when you plan to summit."

We had a lot of cool technology. Network Innovations, one of our best sponsors, covered our satellite Internet and satellite phone costs while we were on the mountain. At base camp, Karen discovered she could get a really strong satellite signal right in the middle of a wide, icy riverbed with Everest as a backdrop, and CNN wanted a live interview during their ten a.m. show. They didn't seem to understand that ten a.m. in New York was nighttime in Chinese Base Camp.

We walked out to the icy riverbed in the dark and set up in the freezing cold air. But after all that, the signal didn't work. We tried, but we couldn't transmit anything.

King Richard and I played cards and watched the one-dollar DVDs he'd bought in Kathmandu. But sitting in the same tent with him should have come with a gas mask. He burped and farted at the same time.

I held my nose. "You need a filter."

He responded by lifting one cheek and firing one onto a pillow, and I have to admit I responded with one of my own. It turned into the War of the Farts, and I definitely lost.

"You wouldn't have this problem if you ate more fruits, vegetables, nuts, and seeds," Dad told him.

"You're not allowed to visit when we get home," Karen teased him. "I'll have to detox Jordan of all this bathroom humor."

I wondered if King Richard would get bored and lonely while we were climbing the mountain. Then we discovered that a longtime friend, Karina, was working with David Breashears to film the story of Dick Bass, the first guy to climb the Seven Summits. They'd gone to the south side of Everest for the thirtieth anniversary of Bass's first ascent of Everest.

When David went back to the States, Karina and her sister, Natalie, decided to join us at base camp.

I was super excited. Karina, a Brazilian ER doc, met Dad and Karen on an adventure race. She had visited us in Big Bear when I was ten, and we'd been like brother and sister ever since.

All King Richard could talk about was how he was going to win the hearts of both sisters.

The weather was 50 degrees and sunny the day Karina and Natalie arrived. Members of the Russian, British, and South African teams were hanging out in front of our tent with us, sipping beer and sharing snacks, when they pulled up in their Land Cruiser.

Karina flashed the most beautiful smile when she saw me. "Little bro, you are taller than me now!"

We'd been waiting at Chinese Base Camp for sixteen days. Other teams spent that time going over their gear, resting for the summit push, and partying. That wasn't our style. We stayed in shape by running up and down hills, even as far as the Interim Camp and back in one day just for exercise.

Karina was still acclimatizing and didn't come along. In the afternoons she did join us for yoga. It was pretty spectacular to be able to focus on Everest while stretching in the warrior pose.

Everyone was waiting for the weather to break. We were getting tired of waiting, but you can't rush things on Everest.

Since we had some spare time, Ang Pasang suggested we hike to a small monastery four miles away.

"Rongbuk Monastery is the highest monastery in the world at sixteen thousand seven hundred feet. About five hundred Buddhist monks and nuns used to live here, but now only about thirty are left," he said. "There are hundreds of meditation caves hidden in the hills."

Prayer flags and carved stones lined a long series of rock stairs leading to a mud building.

I traced the symbols with my finger. "What do they say?"

"*Om Mani Padme Hum*," Ang Pasang told me.

"What does it mean?"

"All of Buddha's teachings are contained in those words. They can't be translated in one sentence."

Then he led us to a tiny monastery carved into the mountain. Unlike Rongbuk, which most climbers visited, this tiny place saw very few Westerners. It felt incredibly special to be there. Ang Pasang asked the sole monk there if we could enter and asked for a blessing to climb the mountain.

The monk granted Ang Pasang's request, and I ducked under a low doorway into the room. There was a table with burning candles and murals of the mountains and of the Mother Goddess on the walls.

The monk prayed for our safe return and poured some kind of holy water from a tiny metal pot into our palms. Ang Pasang signaled for us to drink the water from our palms. Then the monk signaled for us to follow him down a few stairs carved in rock to a small natural cave with a ceiling so low I had to bend over. Even Karen could barely stand up.

It was an amazing underground place. Illumination came from butter lamps on rock shelves and from candles on natural rock tables. The ash had charred the ceiling and walls a charcoal gray. There were photos and money from around the world given as offerings for climbing the mountain. At one end of the tiny room was a small display case containing a seated Buddha surrounded by offerings of seeds and rice and pictures of the Dalai Lama.

"I'm lighting a candle for your safe return," Karina said as she took a long match from Ang Pasang and touched it to a wick floating in a bowl of yak butter.

I lit one for her. Then we all sat huddled together.

"It's so calm and peaceful," Karina whispered.

"Like we're in a sacred cave," I said. "There's definitely a special feeling."

We all sat quietly, absorbing the mood. The monk who had led us was meditating in the corner and must have fallen asleep. I heard a faint snore. He was very old. How many weeks, months, years had he dwelled here seeking enlightenment? I wondered.

Ang Pasang whispered, "We should go now. But first put a handful of sacred rice in your pocket to carry with you on the mountain."

We each took a small handful of the sacred rice. The monk awoke and led us into the upper room, where he tied a thin red cord around each of our necks.

"The *sungdi* scares off demons and ghosts and will protect you," Ang Pasang explained. "You should wear it as you climb the mountain."

The monk draped a long white silk scarf around each of us. "*Tashi delek.*"

"Means good luck. The *kata* is given as a sign of friendship to departing guests," Ang Pasang said.

When we got back to our camp, King Richard made a small fabric bag for my sacred rice and tied it around my neck with the red string. I was armed with a sungdi, rice, and kangaroo testicles, along with my rabbit's foot.

I had all the bases covered. We were in constant contact via e-mail and satellite phone with our friend Steve back in Big Bear. When he let us know that there was a weather window coming, I was ready to go.

Unfortunately, Karina's sister, Natalie, was still having major altitude problems. When she decided to return to Brazil, King Richard, who had never really gotten used to the elevation, took advantage of the ride back across the Friendship Bridge and left with her.

"I'll wait for you in Kathmandu," he promised.

I was really going to miss him. I loved every minute of his silliness.

Karina was sticking around, though. That was good news.

"I want to go with you," she announced that night at dinner. "I've been at high altitude long enough to acclimatize."

Dad tapped his fingers on the table. "That might be possible, but you don't have any gear, snow boots, or oxygen."

"And even more important," Karen added, "no permit."

"I'll try to borrow gear and clothing." She twirled her hair around a finger and smiled. "Maybe I can even talk the liaison officer into giving me a permit."

With her beautiful smile and charm, Karina managed to join another group's permit for Advanced Base Camp, and she seemed to be content with the idea of staying there instead of climbing farther. She asked if she could share my tent up there.

"Yeah, sure, we can share," I told her.

After eighteen days at seventeen thousand feet, waiting for that all-important weather report, we needed to spend a couple of nights at Advanced Base Camp to reacclimatize.

I called Mom to let her know. "We're leaving from base camp tomorrow with plans of making our way to the summit!"

"I'm going to follow you online so I'll know exactly where you are every step of the way," she said. She fell silent for a minute, and then her voice cracked slightly. "I just want you back safe in my arms."

"I will be soon. We won't take unnecessary risks," I promised.

"Then let me know the night before you're going to summit."

"I will. Love you, Mom."

"You too."

In case something happened to me, I wanted to thank all those who'd provided love and support. In a post on my blog I wrote:

> From Advanced Base Camp: here we go. If you have ever sponsored me, ever bought one of my T-shirts, ever attended one of my taco night fund-raisers, or just patted me on the back and wished me good luck, I send you the most sincere thank-you. Today I leave base camp of Everest, and every step I take is finally toward the biggest goal of my life, to stand on top of the world. Every single one of you has made this possible. I feel in some way I have succeeded in just getting this far, but on the other hand I am drawn to do something great. Know that comes from my heart. I hope to make you all proud. Jordan Romero. "It is not the mountain we conquer, it is ourselves."
> —Edmund Hillary.

CHAPTER 26

We were well acclimatized now and hiked to Advanced Base Camp the next morning with the climbing Sherpas and Kumar and Kevin. Karina was hiking with the team that had added her to their permit and would meet us there. Some climbers had dropped trash on the trail, and that drove me crazy. I picked it up and shoved it into my pockets.

Just past the Interim Camp, large snowflakes began to slowly drift to the ground.

By the time we reached ABC, the light flurry had morphed into a full blizzard. We tossed our packs into the tents, which were still there from our first visit, scrambled inside, and zipped the doors shut. A couple of hours later Karina arrived at camp to join me in my tent.

"You guys okay?" Karen called to us.

"Fine!" I told her.

"Jordan's doing great. He's got his gear very organized. I'm impressed," Karina said. She was shivering. "It's *so* cold. How did you stand this when you were a little boy?" she asked.

"I was too focused on my goal to think about it much," I said.

She rolled onto her side and perched on one elbow. "Didn't you ever just want to just say, 'Forget this—I'm done'?"

"Sure. More than once I sat down and cried. There were times when I was totally beat, homesick, and frustrated. I asked myself why I was doing this."

"And why were you?"

"I really wanted to finish what I'd started. It's important to have goals. I feel kind of lost if I don't have something big to work toward."

"So what's after this?"

"I want to encourage other kids to go after their dreams."

Now she laughed. "Little bro, they're not going to want to climb Everest."

"No," I agreed. "They have to find their own Everest. I just want them to know that it's possible."

That was enough serious talk for me. I grabbed one of King Richard's DVDs and popped it into my laptop.

By morning the entire base camp was under a blanket of snow. We woke up to Dad and Karen calling to us to see if we were okay.

"Your tent is covered in snow," Dad yelled. "Better knock some of it off before you try to open your door."

Still in our cozy sleeping bags, Karina and I pushed at

the roof and the walls and heard the heavy, wet snow slipping onto the ground. Finally I unzipped the door wide enough to peek outside. Dad and Karen were lying on their stomachs with their arms crossed under their chins, looking out their door and grinning at us.

There was about a half a foot of snow on the ground.

After a quick good morning we zipped our door shut again. It was cold.

Karina and I were playing cards when Karen called to me, "Jordan, it's time to do some homework."

"Can't. I'm busy right now," I said.

Karina whispered, "No you're not."

But I was. For the last six months I had been training so hard that I hardly had any time to chill with friends. I didn't want to lose this chance to hang with my awesome "sister."

When the sky cleared, Dad and Karen took Karina on a short hike up to acclimatize. I stayed behind to have time alone in the dining tent with Ang Pasang.

He was so powerful that he inspired me to climb better and faster. He sat across from me drinking Tibetan salt tea with butter, which was more like a broth than a tea.

I drank hot cocoa instead. "Do you think I can make it to the summit?" I asked him.

"A month ago you couldn't keep up with me." He stirred his tea, then leaned back. "Now you are one of the strongest climbers on the mountain."

"Seriously? I've never been as fast as my dad and Karen," I admitted.

"You were ahead of them all the way yesterday."

"True, but I think they can still pass me." I sipped my cocoa. "How did you and the other Sherpas get to be so strong?"

"Where I come from in Nepal, we have no roads, no cars. I must always walk, walk, walk, carrying everything I need. I had my baby brother on my back when I was five while my mother worked in the potato fields. When I was older, I took care of our yaks."

"You were a yak boy?" I asked.

He nodded. "Now I earn more on the mountain, but I'm away from my family too long. I miss my wife and children. My wife tells me to quit because many Sherpas have died, but I cannot. I have to take care of my family."

I'd had everything I needed growing up, and he'd had so little. But here we were, sitting together, ready to climb to the top of the world. It was a special moment.

A smiling face peeked through the door. "Ang Pasang?"

"Lhakpa, come in," he said, then introduced me. "This is Jordan Romero."

"Yes, we've all heard about the thirteen-year-old. I wanted to meet him," Lhakpa said, still smiling.

"Lhakpa once held the record for the fastest ascent on Everest," Ang Pasang told me. "He made it from base camp to the summit in just under eleven hours."

"Whoa," I said. "That's insanely fast."

Lhakpa accepted a cup of Tibetan tea. "I heard you live in California. My friend Apa Sherpa and I moved to Utah in 2006 to open an outdoor clothing store with two Americans."

"Awesome. How'd it go?" I asked.

"Not well. Now I lead climbing groups. Apa's on the south side trying to break his own record by reaching the summit for the twentieth time."

I sat in complete awe listening to the Sherpas. The mountain totally belonged to them. They were giants, and most people would never know.

At Advanced Base Camp we kept watching the weather and trying to decide the perfect day to go on up to Camp 1 at twenty-three thousand feet with the intention of summiting in a day or two. A few other teams had already left for the camp, and we were watching them closely.

About midday we got a good weather report from Steve's father-in-law, packed up, and said good-bye to Karina, Kumar, and Kevin.

"I'll see you after the summit," I said.

We climbed along the new route that went up and around the tilting serac. It was a longer route but safer. I kept thinking about saying hi to the Hungarian only minutes before he fell to his death. At least he died doing something he loved, I thought. No one would put themselves through this if they didn't love mountain climbing.

I tried to pace my breathing with one breath per step, but each step was like dragging a freight car up a hill. When I felt this tired, I thought of everyone who was supporting me. I wanted to get to the top for them. Also, the last thing I wanted was to give the critics ammunition. I intended to prove them wrong.

One thing I knew for sure—I felt way stronger going up this time than I had on our first climb. We had acclimatized well.

I reached Camp 1 and immediately crawled into the tent. Some people have trouble sleeping at high altitude, but not me. I always dropped off fast and was the last to wake.

All the teams planned to hike to Camp 2, at 24,750 feet, the following day, but in the morning the wind was so fierce you had to brace yourself against it.

"I talked to other leaders," Dad said. "They're staying here. They don't want to move up to Camp Two in this. No one wants to hike with wind blowing in their faces."

Karen was heating water for breakfast. "The forecast from Steve's father-in-law said the weather was going to improve later today. I think we have to trust that."

"Let's talk it over with Ang Pasang," Dad said. "He's been up at Camp Two in the wind. He knows the mountain."

Ang Pasang joined us in our tent.

"Would you like something hot to drink? Sorry I don't have any Tibetan tea," Karen said, handing him a cup of hot cocoa. "None of the other groups are going to move up today. Seems to us like it's doable. We've hiked in wind before. What do you think?"

"The climb to Camp Two is very steep, but the snow is packed. The trail is on a very wide section of the mountain. It's quite good for hiking," the Sherpa leader told us.

I was still all cozy and warm in my sleeping bag. "What are the chances of someone being blown right off the mountain?"

He smiled. "No chance, especially for someone as strong as you."

"So you think it's safe to go on?" Dad asked.

"Yes, it's better to be up at Camp Two tonight."

We trusted him and set out after breakfast. The altitude was a killer. I had to stop every two minutes to breathe in and out in short controlled bursts to get back to normal. The winds continued and were so loud we could hardly talk to each other. Once Karen and I even lay down on our ice axes when a strong gust came our way. When we arrived in Camp 2 about five hours later, the brutally cold temperatures created a windchill factor of minus 40 degrees. I felt like a humansicle.

Nobody could stay outside in that wind for too long. It was blowing so hard that it took all of us working together to put up one tent at a time—one for Dad, Karen, and me and one for the Sherpas. It was cold, tough work, and we were all tired from the day's hike and being in the wind for hours. But we did what we needed to do to stay safe through the night.

As soon as we could, Dad, Karen, and I crawled into our three-man tent and tried to distract ourselves by spending part of the day talking about the other climbing parties and the stories that each of us and the Sherpas had heard along the way. Ang Pasang told us of a climber who had ascended too fast and was hypoxic from lack of oxygen to his brain. He'd gone totally berserk and tried to kill one of the other climbers. Sherpas had to contain him and get him off the mountain to a lower elevation.

I was glad we had oxygen with us.

The winds pounded us for the rest of the day. Empty tents flew a hundred feet into the air, whirling like fall leaves before disappearing completely.

"What if it does this for days?" I asked.

"There's no rush," Karen said. "We'll wait until it's safe."

We were so close; I didn't mind waiting. "Why do you think we always make the summit the first time we try while others have to keep trying?" I asked.

"Because we're well trained and work as a team," Dad answered. "But we can't control the weather. We have to face the fact that we may or may not reach the summit this time. It might just be a dress rehearsal. It could take a couple of weeks or a couple of years."

I lay down and watched the roof of the tent flap wildly in the wind. Everest was a tough mountain, physically and technically. I told myself that seeing Everest was what it was really all about, that it was okay if we didn't summit.

We used oxygen that night when our bodies were quiet and our lungs sucked less air. The wind was blowing so hard it flattened the tent against us, burying me under the wall. Once again Dad propped himself on one elbow for hours, holding it off me.

It was a restless night. At about two a.m. we heard commotion outside.

Ang Pasang unzipped our door. "The wind tore our tent and is blowing it away."

Dad waved them in with his arm. "Get in, get in. All of you."

We slept like sardines the rest of the night, the Sherpas with their feet sticking out of the door because six people didn't fit in a three-man tent. The wind continued hammering us.

By morning the weather had improved as predicted. Only the occasional gust hit us. Gear and tattered tents were strung out all over the camp. The Sherpas' tent hadn't really blown away, but it had blown down and was damaged. We worked together to repair it and set it back up.

Other teams were beginning to arrive from Camp 1—the ones who had waited out the wind. We had to decide whether to leave Camp 2 for a summit attempt. That led to another conference with Ang Pasang.

"The winds have died down," Dad said. "If no one else is on the mountain, we can avoid long waits in the cold and wind on the Three Steps, the Chinese Ladder, and the summit ridge."

The Three Steps are three rocky outcroppings on the northeast ridge of Everest. Anyone climbing Everest's north face has to navigate the giant rocks.

"It's safer to move quickly," Dad continued. "At ABC your friend Lhakpa recommended going straight past Camp Three to the summit. What do you think?" Dad asked.

"I agree," Ang Pasang said. "Camp Three is not a good place to stay. I think you're strong enough to make the summit from here. We should watch the weather and plan to leave at five p.m."

Leaving in the evening might seem strange, but our plan was to hike all night and arrive at the summit in the morning, giving us plenty of time to walk back down before darkness hit. Unlike on Denali we didn't have twenty-four hours of sunlight to enjoy, and we needed to have daylight on the descent. Climbing down the mountain could be even more dangerous than climbing up.

We prepared our gear, slept, and ate as much as we could during the day. Then we put on every piece of clothing we had so not an inch of skin was exposed to the wind and the cold.

I put on my oxygen mask nearly last and made sure it was sealed tight. It covered everything from the bridge of my nose down to the bottom of my mouth. When I tried to move my head around, the mass shifted under its own weight—a bit annoying, but worth it not to go berserk.

Karen handed me my goggles. I didn't need to protect my eyes from the sun but from the wind and blowing snow.

Putting them on created a constant battle between the goggles and the oxygen mask—both competing for space. If I pulled down on the goggles, they pushed the mask off my face, and I definitely couldn't let *that* happen. When I pushed up on the mask, the goggles rode higher on my forehead, opening a gap that caused them to fog.

I wrapped two bottles of boiling water in neoprene foam insulators and slid them inside my down suit next to Hammer energy bars, string cheese, nuts, and chocolate for a power boost. Getting my crampons on took longer than usual. The buckle was frozen, and the metal was so cold it stuck to my mittens. I finally got to my feet, leaned on my axe, and stared at the northeast ridge of the Mother Goddess of the World.

This was it.

No mind wandering, I told myself. *There's no room for error.*

"Ready?" Dad said.

I nodded.

"Remember," he said. "No mistakes. We know what to do. Summit or not, we stay safe."

Karen and I both nodded. Then, ready to switch on our headlamps as soon as darkness began to set in, we left for the summit with the three climbing Sherpas. After four hours of hard, steady climbing, we reached Camp 3.

Dawa and Karma had stocked the camp with an extra

oxygen bottle for each of us and a stove. We swapped out our cylinders and ate some Hammer bars and cheese while melting snow to replenish our water bottles. I could see why Ang Pasang had said it was best not to stay here if we didn't have to. Camp 3 wasn't what you'd really call a camp; it was more like a 30-degree rocky, icy slope where you could barely pitch a few tents.

Small flakes blew around us as we followed a snow-filled gully on a fixed rope and climbed a steep slope that required an ice axe and crampons. The trail was mixed rock and snow. The wind wasn't as strong now, but we were at a higher elevation, so the temperature was about the same minus 40 degrees. It froze our water bottles even though we'd wrapped them and carried them inside our jackets.

A body in fluorescent-green mountaineering boots lay curled up in a fetal position under a tiny rock shelter.

"That's Green Boots," Ang Pasang said. "He's an Indian climber who was separated from his group in a whiteout. He crawled into that small cave and died."

More than two hundred bodies remained on the mountain because the thin air made it hard to recover them, but this was the first one I'd seen. I wondered if Green Boots had realized this would be his final resting place.

"How long has he been here?" I asked.

"Since 1996," Ang Pasang told me. "Climbers use him as a marker to know how far they are from the summit."

And to remind themselves just how dangerous this is, I thought.

I was climbing behind Ang Pasang now, not missing a beat as we approached the most critical part of the mountain, beginning at 27,890 feet—the treacherous rocks known as the Three Steps.

The First Step was made of large exposed boulders. Climbing it would have been easy in Big Bear, but at this altitude I had to pull hard on the fixed lines and stop every thirty seconds to rest. I couldn't believe how little oxygen I was getting, even wearing the mask.

I was breathing in one small hole and out another, creating a continual hiss that muted everything around me. So I was in my own little world. Very little snow covered the boulders, which made walking with crampons tricky. I had to be careful that my crampons didn't slip on the rocks.

Above the First Step we came to a mushroom-shaped rock with a small depression behind it where we could rest, eat, and hydrate. Breathing oxygen had dried my throat out. Having had nothing to drink since our water froze, I had developed a bit of a stomachache. I tried unzipping my parka to reach the food next to my body, but my hands were cold and the clumsy mittens couldn't budge the zipper. I pushed my goggles up to see what was going on.

The oxygen masks muffled our words, making communication difficult. "My zipper's frozen."

Karen pointed at hers and nodded. Dad too.

The water vapor we were exhaling had to go somewhere. It had dripped onto our zippers and frozen them solid.

Dad motioned for us to check our packs. I couldn't get my buckle open. Everything took so freaking long at that altitude; I felt like I was starring in a slow-motion movie. I draped my arms over my knees, trying to suck more air, as Dad struggled with my pack. He pulled out some FRS concentrate that amazingly hadn't frozen.

Karen had some too and so did he. We changed out our oxygen cylinders for fresh ones. Other climbers had dumped their old cylinders behind Mushroom Rock and left them there forever. We left ours behind the rock with plans to pick them up on our way down.

To reach the Second Step, we had to travel around a fifty-foot snow crest on an exposed traverse of ledges and steep slabs. If they hadn't been at twenty-eight thousand feet and covered in ice and snow, I could have scrambled right up. The lower part was a ten-foot rock we scaled using fixed ropes.

The warm, moist air I was exhaling escaped the oxygen mask and fogged my goggles. Dad and Karen were having the same problem, so we removed our goggles for a while. Blowing snowflakes hit my eyelashes and melted, which was no big deal until they froze my lashes together and sealed my eyes shut! It was totally crazy. I couldn't see a thing and kept trying to clear at least one eye with my mittens. I finally wiped my goggles off and put them back on. It was like peering at the world through a foggy film.

We came to a massive rock wall about thirty feet high — the infamous Second Step. It wouldn't have been that difficult to climb except for the snow, freezing temperature, extreme exposure, and altitude at 28,140 feet.

Four members of a Chinese team of 214 people had been the first to summit the Second Step from the north, in 1960. Fifteen years later the Chinese installed a metal ladder for everyone's use.

While I waited for Ang Pasang to climb it first, I stared at a corpse just below me in the rocks, still in full gear. He didn't look real, more like a wax figure. And that made me sad. He was somebody's son, brother, father, or good friend. I wondered what had gone wrong — a fall, an unexpected storm, not being prepared. The body was another reminder of how dangerous this was.

I clipped in to the fixed line. The ladder was only thirty feet high but dead vertical. A slip meant a deadly fall. The ladder shifted to the left slightly when I stepped on, and my heart jumped. Had the body below me fallen from the ladder and died of exposure? I needed to get myself together, focus.

I moved up one rung, gasping for air, my head pounding, dizzy. I took another step and paused again. I didn't hear anything other than the hiss of my mask and the clank of metal on metal in the thin air. Step, pause. Step, pause.

I reached the top rung and inched three feet to the right onto a ledge, where I sat and waited for Dad and Karen. I was higher than the clouds and could actually see the curvature of the earth with an orange line along it and an arc of white light above. I was catching the first hint of sunrise.

When Dad and Karen reached me, I pointed to the orange line, "Look behind me. The sun!"

Ang Pasang joined us a moment later. "It was good to climb alone today and not wait for a turn on the ladder in the cold," he said.

Once again Dad and Karen had made the right decision in not waiting for the other teams. Good call.

I'd made it to the top of the Second Step and figured the summit was in the bag, but I didn't say a word. I didn't want to jinx us.

I had read that sunrise on Everest would be the most amazing one I'd ever see, and when that bright yellow ball rose above the horizon, spreading rays across the sea of white, I knew that was right. I hoped the sun would warm things up a bit, but I doubted it. Every single part of me was cold.

Soon I was looking at clear blue sky. The sun had brought a positive feeling with it, a new energy. I had no doubt I'd reach the summit.

Before me was the Everest pyramid. I was so stoked to be doing something this big.

We went around an outcropping of rock known as the

Third Step, and then came to a steep ridge. One misplaced step could send me tumbling thousands of feet to my death. Corpses in multicolored down jackets littered the hillside below me, lying frozen in time in the same position they'd been in when they took their last breaths. Some looked like they had just sat down to rest and never gotten up again.

"That's called Rainbow Valley because of the colorful jackets," Ang Pasang said as I stood staring at the open graveyard. "The cold dry air preserves the bodies."

"Like mummies," I said.

For the next hour I followed him up the 50-to-60-degree snowy slope. It was windy and brutally cold. I could only go four or five steps before stopping to gasp for breath, my heart thundering in my temples. We went around another outcropping of small rocks before getting onto the summit ridge. It wasn't particularly steep, but it was totally exposed, with a ten-thousand-foot drop on either side. Yikes!

And then, there it was, five hundred feet away. The summit!

The moment I saw it, I felt like a racehorse that had just been let out of the barn—but still one in desperate need of air. Every movement was in slow motion until I finally stepped onto the summit right behind Ang Pasang.

I did it! It was a most amazing feeling in the world. I'd rehearsed this moment for four years and just couldn't believe I was really here. The sense of accomplishment I felt was unbelievable—even greater than what I'd felt on Denali.

I put my arms out and did a slow 360-degree turn. I was standing on the highest point on earth. I had reached the summit of Mount Everest. Every minute of my training, every missed afternoon hanging with my friends, every single hard choice I had had to make had been worth it to stand on the top of the world even for a second.

I heard a muffled yell and looked back. Karen was holding up her camera and waving me to come down again. She wanted to shoot a video of me summiting.

Oh, man, don't make me do this. It's so freaking cold and windy. But it was such an incredible moment. We had to record it. I plodded two hundred feet back down the ridge. "Ready?"

She nodded. Ang Pasang took the camera from Karen and said he'd get a shot of all of us. We walked together to the summit, one step at a time. On top again, I threw my arms in the air. I was standing in the plume of moisture I'd seen on the summit in every picture of Everest.

The thousands of hours of training, being away from my mom and sister, missing my friends in school—all of that would take time to process. But right then I was having the time of my life on the roof of the world. I stood where Edmund Hillary had stood, remembering his quote:

It is not the mountain we conquer, but ourselves.

And I'd done that. I'd overcome my fears and doubts in order to achieve a goal I'd set four years earlier.

It was the biggest moment of all of our lives.

I knew that behind those goggles Dad's eyes were full of tears. "We did it—made it to the top of the world," I said.

The three of us looked at each other and, with words unsaid, we were proud of our little team. We hugged each other, there on top of the world, sharing the moment.

No one else was summiting from the north today, but I could see a long string of climbers coming up from the south. The top of Everest was no larger than a small dinner table, and we all needed our moment there. I'd been on this mountain for six weeks and only had thirty minutes to stand here. I wanted to store every second in my memory.

I saw the curvature of the earth again and gazed at giant Himalayan mountain peaks in every direction. The entire summit was covered with prayer flags, more than I'd ever seen. A little plastic box had a Buddha figure in it. Super cool.

I wanted to call my mom first thing. Dad removed the mitten from one hand to dial the satellite phone for me. His cold, stiff fingers tried several times to make the connection to Big Bear, California—halfway around the world. Finally he handed it over to me.

I removed my oxygen mask to speak to her. "Hi, Mom, this is your son calling you from the top of the world."

She and her friends went crazy on the other end. They'd been sitting around our dining table all night, tracking me on our website. The red dot had turned green when I reached the summit.

She was sobbing. "I love you! I love it! Now get your butt back home."

The minute I heard her voice, I completely broke down and cried too.

I held up flags for Karen to photograph, then spoke of the boy I'd thought about all the way up here. "I want to dedicate this climb to my eight-year-old friend Nigel in Big Bear, who has a brain tumor. He's the strongest and bravest person I know."

I threw some prayer flags into the air. I was incredibly grateful that we had made it safely to the summit. Now I asked for the mountain's blessing to see us safely home again.

It wasn't until then that I realized that Dad had removed his mask and was blowing on the bare hand he'd used to get the phone ready for me. "It's frozen," he said. "I have no feeling in my fingers. I can't even move them. I don't know how I'll get down the ladder and back to camp."

Most deaths occur on the descent, when climbers are exhausted beyond their limit. How would Dad manage with the use of only one hand? Karen said she'd help him clip and unclip his carabiners on every anchor until he once again had feeling in his fingers.

While Karen helped Dad get his mitten back on, I stepped back to make room for three climbers coming up from the south.

"Congrats, you made it," I said, taking my mask off.

The first one lifted his goggles. "Dude, how *old* are you?"

"Thirteen."

He shook his head. "That is some kick-ass."

"Thanks!"

I was sucking air big-time and put my mask back on. More climbers were arriving from the south, so we started down to make room.

Departing from Camp 2, we had reached the summit in fourteen hours. Lhakpa had done it all the way from the Chinese Base Camp in just under eleven. I decided that X-Men have nothing over the Sherpas. They're real-live superheroes who can climb at unbelievable speeds.

CHAPTER 27

Descending didn't have the excitement and anticipation of reaching the top. It was kind of a letdown after all the training and planning to summit. We'd gone ten hours without food or water, but the FRS concentrate had relieved my cramps and kept me going.

I knew I had to keep my focus on the descent, but already my brain was whirling with ideas of how to reach the final step of my goal to climb the Seven Summits plus one. I still had one mountain to go.

The Sherpas knew my journey to the top of Everest was something special and kept telling me how proud they were to be part of it. They even bragged to other porters on the trail that they worked for Jordan Romero, the youngest person to climb Everest.

Everyone we passed going down knew who I was and congratulated me. They wanted autographs and pictures. That was cool because it told me just how big my accomplishment was, but at that moment all I wanted to do was crawl into my sleeping bag and zone out. I was exhausted, hungry, thirsty, and getting really sick of the annoying oxygen mask. Karen and I decided that we could take off the masks above Camp 3 and be just fine. And we were.

We picked up our old oxygen cylinders at Mushroom Rock and continued on to Camp 3 in just over six hours. We picked up our other cylinders, tent, and stove there and made it back to Camp 2 to spend the night. We were up again at dawn to make our way to Camp 1.

As we approached the camp that morning, we ran into the Seven Summits Russian team and their leader, Alex, who had been one of my few skeptics on the mountain. He greeted us with a smile.

"Congratulations, Jordan," he said. "I never thought you'd make it, and I have to admit I'm amazed. I hope you'll forgive my doubting you. I'd be proud to take you on any mountain you wish to climb."

Wow. That was a big deal coming from him. His team regularly led climbers up the Seven Summits. I'd officially made it into their community.

"Thank you so much," I told him. "I'd be honored."

We didn't hang out long at Camp 1 but made our way steadily down the mountain.

Karina met us just above Advanced Base Camp with hugs and congratulations.

Ang Pasang had radioed ahead that we were on our way down, and I was blown away by the reception at ABC. Everyone cheered as we walked into camp and wanted pictures taken with me. They asked how it had felt to stand on the summit and what I planned to do next. I discovered I was repeating the same information over and over and realized this could be a rehearsal for things to come—no doubt the media would be calling as soon as word spread.

Dawa, Karma, and Ang Pasang joined us in our dining tent for a big celebration. Kumar had fixed a gourmet meal of chicken, yak steak, fried potatoes, Tibetan bread, greens, and fresh apples and oranges. After dinner I noticed that the Sherpas were giggling with one another. They seemed to do that a lot in spite of their hard lives. Something I wished more Westerners could learn.

"For the world record holder on Everest," Kumar announced as he walked through the door carrying a carrot cake with yellow and green frosting, green leaves on top, and yellow lettering that read *Congratulations Team Jordan on Everest May 22*.

How had he baked a freaking cake on rocks at twenty-one thousand feet? Next they popped a bottle of champagne. Who had carried *that* up the mountain? Dad poured some for everyone, but the Sherpas had their own drink. *Chang* was a local brew made from fermented barley, millet, or rice, and it still had grains floating on top.

I stuck with hot tea made from a bag, not the Tibetan salt kind.

We spent two nights at Advanced Base Camp, cleaning up our tents, gathering our gear, and packing for the yaks to arrive and haul everything back to Chinese Base Camp. I was glad to walk back down the fifteen miles into thicker air.

We got another surprise when we walked into Chinese Base Camp. My friend Zanskar and his Dad, Ryan—good friends from Hong Kong—were there to greet us!

Zanskar was my age but three inches shorter and with a slighter build. He was a hot soccer player and traveled to compete. He and his dad had come here just to welcome us back.

Dad and Karen had started making these connections while adventure racing. Now I was a member of the international club too.

Less than an hour after we arrived, I spotted the liaison officer heading toward our camp. "Karen, quick, hide your camera equipment."

"Oh, damn, he's going to confiscate everything," she said.

We tossed sleeping bags, pads, and everything else that was handy on top of the BGAN and video cameras, then went outside to look busy sorting through bags that had just come off the yaks.

The officer stood there in his stiff uniform, arms folded tight across his chest, and glared at me. "Did you make it to the top?"

Nervous sweat crawled along my scalp. "Yes."

"I need to see your cameras," he snapped.

Karen shot Dad a sideways glance. He returned a look that said, *Better do it.*

She retrieved the video camera from our tent.

The officer asked for proof that we had been on the summit. Karen cued up the video and he watched the whole scene of us reaching the summit. He handed the camera back. "That is good. Now I can sign your certificates."

I held my breath until he'd signed each one.

After he left, Dad shouted, "It's official, man! Give me five."

We waited another two days for a car to pick us up. The good news was that we didn't need to acclimatize going back and we could head directly to the Friendship Bridge. Once again people grabbed our bags and started lugging them across on foot.

The moment I stepped across the border into Nepal, a tsunami of reporters and photographers flooded me. I shielded my eyes from the flashing lights. The CNN reporter who'd talked to us in Kathmandu along with twenty others shoved mics in my face, all asking the same questions.

"What was it like to stand on the summit?"

"How does it feel to be the youngest to climb Everest?"

"Was there ever a point when you wanted to turn back?"

"Critics claim no one your age should go that high or do anything that dangerous. What do you say to that?"

"Aren't you missing school?"

"What's next?"

I barely had a chance to answer the first question before about fifty Nepalis arrived and hung kata scarves and marigold garlands around our necks. The scene was exciting but exhausting. When our gear had been loaded into the truck, I smiled and waved good-bye to everyone as I climbed into the van and slid the door shut.

"Whew." I put my head back and closed my eyes.

"Get used to it, buddy," Dad warned.

He was right. News of my climb and photos of me were in all the Kathmandu newspapers. As soon as I stepped onto the street, any street, a crowd formed and followed us for blocks.

Karen smiled. "So what do you think, J?"

"It's a bit overwhelming," I said. "I kind of like it as long as they're not flashing lights in my face."

Our first night back in Kathmandu, we treated ourselves to the five-star Hotel Yak and Yeti only fifteen minutes from Tribhuvan International Airport. The Al Jazeera news station that broadcast in English met us there for a live interview that played all over the world.

We had invited the Sherpas to join us for dinner. Ang Pasang had told us that we must go to a restaurant called the Rum Doodle.

The restaurant was a gathering place for mountaineers. As soon as we walked in the door, we noticed footprints on the walls—large white cutouts with autographs. They were "yeti" footprints, and each one had been signed by a trekker or someone who'd climbed in the Himalayas. There was even one with former president Jimmy Carter's signature—he'd hiked in the Everest region.

Dad, Karen, and I each signed one of the footprints and gave it to our waiter.

When he saw who we were, he led me behind the bar to stacks of wooden boxes. "Edmund Hillary signed this first one," he said, showing me the footprint.

"The *real* Edmund Hillary?" I asked. "The first guy to climb Everest?"

"The very one."

I traced the letters with one finger. This was the signature of one of my heroes.

"We have the largest-known collection of signatures of climbers who've reached the summit," the waiter said, winking at me. "Now that you've made it to the summit, you are a member of the Rum Doodle Club and can eat here free the rest of your life."

I slapped him high five and did my best Schwarzenegger imitation. "I'll be back."

Ang Pasang had done more than bring us to the best restaurant in Kathmandu. He had brought someone with him who I immediately recognized from pictures—Lhakpa's friend Apa Sherpa, who had just broken his own record by summiting for the twentieth time.

"And will you break my record someday?" he asked in a friendly voice.

"No way. Once was enough," I said. "It's a super-hard mountain."

"I didn't start out to set records. I had to go to work at twelve when my father died. I come from the village of Thame, same as Tenzing Norgay who climbed with Hillary, so it was natural that I worked on the mountain," he said.

Apa, Ang Pasang, and the porters on Kilimanjaro all worked to support their families at such a young age. That could've been me. I was so fortunate.

Our PR man, Rob, had scheduled five interviews in New York City, beginning almost as soon as our plane landed. The ABC news show 20/20 wanted to feature us as soon as we got back, and requested video.

"Okaaay," Dad said, "so do we send them footage of the avalanche?"

"It'll come out anyway," Karen said. "And we're fine. Jordan, what do you think?"

"Mom already knows," I said. "And I'd like to go on the air to show all those who criticized us that they were wrong—that we held on despite an avalanche."

We flew directly from Nepal to Hong Kong and on to New York. I was exhausted from jet lag, and being in hot TV studios under bright lights didn't help. At least I didn't have to walk out waving to the audience like on Martha Stewart's show.

Dad, Karen, and I were seated on a couch waiting for *20/20* to begin taping. The opening line was "Should children be allowed to act like grown-ups even if it puts them in jeopardy?" Then Elizabeth Vargas questioned whether the title of being the youngest person ever to climb Everest was worth dying for.

I was so afraid she'd play up all the dangers I'd faced, especially the avalanche, but she gave a very sincere and objective commentary during our video.

She asked Dad about the day I first told him I wanted to climb Everest. "Isn't it a father's duty to say, 'Wait a couple of years'? A lot of people think it was irresponsible."

Dad had dealt with criticism before and during the climb, but this was on national TV and a highly respected program. He remained calm but clearly stated his beliefs and how important they were to our lifestyle. "You want to talk about irresponsible parenting? Let's talk about the million and some parents that are standing in a fast-food restaurant waiting to supersize their kid right now for dinner tonight. That's irresponsible parenting."

She asked if having a Big Mac was as dangerous as climbing Everest. Dad's response was, "Well known to promote disease and early death. Documented. Proven."

Elizabeth was fair with Dad and definitely caring and respectful of me. She let me end by saying how I wanted to encourage other kids to find their own Everest.

"Dream big," I said. "Live life. Do something."

It was our first night back in the States. Interview over,

I could relax and look forward to a big, *healthy* meal. Dad, Karen, Rob, and I were checking out the menu when Karen nudged my elbow.

"Look, J," she said.

I glanced up and saw my mom and sister, Makaela, strolling toward the table. I ran to them, tears pouring down my cheeks. "I didn't know you were coming!"

"We wanted to surprise you," Mom said.

They put their arms around me and the three of us stood there hugging one another and crying.

"I love you!" Mom sobbed.

"I love you too. I missed you so much." I wiped tears on my sleeve. "The hardest part of the climb was being away from you for so long."

Dad and Karen's eyes were watering too as they scooted around the table to make room for all three of us.

"How'd you know where we'd be? How did you get here?" I asked.

Mom squeezed my hand. "When Rob said you were going to stay in New York for interviews, I told him he couldn't keep me away from my son any longer."

"He flew us out here and got us a room and everything," Makaela added.

I looked over at Rob. "Thank you so, so much. This is the absolute best thing you could have ever done for me."

Over the next two days we did interviews on the CBS

morning show, CNN, *Fox and Friends*, and the *Today* show. Justin Bieber was playing an outdoor concert on the *Today* show the same morning I was there. Thousands of screaming girls and their mothers were on the street carrying signs and trying anything to meet him. Then they started screaming for me when my face flashed on a huge outdoor TV screen.

Dad took in the scene and put his arm around my shoulder. "So what do you think?"

"Oh, it's super cool," I said. "But it would get old really soon. Never having any privacy."

I was so excited to get home to Big Bear after being gone two months. A friend picked Dad, Karen, and me up at the airport and drove the winding road from sea level to seven thousand feet. A fire truck escorted us into town, followed by a caravan of cars honking their horns. We were greeted with welcome-home signs, and Big Bear's famous pirate ship, which normally offers tours of the lake, blasted cannon shots as we passed.

A forty-foot crane had an American flag hanging from one arm and an enormous banner on the other: WELCOME HOME, TEAM JORDAN. BIG BEAR LOVES YOU.

Dad, Karen, and I waved to everyone lining the road.

"This is so freaking cool," I said.

This welcome home meant more than all the reporters and TV interviews. Big Bear had put me on the mountain and climbed it with me. I was smiling and waving to everyone.

"I love this place," I said. "I love being back from the snow in this gorgeous weather on a sunny day."

Hundreds of people gathered for a party at Nottinghams Tavern. A poster hung on the wall covered with congratulatory signatures.

"You guys have been the biggest support system," I said to the room. "Thinking about all of you is what kept me motivated to go harder and harder. You guys are the best. Thank you so much for putting all of this on. I couldn't ask for anything better."

A few days later I felt like the big man on campus when a huge number of people turned out again at my school. I received commendations from our top political leaders. Big Bear's mayor even read a statement from Governor Arnold Schwarzenegger.

As a fellow athlete, I commend you for challenging your determination, he wrote. *Your perseverance is the hallmark of a true champion.*

Our school principal told me that even the White House had heard of me.

We gave an Everest slide show, and the kids at school made me feel like a rock star.

A week later NBC called and invited me to be on the Jay Leno show in Burbank. He sent a car all the way to Big Bear for me.

"Man, this is big time," Dad said. "Five million viewers. Aren't you nervous?"

"Not really. I mean I don't think so. He seems like a nice guy."

"A guy who was just at the White House cracking jokes with President Obama," Dad said.

"He'll probably ask about my climb. I've answered the same questions so many times that it's pretty natural."

It turned out that Dad was the nervous one. "Five *million* viewers."

"Would you relax, Dad? You'll make me nervous too."

The chauffeur who picked me up was pretty entertaining. I laughed most of the way down to Burbank. Maybe his real job was to put guests at ease. The show's staff fixed my hair and put makeup on me. I wondered how movie stars put up with people fussing over them all the time and putting that stuff on their faces. Then I waited in the greenroom backstage with the punk-rock band Authority Zero. We exchanged stories about our travels and appearances. Tim Allen was on the show too but had his own greenroom.

When it was my turn, I took several deep breaths. *You can handle this,* I told myself. *Just relax and talk like he's an old friend.*

I walked onstage and took my seat between Jay Leno and Tim Allen. They seemed to be buddies, and the conversation flowed easily. Both were super nice to me during the commercial break.

Many more interviews followed during the summer and into winter—LA news channels, NPR, the BBC, and many international news and radio programs. The Disney Channel came to Big Bear to tape their segment called *The Time I . . .* For me it was "The Time I . . . Climbed Mount Everest."

Fortunately, media events slowed down once school started, and my life returned to normal. I was happy to just hang with friends. Kids in town were proud I'd summited Everest but had become so accustomed to my goal that I was simply Jordan who climbs mountains, just like Casey was Cameron's brother who races bikes.

The three of us hung out at the lake, walked the slackline, and rode our bikes until ski season began. Then we hit the slopes every free minute and worked on new tricks.

I still had one more mountain to climb, but even after trying for a year we couldn't get a permit for Vinson. Antarctic Logistics and Expeditions (ALE) was the only company that flew to Antarctica, and it had a minimum age of eighteen to even board the plane. In spite of my climbing history, they denied all of our requests.

Then my mom really came through. She called one day, super excited.

"Jordan, I just got off the phone with a friend in Tahoe. She knows the CFO of an environmental expedition company who knows somebody who used to live in Antarctica and has contact with the pilots who fly there. The CFO will see what she can do to get you your permit."

Karen also wrote a final letter to ALE asking for a meeting

to discuss my climbing the mountain. She got a phone call from Chile a few weeks later and they said they were willing to discuss it. She went all-out preparing climbing résumés and filling out pages and pages of paperwork about our training, our climbing, and our health.

Once that was submitted, all we could do was wait and hope.

I was afraid my dream of achieving the Seven Summits plus one would have to wait until I turned eighteen. And that sucked. I wanted to finish and move on to another big goal.

Then, finally, the waiting came to an end. Karen got the call. We were in!

After a big round of hugs and high fives, our minds turned to training.

"Better start running with that tire again," Karen said. "You'll be pulling a sled in Antarctica."

I was fifteen now and over six feet tall. All the riding and skiing had kept me in great shape. I just needed to work on those hauling muscles. As much as I hated dragging an SUV tire up and down our steep road every day, I did it until I felt strong enough to tow a truck.

We also did our usual fund-raising in Big Bear, and more corporate sponsors came on board. Without them we never would have reached Antarctica.

I was about to climb my final summit—the cold one.

THE SKIING CLIMB:
ANTARCTICA'S
MOUNT VINSON,
16,050 FEET

AVERAGE NUMBER OF CLIMBERS
PER YEAR: 300

DECEMBER 24, 2011, AGE 15

CHAPTER 28

Before we even knew about the permit problem, we'd scheduled Vinson last because Antarctica is the most expensive place in the world to fly into. Plus there was no way around hiring a licensed guide—everyone had to.

We flew from Los Angeles to Dallas to Santiago, Chile, and finally to Punta Arenas at the very southern tip of the country. Antarctica is huge—the size of Australia and Europe combined. To get there from Chile took four and a half hours, with nowhere to land in between. There was only one type of plane, a Russian cargo plane, that held enough fuel to be able to turn around and make it home if conditions were such that the plane couldn't land. The fuel cost for each trip was huge, so the plane didn't fly without a full load of passengers and cargo. If the plane were to run low on fuel, the pilot would have to continue on no matter what the conditions. You either made it or landed in the ocean.

I understood the danger but wasn't going to let it get into my head. There was no sense in that. It ruined the journey.

The go-ahead for departures depended upon this Australian dude who did the weather forecasting and had never been wrong in more than seven years of letting planes know it was safe to fly. ALE told us to be ready for the call at six a.m. on December 15, but the go-ahead didn't come; nor did the calls for ten a.m. or three p.m. departures.

It was sunny in Punta Arenas, and we were in shorts and flip-flops waiting for the go-ahead to fly to the coldest place on earth.

The next day we were finally called out to a Russian Ilyushin IL-76. It was an enormous plane. There were only about forty seats, no windows other than over the emergency exits, and just enough insulation to keep birds out. The whole back end was about seventy-five feet of cargo space.

Dad was the last to climb in and sat down all excited. "When they filled this sucker up with fuel, the wings dropped until they were almost touching the ground."

The flight attendant gave us each a wad of cotton for plugging our ears and two pieces of white bread with a piece of mystery meat slapped in between. As heavy as the bird was, the wind still had its way with us. We rocked and bounced and were knocked from side to side for four hours.

Finally, the pilot announced, "We just crossed the Antarctic Circle at a latitude of sixty-six degrees south. We'll be landing at the southernmost end of the Ellsworth Mountains at eighty degrees south."

Carstensz and Kilimanjaro were near the equator, and Denali at a latitude of 60 degrees north. Now I was going at far as 80 degrees south. Pretty amazing.

One of the mountain guides came down the center aisle to check on our seat belts. "Make sure you pull them snug. We'll be landing on ice and can't use brakes."

The plane touched down with a definite thud and coasted to a stop, using the reverse thrust of the powerful engines on a three-mile runway, in what felt like fifteen minutes. We climbed down metal stairs into howling wind and a temperature of minus 40 degrees. If someone had told me I'd landed on another planet, I would have believed him. It was an insane landscape. There was ice as far as I could see, and it was a beautiful transparent blue. There was no vegetation, no color—nothing but ice and snow.

The air in Antarctica has zero water vapor and zero dust. You can see for hundreds of miles, so distances are hard to figure out. Plus the weather can turn on you at any second.

The ice runway was like transparent polished marble with Vaseline smeared all over it. There was absolutely no traction, and I didn't have my ice legs yet. I slipped and slid my way toward a Ford Excursion, feeling about as graceful as a penguin on stilts.

I looked at my altimeter. "It's as cold as the summit on

Everest, but we're only at thirty-three hundred feet."

"The atmosphere's thinner at the poles," Dad said. "Less oxygen per breath. It will seem two thousand to three thousand feet higher."

Two guys tossed our gear on top of the Excursion, which had been rigged for ice, and told us to climb in. Then we drove over the massive glacier for about half an hour. There were rugged dark peaks and snow and ice everywhere I looked. I was psyched to finally have my skis with me on a climb.

"How deep's the ice?" I asked our driver, a mountain guide from Colorado.

"Dude, you've got a five-thousand-foot base."

I leaned back. "That's so sick."

ALE'S Union Glacier Camp is eighteen hundred miles from the southern tip of Chile and just over six hundred miles from the South Pole. It only operates during the Antarctic summer—winter in North America. During the long, harsh Antarctic winter all the camp's structures and machines are disassembled and buried to protect them from the snow, ice, and wind.

The camp was amazing—there were huge kitchen and dining tents, housing for pilots and maintenance crew, a medical tent with a full-time doctor, and control rooms for an air-traffic controller.

Given how far we were from civilization, I was surprised by the number of other climbers and South Pole trekkers at

Union Glacier. The place was overrun with them. Karen asked what was going on.

"It's the one hundredth anniversary of the race to the South Pole," a man told us.

That made sense. Soon we learned that all the descendants of Roald Amundsen, the Norwegian who first discovered the South Pole, were there, along with scholars and historians. Teams were re-creating his trip, even down to stuffing their jackets with hay for warmth. It would have been cool to connect with some of them, but we got notice that we would be on the first flight out in the morning to Vinson Base Camp.

ALE was the only airline into Antarctica, but climbers could hire other guiding services for their trips once they were there. Groups not using the ALE guides had to put up their own tents and cook for themselves, but groups like us traveling with ALE camped and traveled in comparative luxury. Our gear was sitting in front of permanent tents with our names on them.

One of the first things ALE gave us was a brochure about refuse restrictions. The rules were even stricter on Antarctica than on Aconcagua or Denali. The temperature hardly ever rose above 32 degrees, so anything left behind would freeze and remain there forever. Everything had to be carried out and flown to Chile, even our urine.

"Gross!" I said. "During our return flight the cargo area will be filled with our *stuff*?"

Karen snickered. "We each get three bags that contain, and I quote, 'Poo Powder, which quickly turns waste into a stable gel for easy transport and safe disposal, plus neutralizes it to eliminate unpleasant odors.'"

I guess it made sense. When you walk a dog, you pick up after it. So why not after yourself? I liked the idea of keeping the continent clean.

"Check out the bathroom," Dad said.

There was one place to poop and another to pee with a big sign that said DON'T YOU DARE MIX THE TWO. There was even a separate place to spit out your toothpaste.

The next morning I was so eager to get started that I went to breakfast early by myself. Scott Woolums, who'd led Johnny Strange on Denali, was sitting in the dining tent.

"What are you doing here?" I asked.

"I saw that you'd made it up Everest, and I wanted to guide the youngest kid ever to climb the Seven Summits up his last mountain."

I knew Woolums had climbed the Seven Summits multiple times. I couldn't imagine a better guide to the top of Vinson. "Excellent! How many times have you done all seven now?"

"I finished my fifth complete round in October, but you'll top that."

I sat across from him. "No. I'm good with just once."

"I led Johnny up Vinson too, but I suspect you've heard about that."

I nodded. "He skied to the South Pole last January and is planning to ski the North Pole too." In the late nineties a British adventurer had done the same thing after climbing the Seven Summits and had named it the Grand Slam.

Scott leaned forward with his elbows on the table, hands clasped. "You going for that record too?"

Dad and Karen had just come in, and they heard Scott's last question. "We're thinking about it," Dad said. He gave Scott a high five. "Glad to see you."

"We heard from the office in Salt Lake that you might be guiding us," said Karen, "but they couldn't confirm it till we got here. We're glad you're going to be with us; what's it going to be like?"

"It's similar to Denali, but four thousand vertical feet shorter, so we don't need to spend as much time acclimatizing," he said. "It's a shorter expedition. So fewer supplies and a lighter sled."

"So an easier mountain?" I asked.

Scott nodded. "Except for the blasted frigid weather. Weather's the enemy here."

"I am *so* ready."

Scott leaned back in his chair. "Not for a couple of days. There are high winds and complete cloud cover above. We've got plenty of time scheduled here, so we'll wait for just the right weather window."

That was a bummer, but I trusted Scott. He had an air of

confidence that made us aware that he really knew his stuff. He had climbed Vinson a whole bunch of times.

After breakfast we had a spectacular one-hour flight on a Twin Otter plane. Even the mountain peaks looked like they were buried in ice. The plane landed on skis, bouncing along until it finally came to a stop. Base camp was at seven thousand twenty feet.

Again, ALE had our tents ready, plus a dining tent and a kitchen, too. Once we got settled we met Scott in the dining tent for a cup of tea.

Scott grinned. "You guys want to ski today?"

Did I want to ski? Did dogs want bacon? Yeah, I wanted to ski Antarctica.

Scott took us up a small pitch to check out our skills. It was easy and we totally aced the slope. He smiled and gave an approving nod. "Okay, we can go higher."

Three hours of skiing uphill, or skinning, wasn't easy. Our skis made it possible for us to climb uphill without sinking into the snow, and the skins we put on them kept us from sliding backward, but it still wasn't my idea of fun. Not until I reached the top of a huge hill and looked out over nothing but absolute white. It was like winning the lottery.

Dad is an awesome snowboarder, but more like a giraffe on skis. He'd carried his snowboard up in his backpack for the trip down. He wouldn't have been able to keep up with us on skis.

Karen has been a ski racer and ski coach for most of her

life, so she helped Dad out and carried his skis down the mountain. We pulled the skins off our skis. Scott pushed off first, Karen followed, and I jumped right behind her, carving my own sweet tracks.

I swished down what looked like fresh, fluffy powder—only it wasn't. Snow rarely falls in Antarctica. I was skiing on this crazy, creamy snow that had blown here from somewhere else and never melted.

There were heavy winds again the next day, so Scott asked again, "You guys want to go skiing?"

"Are you kidding? I asked. "Most definitely."

So up the hill we went. While other less-experienced teams were busy practicing with ropes and crampons, we were playing in a snowy wonderland and having the time of our lives. We swished past them, climbed back up, and skied down again.

The guides in our camp had constant communication with Union Glacier and received a detailed weather report and forecast at least twice a day. Finally, at dinner one night, Scott told us that the weather forecast was exactly what we wanted.

"We can leave for Low Camp tomorrow," Scott said.

ALE provided small plastic sleds we hauled up the mountain with a rope attached to our packs. The loads on them were much lighter than those we'd had to haul up Denali because most of what we needed was already at one of the two camps on Vinson. Two ALE rangers were responsible for keeping the ALE camps stocked all season.

This was definitely luxury travel compared to our treks up other mountains. The chef at Union Glacier made amazing meals, froze them, and sent them up to Vinson Base Camp on the Otter. The cook at Vinson Base Camp just had to boil the sealed packages in water.

After we'd packed our sleds with personal items, we were ready to go. We clicked into our skis with the skins on and headed to the snowy trail marked by tiny orange flags.

The glacier climb wasn't that steep, but crusty, windblown snow made it awkward to pull sleds. We'd roped up because of crevasses. You never knew when something could go terribly wrong. At first it was a bit tough managing the skis and poles, sleds, and a rope, but eventually I got the hang of it.

Good luck had accompanied our quest of the summits from beginning to end. We'd had no major accidents like falling into a crevasse or getting lost in a storm. No frostbite. Breathing had been difficult at times, but none of us had ever experienced the kind of serious altitude sickness that had forced so many of our friends to turn back.

Climbing Vinson, I realized that it was more than just luck. It was our training. We'd worked so hard to make sure there would be no drama on our climbs, and that had seen us through.

I was a very different person today than I had been when I'd first told Dad I wanted to climb the Seven Summits. People were always surprised to discover my age. I'd grown up a lot on those mountains. I didn't feel like a boy any longer. I felt like a man. The mountains had given me that.

I was lost in thought when Dad signaled me to catch up to him.

"The glacier reminds me a little bit of Everest," he said. "The ice is solid but doesn't really act that way."

"Yeah, I can't see it moving but I feel it somehow," I agreed. "It's really hard to judge distance with no landmarks, too. It's just snow and more snow. I spotted an ice chunk and thought I'd be there in ten minutes. It's been an hour and we still aren't there yet."

When we finally reached Low Camp at 9,100 feet, a team that had been traveling just ahead of us was busy digging a hole and building snow walls.

"Guess they didn't sign up with ALE," Karen said, and waved me over to her. "Check this out."

Our guides had dug a hole about five feet deep in the snow and set up a really awesome round, circuslike tent over the top of it. We walked down a few steps and then were able to stand up inside. It reminded me of crawling into that meditation cave near the Tibetan monastery, only this one had shelves and benches made from snow instead of rock and the roof was much higher. Our kitchen/dining/meeting room was a great place to chill no matter what the weather, kind of like an underground igloo.

We planned a rest day there to acclimatize, so I stayed up watching a video on my iPod until one a.m. The sun only rises and sets once a year at the South Pole, so it was circling the horizon with this really soft glow. The light was like nowhere else on earth because it was so free of impurities.

We skied nearby hills most of the next day, over what looked like sand dunes covered with snow. It couldn't have been any more different from the Carstensz jungle, and yet both are among the most beautiful places I've ever seen.

High Camp was about one mile straight up from where we were. It was much too steep to ski or pull sleds. I was a bit sad to leave my skis behind. We stuffed enough personal items and food into our packs to last three days in case of bad weather and hiked to the base of a 45-degree wall. From there we'd have to climb 2,300 feet using fixed ropes. There were several teams ahead of us, moving up at a tortoise pace.

"Imagine a crowd like this on the Chinese Ladder on Everest," Karen whispered from behind me.

I spoke quietly over my shoulder, trying not to offend anyone. "Yeah, one word—frostbite."

The guy in front of me must've heard us, because he looked back. "Are you the kid doing the Seven Summits?" he asked.

I nodded.

"Go ahead and clip past us," he said, indicating himself and his three teammates.

"Really? Thanks!" I felt kind of bad making them wait,

but we were definitely moving faster than they were.

We eventually made our way around more generous climbers and moved to the front of the pack to reach the High Camp at 12,385 feet. Hot tea and lunch waited for us in the same kind of underground snow room. We learned from rangers that two teams had been stuck there for three days in horrific winds.

Dad cupped his hands around hot tea. "I don't want to stay here any longer than we have to. It's too dang cold," he told Scott.

Karen poured herself a cup. "The summit's not even as high as the Everest base camp, and we used a hypoxic tent up to fifteen thousand feet. You said it yourself: Weather's the enemy here."

Listening to them, I remembered how the challenges of climbing Everest constantly reminded me not to screw up. Lose focus on a narrow exposed ridge and you were done for. Here, on the relatively gentle slopes, I found myself concentrating more on the beauty around me. It was possible I was underestimating the cold. Lose a mitten and your hand could turn to stone and you wouldn't be able to zip your jacket or cover your face. Dad understood that after his Everest ordeal.

I was with him and Karen on this one. "Let's summit tomorrow."

The other teams at High Camp weren't ready to climb, so the next morning we had the entire mountain to ourselves—

just the way we liked it. We set out wearing light fleeces on a balmy 30-degree day. Roped together, we climbed an easy ice slope to the base of the triangular summit pyramid. From there we had to choose whether to take a short steep slope to the west ridge or the longer but easier trail to the east.

Steep and fast—that was our style.

I was in my groove. I was out in nature, surrounded by ice, snow, and blue sky, with mountain peaks just waiting to be climbed. I realized how small I was in the greater scheme of things, but I was confident I could hold my own as long as I respected the mountain. I remembered Samuel's words from that very first climb on Kilimanjaro: *The mountain wants you to climb it.*

We hiked a beautiful, slender ridge toward what we thought was the summit, but Vinson is such a huge, complicated mountain that the summit hides itself.

"We've got another quarter mile to go," Scott said. "Take a minute to hydrate and catch your breath."

"Got it," I said. But really, my heart was ready for a summit run.

I was used to climbing above the clouds and had to keep reminding myself that the huge expanse of white on the horizon wasn't clouds, but ice and snow. At one p.m. on Christmas Eve I stepped onto the summit—six years after my first real climb up San Gorgonio with my brand-new ice axe.

"I did it!" I yelled. I stood on the roof of Antarctica,

staring in every direction at a landscape virtually untouched by humans. I experienced that same thrill I felt on the top of every summit—only this was even better. I had climbed all Seven Summits (plus one) and had stood on top of the world on every continent on the planet.

I had set myself a big goal. It had taken years of hard work, but I'd finally achieved my dream. Getting here was worth every setback, every disappointment, every time I'd fallen to the ground crying that I couldn't make it.

Dad gave me eight high fives, one for each summit. "You made it, buddy! I love you."

"Love you too." I hugged him and Karen long and hard. "I never could've made any of this happen without you. I'm so, so grateful."

Next I called Mom. "Merry Christmas, Mom. I'm standing on the summit of Mount Vinson overlooking a huge ice shelf only seven hundred forty-six miles from the South Pole."

"I love you," she said, and I could hear her tears of joy in the background.

"Love you more."

The wind turned bitter cold, and it actually started snowing! The timing couldn't have been more perfect, because we were ready to head down anyway.

We took the easier ridge to the east for a straightforward and fast descent and a change of scenery. When we arrived in High Camp, all the other teams were waiting. They knew this was my eighth summit and cheered and crowded around me. One after another they hugged me and wanted pictures taken. It felt super good being supported by people who truly understood the challenges I had faced.

Earlier we'd seen another team coming up behind us, but they'd disappeared. At camp we discovered that when the wind had blown in, their guide had told them to stop and put on their down pants. But one of the men didn't have any, so they'd all turned back.

"Here, bro, borrow mine," Dad said. "You've got to go on. The view's spectacular."

That's my dad. Always willing to help out.

High Camp was a cold, blustery place. After we'd had something to eat, I looked at Dad and Karen and knew instantly that we were on the same page.

We all turned to Scott.

Karen pulled her colorful Buff up over her neck and chin. "Let's get out of this wind."

"Let's go," Scott agreed.

Rappelling down the fixed ropes with a heavy pack was tough work. I kept looking at the slope, wishing I had my skis, but it was too steep even for me.

We made a similar decision at Low Camp, where we had left our skis.

"Okay, stay here or go all the way to base camp?" Scott asked.

Our energy level was high enough to keep going.

"Let's go," we all said together.

We stopped only long enough to have some food and drink.

"Now let's *ski*," I said. "It's gonna be great to ski all the way to the bottom."

Dad rolled his eyes. "I'll have to ski. Can't snowboard pulling a sled."

We broke camp, loaded the sleds, and put on our skis. Without King Richard's PVC to keep the sleds in line, they were all over the place. As long as we went fast enough, they couldn't catch us.

Scott and I were out in front, having a blast, whooping it up on four to six inches of fresh powder. It was like skiing on a cloud, because the earth and sky all blended together. Dad looked ridiculously funny because he was so tall and lanky and his skis were almost in a wedge. His sled was wiping out all the orange flags marking the trail. Karen finally tied a rope from herself to the back of Dad's sled so the sled wouldn't run him over.

Scott had radioed ahead to the base camp manager to let him know we were coming. We arrived to wild applause and cheering.

Everybody kept asking, "You made it to the summit how quickly?"

A wonderful champagne toast followed that brought tears to all of our eyes.

We posed for pictures with everyone and even signed a few autographs.

After a fantastic Christmas dinner, Scott walked over to our table with a surprise. He handed me a bowl and then gave one each to Dad and Karen before taking the fourth one for himself.

"World-famous antarctic ice cream," he said. "It's an extremely rare treat when it's made from fresh snow." He laughed. "Which we don't often get around here." He dripped a circle of honey on top of mine, added fresh berries, and raised the bowl for an ice-cream toast. "To the boy who inspires us not only to dream big but to set our hearts on achieving those dreams."

I was extremely touched by this man who'd done what I had, only five times more.

We'd reached the summit and come down faster than other teams, so we had to wait. The Twin Otter to Union Glacier wouldn't fly with just three people. This gave us two more days to ski and hang out, which was totally sweet.

News of my finishing the Seven Summits had spread quickly through the media. TV stations couldn't wait to get the story. From right outside our tent at Vinson Base Camp I did phone interviews with the BBC, *Good Morning America*, NPR, the *Today* show, and a couple of other stations. With so much publicity, I wondered what it was going to be like when I got home.

We made it back to Union Glacier on a sunny 20-degree day. The staff had taken time off to celebrate the holidays. They'd put up a volleyball court and made furniture out of ice and snow. Everyone was in shorts. Diving after balls on ice in bare skin looked much too painful for me. I kept my long pants on.

"C'mon, J Man. You too, Karen," Dad called. "We're forming a team with three Russians to play against the Argentines."

"Oh, yeah, I'm a great blocker," Karen joked. She was definitely height challenged, but she is also stronger than most men. We'd measured head to head when I was nine and we climbed our first mountain, but I'd shot right past her to six feet. Dad still had a couple of inches on me, and it helped that he used to play beach volleyball. He was freaking awesome and got lots of high fives from our Russian teammates.

I'd been so excited to climb Vinson because it was my last summit, but I really hated missing the Big Bear ski season. Getting to ski as much as I did on Antarctica made up for it somewhat.

The big bird hadn't arrived from Punta Arenas to pick us up yet. We got up very early and hiked up a steep mountain close to the camp. We'd just reached the top when a call came in saying the plane would be there in an hour.

"If we don't get back down," Karen said, "we could be stuck here for a week."

We made record time skiing down the mountain, spraying snow behind us like white veils. The other groups who would also be leaving that day had already eaten and packed their bags. We hurriedly marked our luggage and tossed it in a truck. All of us were herded like cows into an open trailer behind a snowcat and stood for the next five miles in the freezing cold.

I spotted the IL-76 approaching the blue-ice runway. As big as it was, the plane looked like a gnat against Antarctica and reminded me again just how small I was in the universe.

CHAPTER 29

As soon as we made two phone calls from Vinson, one to Mom and one to our new PR guy, Clay Abney, news of me being the youngest person to scale the Seven Summits went through the roof, but the worldwide coverage still wasn't as crazy as it was after Everest.

Newspaper articles, radio interviews, and TV appearances were largely positive. The critics had backed off because I'd proven them wrong. We were home safely with no broken bones, no frostbite, and no major disasters. At age fifteen I'd experienced more physical environments, cultures, religions, and ideas than most people do in an entire lifetime. I was incredibly thankful for that. It made me aware of how similar humans are everywhere, and you can't learn that from books.

The day after returning home, we were off to New York again to appear on the *Today* show. When Ann Curry interviewed us, Dad said, "I'm the proudest father on the planet to have a fifteen-year-old son with goals. And he didn't turn ninety degrees or a hundred eighty degrees away. He stayed fixed on it."

She looked at me. "But there were times—I know I've read about them—when you were thinking, 'I want to quit this thing. I don't want to keep doing it.' But your parents kept encouraging you to get back on track when those times happened." She looked at Dad and Karen. "How did you know to keep pushing him?"

Karen said, "It's a fine line for a parent to work with a kid to push just hard enough that they do something great and feel good about it. But not push them into something they don't want to do."

"We live in Big Bear, California," Dad added. "We live, eat, and breathe this stuff. This isn't a weekend sport for us. It isn't a little recreation. It's our lifestyle."

Ann asked me, "What do you want to do next?"

"My main goal is to still keep inspiring kids. I want kids to be fired up on goal setting and to find their own Everest. To know that anything is possible."

I was on Fox News the next day and CNN the one after that. When asked if I was going to continue climbing, I told them we were considering doing the Grand Slam and that I eventually wanted to work in the outdoor industry.

Meeting new people was fun, but I didn't want to be a celebrity. I was happy to get back home and just hang with friends, ski, and work toward getting my driver's license. The media died down after a few months, but there was a constant barrage of e-mails and requests for me to visit schools and do more interviews. Almost everyone was supportive, which made me feel really good.

I was so goal oriented that I needed to come up with something—something big—to focus on. I kept seeing kids who were not just overweight but downright obese. They were into junk foods and sodas and spent too many hours in front of TV and video games.

I decided to try to use my experiences to inspire other kids to live a healthy lifestyle and to pursue their dreams—even dreams that seemed impossible.

Following the plan of the climber we met on Whitney, we decided to do our own fifty-state tour we called Find Your Everest. We actually began in New England the summer before Vinson, but I hoped to continue now that my summit quest was complete.

Europa Sports, the parent company of NOW Energy Bars, loaned us a Sprinter motor home to drive across the country. Maine was the first stop on the 2012 tour because it's the northeast corner of the country and I'd never been there before. The forecast for the day of our hike was pretty sketchy.

"Hey, we've climbed Everest," Karen said. "A little rain's not going to stop us from reaching Mount Katahdin."

The owners of the campground we stayed in had heard

about me and were so excited that it made me a little embar-
rassed. They invited us to dinner and treated us like royalty.
Their son Ryan and his friend Noah were my age and outdoor
types. We hung out all day, and it was great making new friends.

"Want to climb with us tomorrow?" I asked them.

"Man, that would be totally cool," Ryan said.

The next morning the five of us hiked 3.3 miles to Chimney
Pond and continued up another 2.2 miles to the summit of
Mount Katahdin, elevation 5,268 feet. Rivers were running
high, and water poured down parts of the trails. Hiking up
waterfalls was a definite challenge.

I shook water off my jacket and told my new friends, "I
think this is the wettest climb we've done."

Compared to the Himalayas the Appalachian Mountains
weren't exactly extreme, but the weather could be. Mount
Katahdin was like a big wet beast. We left the next day for
Mount Mansfield in Vermont, then on to New Hampshire's
notorious Mount Washington and more wicked weather.

In each place I spoke to hundreds of kids. Hearing them
cheer as I came onto the stage made me feel really good that
I might be able to inspire them. This was my new dream and
equally important as climbing the Seven Summits, because I
just might be able to change someone's life for the better.

I started by telling them that the most important thing was
to live a healthy lifestyle, get outdoors, be active, and enjoy
nature, plus spend time with their families.

After Karen gave a slide show of the summits, I told kids, "Don't be afraid to aim high, and know that you don't have to do it alone. Find the support wherever you can. In the beginning, I wasn't sure what my dad and Karen would think. Would they go for it? I was a nine-year-old geeky kid. So I did research, told people, made a plan. And you can too. Just believe in yourselves."

Kids always asked, "Did you ever think about quitting?"

"Yeah, sure I did, but I never gave up. My dream was climbing the Seven Summits. That was huge, and sometimes it just felt too big. So I had to look at the summits one at a time. And then even a single mountain—like Everest—felt too big. You have to break things down into smaller steps. Don't ever let the size of your dream overwhelm you. Follow it one step at a time without losing sight of the goal."

"How long did it take you to accomplish yours?" someone would always ask.

"Six years. But you know, the longer you have to work at something, the more rewarding it is in the end."

"What if you fail?"

I walked back and forth across the stage, trying to make eye contact with everyone. "Nothing can stop you if you want it badly enough. Celebrate small victories. Keep working on your plan. It's just as important to step backward sometimes as it is to step forward. But never let up. Climbing is a great metaphor for life. Up, down, and around."

I stood next to Karen. "I'm proof that you've got to tell your family what you want to do. Surround yourself with a support system. Then anything is possible. And I do mean anything."

I moved to center stage for the final part of my talk. I always asked my audience to bring index cards with them.

"Take the three-by-five note cards you brought today and write down your goal. Aim high. Whether it's to climb a mountain, play football, take a trip, or even get better grades in school."

After they had done that, I gave them another task. "Hold on to your cards and take them home to share with your parents, teachers, or anyone who might support you. Then remember to be patient. It may take time.

"Okay, now everybody stand up. Shut your eyes. Hold that index card up to your heart. Think about your passion, your dream. Think about how you are going to make it happen. Think about the steps you are going to take. Think about the people who are going to help you. Then, with your eyes still shut, I want you to take a deep breath and then—keep your eyes shut—take one small step forward."

I paused while the entire audience took a step. It touched me deeply every time this happened. In my most enthusiastic voice I said, "There you have it. Congratulations, you are now one step closer toward reaching your goal.

"Find *your* Everest."

I was incredibly grateful that my goal of climbing the

Seven Summits had put me in the position of being able to talk to kids about achieving their dreams, and I hoped my experiences would inspire them.

If climbing the tallest mountain on each continent taught me anything, it was this: With the right support and training, you can do anything you set your mind to do.

I am lucky enough to have a family that is willing to help me make my dreams come true. With their help and encouragement, there's no limit to what I'll be able to accomplish in the future. I can't wait to find out what that will be.